Video Games

An Introduction to the Industry

Andy Bossom & Ben Dunning

Fairchild Books
An imprint of Bloomsbury Publishing PLC

BLOOMSBURY

LONDON · OXFORD · NEW YORK · NEW DELHI · SYDNEY

CONTENTS

1
VIDEO GAMES: PAST, PRESENT, AND FUTURE

4
LATERAL THINKING

5
GAMES AND SOCIETY

2
WHO MAKES GAMES?

3
GAME TECH

6
THE BUSINESS OF GAMES

IT IS STILL SURPRISING WHEN PEOPLE ARE SHOCKED TO DISCOVER HOW SIGNIFICANT THE VIDEO GAME INDUSTRY HAS BECOME IN THE GLOBAL ECONOMY

FOREWORD

IAN LIVINGSTONE CBE

Co-founder of Games Workshop, co-author of Fighting Fantasy gamebooks and former Chairman of Eidos plc.

Part of what makes us human is our ability to devise, construct, and play games. We get sweaty on sports fields, furrow our brows over crosswords and, during holiday periods, the bravest amongst us play board games with our families.

However, in the emergent digital age of the early twenty-first century our playtime now frequently takes place in the virtual worlds of video games. In some respects, contemporary life has itself become a game; the "gamification" of the everyday. A new generation of portable devices littered with apps encourages us to compete, record and engage with each other through social networks that we embed into our daily routines.

The video game industry is relatively new compared to its peers in the global entertainment sector but has grown rapidly in the last forty years, now rivaling them in both financial terms and as a creative force. Having been largely pioneered by enthusiasts in garages and bedrooms, from what was essentially a hobby, video games quickly became a phenomenon and a career. The industry's early years are still considered a golden age of creativity and originality. More recently, a new expressive spirit has returned to game design, aided by the Internet, its related technologies, and cheaper, more accessible computing. These factors have made the creation and distribution of games accessible once again allowing the aspirational enthusiasts the opportunity to be involved in game creation. It is a great time to be involved in this exciting industry.

The games industry is at the forefront of contemporary entertainment but video games are still perceived by some to be a niche pursuit.

Research tells us that video games are played across the age spectrum and in every strata of society permeating all walks of life as well as businesses large and small. The diversity of player demographic is reflected in the breadth of narrative content produced by the industry.

It is still surprising when people are shocked to discover how significant the video game industry has become in the global economy, arguably becoming the most creative and immersive playground that the modern world provides. A working life spent in video games is now a sought after career providing varied opportunities and employment for a great number of highly skilled artists, designers, programmers, and creatives from many disciplines.

The future of video games is assured but in order for the industry to evolve and continue to create skilled employment, more people need to be informed, enthused, and educated about its potential. This book has an important role to play in this. It ties together the video game industry's varied strands, exploring its structures, technology, context, and broader relevance. It provides a concise introduction to students, educators, and the general public. Built around the voices of those who know most about the industry: its creative designers, artists, producers and coders, it combines sound advice with illustrations of the visual richness and inventiveness of the medium that are so often overlooked.

It's a refreshing approach.

INTRODUCTION

Video Games: An Introduction to the Industry aims to provide an expansive, relevant, and engaging introduction to the world, context, and business of video games to empower the reader and to open their eyes to its diversity and significance with a lateral exploration of this global cross-cultural phenomenon. It is filled with full color examples of this exciting visual medium alongside interviews that give insight into the creative processes involved in making games, the global businesses behind big budget productions, console and online markets, web and app gaming, company structures, business models, game genres and the (re)emergence of the indie game scene. Each chapter is supported by interviews and comment from industry.

The video game industry is vast and there are many aspects to it, therefore it presents a challenge to those of us wishing to distil its breadth and depth. This book should be seen in this context. It is an introduction that is aware of its limitations, but also aware that there are very few starting points for those people who wish to know more about this industry and how to prepare for a potential future within it. This book is for those people.

From their obscure beginnings in the early 1950s, video games have blazed a trail from laboratory to arcade to living room to become a commercial behemoth in the twenty-first century; a long way to come in sixty years. What was once considered a pastime for mostly male, tech-obsessed nerds the video game cannot now be ignored as a passing fad or another frivolous, adolescent pastime. Instead, gaming has taken a place at the forefront of contemporary global culture and in the process become an economic driver around the world. The industry's spectacular growth means that it is generating more revenue than the combined might of the music and film industries and is now, arguably, more culturally pervasive than these established popular media types.

Video games have been both elevated and ridiculed by the press, but as a digital art form they go from strength to strength. Their ability to capture, enthrall, and communicate to millions using both simple and complex ideas is now recognized by critics and academic institutions, and a paradigm shift in societal attitudes is occurring. This is typified best by the decision in 2013 of MOMA, the Museum of Modern Art in New York to acquire twelve titles for its collection including the 1970s' arcade game classic: *Asteroids*.

Video games are rooted in the thoughts and desires of our complex cultural and biological past. The human need to interact in a multiplicity of ways is in part fulfilled through engaging in personal challenges, competition with others, the acquisition of knowledge and conflict (simulated or otherwise). These activities require us to formulate strategies that satisfy our primal urge to solve puzzles; the evidence for this can be traced back to the origins of civilization.

From smartphone based snackable content to the hours of screen time spent in front of the latest AAA games, we now take our gaming leisure time for granted. In the unlikely event that the

sum of all our fears comes to pass, and we are all subject to a dystopian social breakdown—regularly expressed in popular media (see *Walking Dead* image 0.01) —video games are here to stay in one format or another. This is of course not surprising. The accessibility of multi-format, multi-generational gaming libraries available via the Internet, mobile free to play, rental, or simply trading in old for new on the high street, gaming has made video games as disposable or throw away as any product in a decadent and affluent culture. But, if we take a moment and give a cursory glance at the core mechanics of what we invest a proportion of our leisure time in, we can see an astonishing legacy of gaming structures and strategies that span across cultures and millennia.

KEY TERM

AAA TITLE
Video games of the highest quality combined with the biggest budgets raking in the largest revenues. Titles and franchises such as *Hitman*, *Battlefield*, *Halo*, and *Killzone* fit this description. This definition doesn't usually apply to the indie scene although some games have crossed over from small entities in to super brands of their own, such as *Minecraft*.

CHAPTER SUMMARIES

1
Video Games: Past, Present, and Future

This serves as a brief introduction to the context of the video game industry: where it came from, where it is currently, and where its future may lie. It provides a broad base of information that covers the ancient history of game concepts to the amazing array of game types available to players today. In order to understand the contemporary video game industry and its contexts, it is important to examine what has gone before, whilst recognizing the creative shoulders and collective effort upon which the next generation of game makers will stand.

2
Who Makes Games?

Starting with a description of the many different roles that work together to create video games, this chapter goes on to showcase some of the people who make games, giving them the opportunity to discuss their roles and the processes involved in making games. These interviews provide valuable insights and advice from a wealth of experienced video game industry professionals, who have worked across a range of laterally aligned positions. They offer useful reflections of daily practices and share their acquired knowledge of the industry.

3
Game Tech

This chapter is an exploration and primer concerned with the technology upon which the game industry is based. It discusses both the past and the present of some of the consumer technology used in gaming, including the common platforms on which games are played. It also discusses aesthetic and design thinking for games, combined with a look at the software that powers our games and which allows developers to efficiently produce new products.

4
Lateral Thinking

The world of games is much broader than the simple act of playing them. They are both art and the subject of art. They are the center of communities that exist not just in small localities but also globally. This chapter deals with the broader question of where video games sit in the world we inhabit now, and how the boundaries between what is a video game, and what is simply a game, are being broken down by new technologies and the repurposing of long-standing ideas.

5
Games and Society

The video game industry does not exist in a vacuum. Games have an impact on and are influenced by concerns and questions outside and within the industry. In this chapter we look at and discuss a range of issues including the establishment of the regulatory environments that control who games can be sold to; and also tackle questions about what responsibilities the industry has, and what themes and biases might exist within it.

6
The Business of Games

In this chapter, you will find information and statistics about the business side of video games. It discusses funding methods and monetization models, and the significant impact mobile gaming has on the modern industry, which has allowed the industry to drop its reliance on traditional demographics. It also covers how the stories in our games are tied into the larger cross-media franchises and how these and other branding efforts keep us playing and asking for more.

1.1

Minecraft: Ziggurat
An indicator emphasizing the scale of collaboration in organized societies past and present.

1

VIDEO GAMES: PAST, PRESENT, AND FUTURE

TOPICS COVERED
Origins of Play / A Brief History of Video Games /
The Age of the Console / Twenty-First-Century
Gaming / Game Genres

The origins of the video games we play today are simultaneously complex, because of the evolution in technology required to play them, and primitive due to the ancient potentially timeless mechanics. These mechanics have been adapted from a rich heritage. This chapter explores how game ideas and strategies stretch back into antiquity, our shared history of learning through play.

ORIGINS OF PLAY

Both simple and sophisticated games have been played for thousands of years; their origins dating back to the birthplace of civilization—Ancient Mesopotamia—an area defined by the Tigris and Euphrates rivers and roughly equivalent to present day Iraq, Kuwait, north-eastern Syria and parts of southern Turkey. Comprised of city-states such as Uruk, Akkad, and Ur (others existed) these are considered the first incarnation of what we would define as a metropolis; huge permanent and organized communities, which represent a significant economic, cultural and political hub. This is where we find the first ever example of a recorded game, the Royal Game of Ur.

The Royal Game of Ur

The Sumerian city-state of Ur was established as early as 4000 BCE. In the 1920s archaeologist Sir Leonard Woolley led an expedition that retrieved remnants of the Royal Game of Ur (see image 1.2) from a gravesite, which currently reside in the British Museum in London, UK.

The earliest records of the Royal Game of Ur being played are contained in tablets that date between 4000 and 3500 BCE. These ancient records of the game were written in one of the oldest systems of writing, known as cuneiform script, an early form of representation made up of rows and columns of triangular wedge-shaped indented marks on a clay tablet.

It describes a two-player game where each player competes to race their pieces from one end to the other over the twenty-square rectangular board. The board was made from natural materials like wood and sometimes decorated with inlays of shell, red limestone, and lapis lazuli. This long board had twenty squares made of shell, in a 12, 2, 6 linear configuration: five of the squares have flower designs whilst others are detailed with circled dots.

1.2
The Royal Game of Ur

1.2
The Royal Game of Ur

The remaining squares have various designs utilizing five-dot configurations.

The importance of decoration and illustration are evident in the game's design. Over 6,000 years later and things remain the same: a key component of the gaming aesthetic had been established, which was fundamental in helping to engender a level of desire and elicit an interaction.

China: Wei Qi

The board game Wei Qi, or Go originated in China around 2200 BCE. It appears to be a simple game, which is still widely played across Asia. It has few rules, but remains a complex and challenging strategy game for two players. It is played on a square board table, called a "Go-Ban." The game mechanic is based on tactically controlling the movement of pieces on the board, to capture your opponent's pieces, take territory and dominate your opponent's ability to establish a stronghold.

1.3
Senet Game

Egypt: Senet

The Senet game (see image 1.3) also known as "Passing" or "The Game of Passing," dates from 1500 BCE in the pre-dynastic period, having its origins in Egypt where it is still played today. It has a similar appearance and game dynamic to Ur. It is played by two people using a long narrow board of three parallel rows each having ten squares.

Each player starts with seven pieces, often fashioned from knucklebones or twigs. The object of this game was to ensure that all your pieces safely traveled the board from one end to the other, navigating the squares, which represent good or bad fortune. To play the game you must block your

1.4
A Go-Ban (playing surface)
Despite its simplistic appearance it bears many similarities to RTS (Real Time Strategy) games where dominating territory and the other player's ability to function with the pieces at their disposal is a key game mechanic.

opponent's pieces and ensure safe passage for all seven pieces to the other end of the board before your opponent.

A hundred years later in 1400 BCE and Mancala or "Wari Boards" appears. The name Mancala is derived from the Arabic meaning, "to travel." It is a mathematical thinking strategy game still played in Africa. Each player attempts to outwit the other to achieve a high score. The aim is to capture the majority of your opponent's seeds or pebbles, collecting from a finite amount to win.

We see many puzzle or counting games in the recent trend of smart device app gaming. The uses of counter combinations in fast moving games challenge the player to achieve a high score. This game genre is defined by time-based constraints, solving condition-based play or a unique goal set by the level. For example, games like *Candy Crush Saga* explore many grid-based gaming variables or constraints to vary each puzzle level.

1.5
Hnefatafl
A traditional set
made by Vlodarius.

Scandinavia: Hnefatafl

The Norse game Hnefatafl (see image 1.5) pronounced *nef–ah-tah-fel*, meaning "King's Table," dates back to around 400 CE, the beginning of the Dark Ages of Northern Europe; despite many similarities, Hnefatafl pre-dates chess by hundreds of years. The rules of the game can be found in a handful of ancient Norse manuscripts such as The Saga of Fridthjof the Bold. An easily portable game, which could be played on a linen board, it traveled widely with Viking explorers. Remnants of the game have been found as far away as Ukraine.

This sophisticated Scandinavian tactical warfare game was designed to pass on and test strategic concepts of battle, particularly against a greater opposing force where ideas of defense, survival and counterattack are of great importance. It is a two-player game where the player can either play as the surrounding attacking force or choose to defend, counter and escape to one of the four corners on the board known as Thrones.

Survival games are an extremely popular video game genre and survival games where wave after wave of phased attack of NPCs (non-playable characters) attempt to kill you, make for intense and enjoyable gameplay. Variations in game modes such as Capture the Flag, Search and Destroy, Headquarters, Team Deathmatch, King of the Hill, Domination or Last Man Standing found in enduring franchises like *Call of Duty*, are regular additions to the standard campaign gameplay menu.

In these game modes, we can see a shared gaming mechanic with ancient board games like Tafl. The enduringly popular zombie sub-culture has also been revived through survival horror titles such as the *Left 4 Dead* franchise. DLC expansion packs (downloadable content) such as *Call of Duty Rezurrection*, with remastered levels, reuse, and reinvent the primary arena. Expandable additions of the core game release extend a title's playability and the profitable shelf life of the franchise.

India: Chaturanga

The game Chaturanga was invented in India around 700 CE. It inspired several derivative incarnations such as Shantranji, Shogi, Makruk, Janggi and Xiagqi, also known as ancient chess.

During this period, Chaturanga was played in Persia and enjoyed popularity across the Muslim world, eventually traveling from North Africa to Europe. Now more commonly known to western cultures as chess, it is probably the most well-known and well-regarded two-player strategy board game. International chess masters are lauded for their mental capacity and ability to strategize many moves ahead.

In this turn-based game, each side has sixteen pieces, from lowly infantry to prized pieces that have a range of different abilities and functions. Hailing from India, Chaturanga did not have a queen but a vizier, who would have led the armies for the king. Centuries later the queen was added to the European version of the game.

The tradition of turn-based strategy computer games dates back to classics such as the 1985

game *Gauntlet*. Action Real Time Strategy (A-RTS) and role-playing games (RPGs) (see pages 40 and 44), offer a range of playable characters who have specific skillsets, powers or strengths. These can be employed to overcome challenges or obstacles.

The *Age of Wonders* series by Triumph Studios (see image 1.6) has been a dynamic proponent of turn-based gaming. These kinds of games allow the player to pursue one character arc over another, potentially varying the gaming outcomes. Over time the player in their role is able to increase their character-specific strengths, develop new skills, gaining new items whilst actively advancing the story in a unique way.

An expansion of this mechanic would be squad-based games like *Team Fortress* having parallels to the breakdown of game pieces with differing strengths, functions and abilities. Choice allows the player to engage in the game in a variety of ways exploring different outcomes. These are often expressed in a handful of character types, nine in *Team Fortress'* case: Heavy, Pyro, Medic,

Engineer, Demoman, Scout, Sniper, Soldier and Spy. Each character type specializes in a certain kind of gameplay with specific skills and weapons. For example, Scout is fast and is useful in completing objectives, but his speed is balanced by being weaker and more vulnerable. In a team context, as Scout goes forward to complete the objective, Sniper or Heavy would protect from a distance by laying down fire and killing the opponents from a safer distance.

Nine Men's Morris

During the early Middle Ages, Nine Men's Morris rose to popularity particularly in medieval England. The game dates back to ancient Egypt and was played by the Romans. Having twenty-four points and intersections it is sometimes described as "noughts and crosses for adults." It can also be played in a 3, 6 or 12 configuration depending on the size of the grid and desired level of complexity. It is notably mentioned in Shakespeare's sixteenth-century play *A Midsummer Night's Dream* by Titania in Act II, Scene 1 (c. 1595).

1.7
Libro de los Juegos
A 1283 painting depicting
the Nine Men's Morris game.

Twentieth-century Europe

Many ideas have been re-appropriated, experiencing an evolution in the twentieth century as board games' popularity reached an all time high, being advertised globally in every medium. For example, the board game Risk was released in 1957 in France as *La Conquête du Monde*, a turn-based strategy game about occupying territory and eliminating your opponents.

From board game to tabletop, a grand extension of the strategy game concept was developed by Games Workshop (UK 1975) with the Warhammer role-playing game (1983). Based on scaling up battle interactions, the game employed fantasy narrative streams, character types (manufactured by Citadel Miniatures) and battle scenarios. The alternative emergent gaming scene was additionally underpinned by *White Dwarf* magazine.

More recently board games such as Settlers of Catan by Klaus Teuber (1996), a resource management and trade board game, has attracted several awards for its engaging game mechanic and multiple narrative variants. Like Warhammer, it has become a transmedia product crossing over into digital formats for tablet, PC and console.

Many game mechanics in modern computer games are older and far more tried and tested than we might have initially appreciated. Grid-based strategy systems commonly employed in RTS (real-time strategy) turn-based games compel the player to explore deeper thought processes and to weaken their opponent's position. Orchestrating an opponent's defeat, coupled with the desire to conquer, is at the core of computer games across the decades. This can be seen in the indie game *The Castle Doctrine* (2014).

1.8
Space Marine Centurion Squad
These figures are from Games
Workshop's Warhammer
40,000 table top game.
Painted by Wermilion.

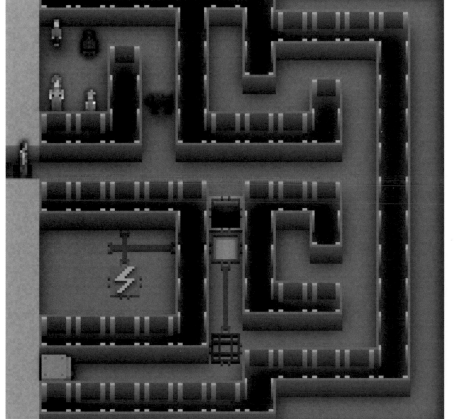

1.9
The Castle Doctrine
Players build a complex home
security system to ensure a
miserable death to unwanted
visitors. Protect your family or
they will inevitably die. *The Castle
Doctrine* context plays on the
palpable fear that armed robbers
will one day come to your house
and you have no choice but to
arm now in an attempt to protect
yourself against the unknown
horrors that await.

A BRIEF HISTORY OF VIDEO GAMES

What are Video Games?

The definition of a video game can get bogged down in academic debate as to what exactly "games" are, not just video games. It is not our intention to over complicate matters therefore to keep things simple we shall use the *Oxford English Dictionary* definition:

A GAME PLAYED BY ELECTRONICALLY MANIPULATING IMAGES PRODUCED BY A COMPUTER PROGRAM ON A MONITOR OR OTHER DISPLAY.

In the Lab

The technological developments upon which the video game industry is founded began in the mid-twentieth century. At the medium's inception, games were a scientific endeavor because computers existed largely in labs. Once computer technology became cheaper and small enough to enter the home and the arcade, the roots of the video game business, as we know it, were established.

In 1952, Alexander S. Douglas created noughts and crosses on the EDSAC (Electronic Delay Storage Automatic Calculator) computer, the first computer built to enable others to solve complex calculations. As part of his PhD at Cambridge University, UK, the computer game formed part of Douglas's dissertation into human–computer interaction (HCI). Other technologies were in development but *noughts and crosses*, also known as *tic-tac-toe*, is the first instance of computer programming being used to define a gaming mechanic. Douglas's research birthed the notion that interaction with computers can be re-purposed towards either strategy simulation or competitive entertainment, rather than for function-driven analytical mathematical calculations. At this point, the purpose of the computer changes forever. No longer are they machines solely defined by an ability to compute controlled arguments, but computers are now devices that can respond to the real-time variables of human input in a competitive simulation.

The first proto computer games begin to appear in America in 1958. Whilst researching at the Brookhaven National Laboratory, nuclear physicist William Higinbotham (who had previously helped develop electronic components for the first nuclear weapon or atom bomb) created *Tennis for Two*, the inspiration for *Pong*, which appeared two decades later. *Tennis for Two* was a two-player game in which the competitors had to direct a bouncing green dot on a black background with wire connected dial paddle controllers, viewed on a 5-inch oscilloscope screen.

In 1962, this electronic game was closely followed by *Spacewar!* a two-player spaceship shooting game where players controlled their ship using the computer keyboard. Originally conceived in 1961 by Martin Graetz, Stephen Russell, and Wayne Wiitanen, it was fully realized in 1962 on the DEC PDP-1 (with the assistance of Dan Edwards, Alan Kotok, Steve Piner, and Robert A Saunders) at the Massachusetts Institute of Technology (MIT).

1.10
EDSAC, 1952
The Electronic Delay Storage
Automatic Calculator was the
size of a large room.

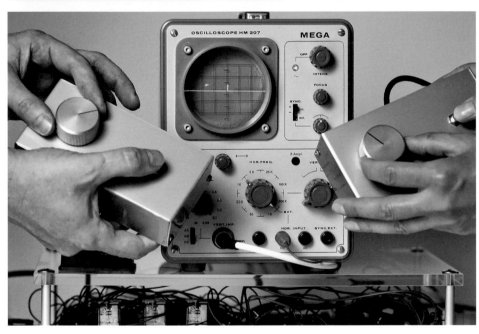

1.11
Tennis for Two, 1958
The original two-player
game; played on an
oscilloscope, an electronic
testing device for visually
describing signal voltages.

It is here that the familiar aesthetic of the computer game begins to appear with its triangular spaceship shooting missile dots towards other objects.

First published in 1963, ASCII (release x 3.4) the American Standard Code for Information Interchange, was developed from telegraphic codes used for communication, but it later became another programming milestone in game development. Initially games exploiting the code were played on mainframes before reaching the home. In 1970, British mathematician John Conway created a zero player game in ASCII—defined by creating generative outcomes—called *Game of Life*. The game allowed the user to work with an orthogonal grid of square cells, entering initial conditions (alive or dead), which then in turn determined how the game would evolve from its initial state. Advanced players could create patterns as the game evolved. ASCII saw a resurgence in popularity in the 1980s spawning games such as *Rogue*, originally created by Michael Toy and Glenn Wichman in 1980.

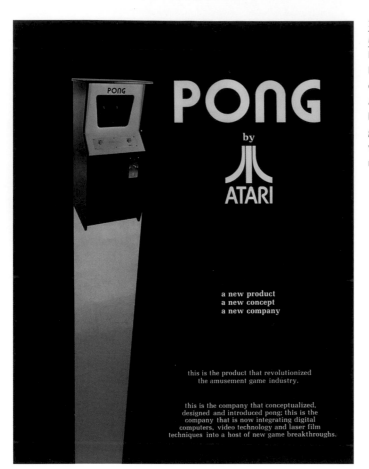

1.12
Pong led the way
In 1972 Nolan Bushnell and Ted Dabney founded Atari. They enlisted the help of a developer, Allan Alcorn (widely considered to be one of the fathers of computer games) to create a coin-operated video game. It took him three months to finish the game.

The Arcade

These mid-twentieth-century prototypes, created with room-sized computers, are the pioneers preceding the cultural entertainment industry explosion that was to become the 1970s computer arcade. In the early years, unless you were a computer science researcher, playing video games was something you did outside of the home; you had to visit an arcade. From the outset, video games were frequently designed to be played by more than one player. Despite the persistent stereotype of a lonely, usually male, individual staring at a screen in a darkened room, these games were conceived and marketed as social experiences, just like their board game siblings.

Pong was released as an arcade machine in 1973, once Atari had successfully secured funding for this new and as yet untested entertainment venture. It proved to be an instant success and an unmistakable landmark in entertainment history, as well as the beginning of social computer gaming.

Pong was believed to have been inspired by the Magnavox Odyssey technology showcased in 1972, which Nolan Bushnell attended. In 1974 after *Pong*'s subsequent arcade success, the game's similarity led to the first ever video game lawsuit in patent infringement against Bally-MidWay, Seeburg, and Atari.

Years later, 1978 saw the release of one of the most enduring and influential arcade games ever made: Taito's *Space Invaders*. This was followed swiftly in 1979 by another legendary arcade game: *Asteroids*, released once again by the fledgling Atari. Its triangular spaceship design and use of minimal vector graphics were directly influenced by its 1962 forerunner *Spacewar!* which Nolan Bushnell had greatly admired. These two epic space games tapped into the zeitgeist as the space race, which had been under way for a decade, was igniting imaginations. This period, now recognized by many as the golden age of computer games, marked the rapid proliferation of arcade machines across North America, Europe and Asia.

THE AGE OF THE CONSOLE

> **IT WAS THE ORIGINAL HOME SET UP: TWO PLAYERS COULD BE ENTERTAINED BY A RANGE OF GAMES AND EDUCATIONAL PROGRAMS ON THE HOME TV SET, AND IN COLOR TOO!**

The 1970s also saw the emergence of home computing and the first games console entertainment systems, the first of which was the Magnavox Odyssey, released in 1972. Created by Ralph Baer, this console heralded the beginning of a new era in home entertainment.

It was the original home set up: two players could be entertained by a range of games and educational programs on the home TV set, and in color too! There were sixteen game titles available for the Magnavox and it sold an impressive 300,000 units. It was not until five years later in 1977 that the first market competitors appeared. It was the year Apple introduced the Apple II home computer and Atari released the legendary 2600-cartridge system. The Atari 2600 sold 30 million units. The public's voracious appetite for home entertainment systems had taken hold. The 1980s became a period of rapid expansion; many companies released their own incarnation of the video game console, all vying to produce the market leader, all wanting to be king of the home entertainment console.

The emergence of 8- and 16-bit computing from notable market leaders transformed gaming in the home as hardware became affordable. Computers such as Commodore with the VIC 20 (2.5 million units sold in 1981) and C64 (20 million units sold in 1982), Sinclair ZX Spectrum (5 million units sold in 1982), BBC B Micro (1 million units sold in 1982), Amstrad CPC 464 (2.5 million units sold in 1984), Apple Macintosh (22 million units sold in 1984), IBM PC/AT (50 million units sold in 1984), Atari ST (6 million units sold in 1985), and latterly the Commodore Amiga A500, favored for its brilliant graphics and its ability to multitask (5 million units sold in 1985) led the way in this home computing revolution. In spite of IBM's extraordinary success in the 1980s, the computer that led the way as the video game platform of choice was the Commodore C64.

This was the decade of numerous original titles and game design innovations, featured across a range of platforms. Games such as *Jupiter Lander* (1981),

Manic Miner (1983), *Congo Bongo* (1983), *Chuckie Egg* (1983), *Jet Set Willy* (1984), *Dungeonmaster* (1985) and Sid Meier's *Pirates!* (1987), *Shadow of the Beast* (1989, rebooted for the PS4) and many more, inspired a generation.

A significant gaming landmark, not just for the 1980s but also in gaming history, was the release of *Elite* (1984). This deep space exploration and trading game created by David Braben and Ian Bell is considered the first ever "sandbox" open world game. Starting out on an Acorn Atom and a BBC Micro, the London-based duo managed to program eight galaxies into this concept game. The scale of this non-linear gameplay experience was an extraordinary leap in video game storytelling, creating its own genre and redefining what was possible with this new technological medium. Its success was additionally enhanced by its unique use of engaging 3D (three dimensional) vector graphics (see Crowdfunding page 174).

After a decade of expansion, echoing the mania of the nineteenth-century gold rush, the games industry faced rapid contraction in the 1990s. Many manufacturers were not in step with the fast pace of change and need for innovation. The remaining console manufacturers, now reduced to a handful of core brands, such as Sega Saturn (10 million units sold in 1994), Nintendo N64 (35 million units sold in 1996), Sony PlayStation (102 million units sold in 1994), 3DO (1.5 million units sold in 1993) and Atari Jaguar (250,000 units sold in 1993). This was to be Atari's last home entertainment console.

Console Core

At the turn of the decade the three big console providers remained Sony, Nintendo and Sega, as the manufacturers released their sixth-generation platforms. In 1998 Sega, in an attempt to beat the competition, released the Dreamcast before Sony and Nintendo spawned their next generation. Despite being an excellent product and selling 10 million units and having 500 game titles, Sega misjudged the market. Poor sales led to Sega's demise as one of the console legends. It left hardware behind and survives now as a developer and publisher. By comparison, the Sony PS2 went on to sell over 150 million units, Sony PS3 over 80 million units (November 2013, ongoing) and now the PS4. Whilst Microsoft Xbox (2001) sold 25 million units, the Xbox 360 sold over 80 million units (October 2013, ongoing) and has now released the Xbox One. Put simply, longevity in the console market is as much about quantity as it is about quality, both are needed for continued success and if the next iteration innovation does not capture the gaming public's imagination, it could be the end of your business. (See Twenty-First-Century Gaming, which looks at Ouya, Steam Box, and Mojo consoles on page 30.)

PLATFORM GENEALOGY

For more information about gaming hardware, see Chapter 3 Key Technologies, page 78.

SOURCES:
THE ENCYCLOPEDIA OF GAME MACHINES 1972-2005, TECHRADAR.COM

Key:

CONSOLE NAME
RELEASED
UNITS SOLD

1ST GEN

2ND GEN

3RD GEN

4TH GEN

5TH GEN

6TH GEN

7TH GEN

8TH GEN

MAGNAVOX
1972
300K

ATARI 2600
1977
30M

APPLE II
1977
5M

SINCLAIR ZX81
1981
1.5M

COMMODORE VIC 20
1981
2.5M

PHILIPS G7000
1978
2M

MATTEL INTELLIVISION
1980
3M

TEXAS INSTRUMENTS TI99/4A
1980
2.5M

TANDY TRS 80
1977
1M

CBS COLECOVISION
1982
4M

SINCLAIR SPECTRUM
1982
5M

COMMODORE C64
1982
20M

AMSTRAD CPC 464
1984
2.5M

SEGA MASTER SYSTEM SG1000
1983
10M

NINTENDO FAMICON NES
1983
62M

ACORN BBC B
1982
1M

ATARI ST
1985
6M

APPLE MACINTOSH
1984
22M

IBM PC/AT
1984
50M

COMMODORE AMIGA
1982
5M

NEC PC-ENGINE
1987
7M

SEGA MEGA DRIVE
1988
30M

NINTENDO SUPER NES
1990
50M

NEO GEO
1990
1M

ATARI JAGUAR
1993
250K

SONY PLAYSTATION
1994
102M

SEGA SATURN
1994
10M

NINTENDO N64
1994
35M

3DO
1993
1.5M

SONY PLAYSTATION PS2
2000
150M

XBOX
2000
25M

SEGA DREAMCAST
1998
10M

NINTENDO GAMECUBE
2001
21M

SONY PLAYSTATION PS3
2006
55M+

XBOX 360
2005
58M+

NINTENDO WII
2006
90M

SONY PLAYSTATION PS4
2013
20.2M

XBOX ONE
2013
10M

NINTENDO WII U
2013
3.3M+

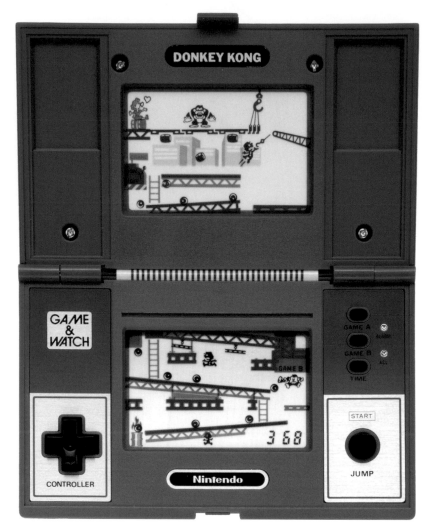

1.13
Donkey Kong (1982) Nintendo Game and Watch
This dual screen handheld gaming device was the "must have" of its day and remains highly prized by collectors. Mario, Nintendo's iconic character started life as Jumpman in the original arcade version of *Donkey Kong* in 1981 and featured again in this handheld version. Designed by the legendary Shigeru Miyamoto, *Donkey Kong* was a huge hit with over 60,000 arcade cabinets sold. Its sequel *Donkey Kong Jr.* arrived in the arcades in 1982 and Jumpman was reborn as Mario.

1.14
Nintendo Game Boy
The original release of the Nintendo Game Boy created a cultural shift in portable gaming. It imported the classic D-pad and two-button interface of the Game & Watch series begun nearly a decade earlier: 1,200 games were released, with some 120 million units sold. The lack of a color screen did not dent its popularity.

Handheld and Mobile

Whilst the expansion and demand for video gaming in the home was going from strength to strength, another phenomena was soon to arrive on the scene, the handheld gaming device.

Portable gaming technology began to emerge in the 1970s but boomed in the 1980s. It was seen as a low-cost alternative to computers and consoles. Nintendo released *Ball*, the first of the landmark Game & Watch series of LCD handhelds in 1980. These single-game machines were a huge international success and helped make Nintendo the dominant player in the new handheld market as well as cement Nintendo's place in the upper echelons of the video gaming industry.

Throughout the 1980s, Nintendo produced a variety of titles and design variations including: *Chef* (1981), *Crab Grab* (1984), *Tropical Fish* (1985), *Climber* (1986) and *Bomb Sweeper* (1987). Their established arcade franchises like *Donkey Kong* (1981), *Super Mario Bros* (1983) and *Zelda* (1989) were also released in portable versions. The use of established arcade franchises helped drive consumers toward this new platform.

Many manufacturers tried to get into the new portable marketplace by creating their own interpretation of the portable gaming device as interest in portable gaming grew. Grandstand, a manufacturer based in the UK, released *Astro Wars* in 1981. The physical design of the device took its cues from arcade cabinets but scaled down to a portable size. Both the game and the design of the product were an effort at mimicking the design and success of the Namco arcade hit *Galaxian*, released in 1979.

Japanese company NEC PC began creating compact handheld cartridge-based gaming devices called the PC-Engine in 1987. They developed several variants of the PC-Engine including: the color display GT (1990), flip LCD screen LT (1991) and the PC-Engine Duo-RX (1994). Although slightly larger than its competitors, the PC-Engine's strength was its superior graphics and sound combined with coin-op conversions of classic arcade games like *R-Type*, *Galaga 88* and *Bomberman*.

In 1989, Nintendo began its Game Boy cartridge-based handheld franchise that shipped with the seminal Russian puzzle game *Tetris*. The shift in accessibility brought about by the Game Boy's success, transformed our understanding of video games and their place in day-to-day life. They

> **“**
>
> **FROM ACCLAIM TO EIDOS, INFOGAMES, UBISOFT AND KONAMI RIGHT UP TO THQ, ELECTRONIC ARTS AND MATTEL—PRETTY MUCH EVERY MAJOR THIRD-PARTY PRODUCED GAME BOY GAMES.**
>
> Winnie Forster, Game Machines
>
> **”**

were no longer tied to the living room TV or study computer, they could go anywhere and be played at any time. The Game Boy went through many iterative redesigns: the Super Game Boy (1994), Game Boy Pocket (1996), Super Game Boy 2 (1996), Game Boy Light (1998) and in the same year the Game Boy Color. It is worth mentioning that the success of the Game Boy from the mid-1990s onwards was significantly aided and boosted by the *Pokémon* game franchise. The other notable competitors were Sega who launched the Game Gear in 1990 (300 games, 11 million units sold) and the Atari Lynx in 1989 (see image 1.15). Despite their specifications being greater than the Game Boy, the Game Gear having thirty-two colors with classic games conversions like *Space Harrier*, both were bulkier, consumed batteries faster and could not compete with Nintendo's massive library of game titles.

By the end of the 1990s, others had joined the handheld market including the Neo Geo Pocket (80 games and 2 million units sold) and Bandai WonderSwan, whilst Nintendo released its Virtual Boy headset and controller (22 games and 1 million units sold) bathed in the hype of virtual reality from its 3D stereoscopic graphics.

In the new millennium, Nintendo released a new wave of handhelds starting with the Game Boy Advance (800 games and 80 million units sold) and the Advance SP with its clamshell flip screen design and rechargeable battery. This was followed in 2004 when Nintendo released another handheld, the DS range (1,000 games and 135 million units sold) that completed the revival of the dual screen layout of the Game and Watch series.

Sony joined the handheld market with the PlayStation Portable (PSP) in 2004. It employed faster and smaller processors with increased memory and capacity signaling a sea change in the quality of graphics found up until then. These improved graphics, combined with a larger screen display, significantly enhanced the gaming experience.

While Nintendo has continued to be the big name in portable gaming, Sony is a credible competitor. These two heavyweights define the handheld market and continue to produce iterations of their flagship handheld gaming devices.

By the turn of the millennium, cell phones had become part of mainstream culture. Handsets shrank in size while their functions and capabilities increased with each new model. From the late 1990s onward, games were a common preloaded feature. One of the most famous of these was a version of *Snake*, which was introduced by Nokia with the 6110.

A technological convergence occurred in 2003 when the dominant mobile phone brand Nokia released the N-Gage to compete in the handheld games market. Despite largely lackluster reviews and limited commercial success, it marked a technological convergence and a breach of the formerly isolated market of handheld gaming devices. The ubiquitous cell phone was now a game machine.

Despite the relative failure of the N-Gage, another phone brand, Sony Ericsson, released its own hybrid handset in 2011. The Xperia Play combined cell phone with the PlayStation gaming franchise. In the same year Sony also released the PS Vita into the handheld market while Nintendo released the 3DS, indicating that the two manufacturers still see some future in dedicated handheld gaming devices.

Mobile has become one of the central formats for twenty-first-century gaming. Games designed for mobile and web-centered formats are generating huge amounts of money as games attract previously untapped market demographic.

Video games are now part of the cultural mainstream, although arguably they are still not accepted as such, and mobile gaming is commonplace, possibly the *de rigueur* pastime of the millennial generation. The ascendency of the smartphone and other touch-screen technology that supports its own gaming ecosystem is now the main challenger to the established order of the dedicated handheld gaming platform, as well as the traditional gaming platforms of the home computer or console. (See Twenty-First-Century Gaming, page 30.)

The New Indie

In the current industry cycle, the game designer has the ability to initiate self-directed projects without the backing of a large publisher, having access to online platforms, which have opened the way to a wide user base. This allows the creator to present work in progress, engendering further support through vessels such as STEAM Green Light (an online gaming hub), or early access Beta Keys along with crowdfunding websites (see page 174). This has led to and made space for many new expressions in game design. The Internet has opened up the marketplace to a new range of customers who may not have previously been able to afford to buy multiples of expensive Next Gen titles. The reemergence of a strong, supported indie scene is an encouraging vibrant expansion of the video games industry with new kit and hardware being produced to cater for it (see Key Technologies page 78).

A VERY BRIEF HISTORY OF THE COMPUTER

Inventor and mathematician Charles Babbage was the first to attempt automated computations in London, which set the stage for things to come.

- **1837**
  The Babbage Difference Engine.
- **1840**
  Analytical Engine, also designed by Babbage.
- **1873**
  Christopher Sholes developed the Qwerty keyboard.
- **1943**
  Thomas Watson (chairman of IBM) said: "I think there is a world market for maybe five computers."
- **1945**
  Grace Hopper recorded the first computer bug (a moth stuck between the relays).

1.16

Sony PSP

The Sony PSP (500 games and 50 million units sold) redefined handheld gaming and controller design. Like the DS, it took its cues from the existing aesthetic of its home console.

TWENTY-FIRST-CENTURY GAMING

Current and Emerging Trends

The public appetite to be mesmerized by new worlds, meandering metanarratives and extraordinary vistas, packaged to the player in ever more elaborate cutscenes (a cinematic device used to progress the storyline) does not abate. Expectations of AAA gaming titles are increasing in line with those of the movie industry: bigger, faster, and accompanied by more explosive action than ever before.

Advances in 3D modeling and animation, facial recognition, dynamic environment interaction (sixaxis, motion sensors) along with improvements in virtual reality (Oculus Rift) technology has led gameplay to become more tangible. The lines between fantasy and reality are becoming blurred. Gaming has become as much about who we want to be and identity, as it is about brand or franchise loyalty.

In the last decade, the video games industry has undergone a significant shift and a partial redistribution of power has taken place. Success and financial rewards can be achieved not only by the pan-national corporations, but also by online start-up companies who resemble the small pioneering garage-based businesses of the 1970s and 1980s where it all began.

Before the turn of the millennium, the publishing giants controlled the release and distribution of video games titles across formats.

They also funded and published the vast majority of video games. Presently the gaming community is re-imagined and indie development teams are no longer beholden to the large publishers to fund their projects, although this is still a significant part of the business of games.

The latest iteration of console development has now entered the eighth generation of video game consoles with the launch of the Sony PlayStation PS4, Microsoft's Xbox One and the Wii U. PlayStation and Xbox, seeing the power of social networks have invested heavily in including social functionality and connectivity to their products, linking live gameplay to online formats such as Twitch TV. For the PS4 the new controller includes a share button to instigate the recording, allowing players to instantly share progress, achievements, battles and losses with others.

VIDEO GAME DOCUMENTARIES

- *THE KING OF KONG: A FISTFUL OF QUARTERS (2007)*
- *SECOND SKIN (2008)*
- *ALL YOUR HISTORY ARE BELONG TO US (2009–2013) (SERIES)*
- *INDIE GAME: THE MOVIE (2012)*
- *MINECRAFT: THE STORY OF MOJANG (2012)*
- *GROUNDED: THE MAKING OF THE LAST OF US (2013)*
- *HOW VIDEO GAMES CHANGED THE WORLD (2013)*
- *FREE TO PLAY (2014)*
- *FROM BEDROOMS TO BILLIONS (2014)*
- *OUTERLANDS (2015).* **A CROWDFUNDED SIX PART TV SERIES ABOUT THE PEOPLE AND CULTURE OF VIDEO GAMES**

Indie Publishing and Online Hubs

If we look back to the golden age in gaming history, we can see a cyclical link to the practice and ideology of the early 1980s "homebrew" programming enthusiasts and the rise of the twenty-first-century indie game developer. Video gaming cult classics were sometimes written in days, what we now call "game sprints," then self-published and distributed on tape cassettes by post. Advertising was often a tiny advert on the back of computer magazines. However, in the twenty-first century the distribution methods of indie games have changed considerably.

This new wave of indie game development is partly a consequence of low-cost computing, ease of access to powerful and affordable design software, and the emergence of freeware or open source software tools. Indie developers, both individuals and micro teams, have been able to define a space in the commercial games industry where they can set their own agenda.

Consumers desiring variety are keen for a bargain and are increasingly looking beyond the established providers to independent retailers such as Steam or The Humble Bundle. These offer gamers weekly and seasonal deals to purchase license keys or DLC items online at a fraction of the retail cost.

Narrative Interventions

Another adjunct in contemporary gaming is the video game as interactive narrative experience. As designers look for new ideas, as well as revisit pre-existing ones, narrative depth in games is becoming more commonplace. With greater frequency, games are focusing on subtlety in story and character with titles such as *Dear Esther* (2012) conveying a poetic vision rather than the traditional fare of conflict-based action. Other games such as *Gone Home* allow the player to view the everyday lives of others and equally offer a far gentler, non-violent experience.

Point and click choice-based narratives are not new. Originating in the 1960s with text based adventures like *Hamurabi* (1968) and later *Zork: The Great Underground Empire* (1977), the format is now re-emerging as interactive living book gameplay, offering the player variety in pace, stimulation and experiential outcomes.

Video games as extensions to comics and graphic novels are also being explored. *The Wolf Among Us* (2013) and *The Walking Dead* (2012), both by Telltale Games are two serialized interactive stories that are pushing this transmedia coupling. Bill Willingham's DC/Vertigo comic series *Fables* is the basis for *The Wolf Among Us*, a five episode video game prequel to the comics that allows the player to interact with the story at key moments in the narrative. At significant waypoints, players are presented with a multiple-choice panel offering several interactions or choices of conversation with non-playable characters (NPCs). Whatever the player selects will lead to divergent storylines and altered outcomes as the game proceeds. This method has strong echoes of the *Fighting Fantasy* series of role-playing books that were first published in the early 1980s. These transmedial products deliberately cross formats, attempting to find new ways to engage consumers and players.

The language and ideas behind video game narratives are steadily having a greater influence on other forms of media, especially TV and film. There have been many films based on video games, which have fallen short of representing the medium but Doug Liman's 2014 movie *Edge of Tomorrow* is one of the best screen depictions of the core mechanics and common cycles of gameplay: play, die, and respawn.

Mobile Gaming

Smart touch-screen devices have assisted the charge of indie gaming by igniting a public appetite for apps and mini games. It would be easy to disregard these games as smaller undertakings, but in a short period, smartphones and tablets have made serious inroads into the handheld gaming market previously dominated by the international video game franchises. In the gold rush for mobile riches, the app game market has exploded but this has not led to automatic success for developers. A situation now exists where multiple variants of the same game type are on offer with many games and developers lacking visibility in the market either through creating a poor product or not having a strong marketing strategy and budget. To illustrate the sums of money now involved in mobile gaming, Hope Cochran CFO King Digital Entertainment plc (the casual and social games company), when speaking at a Deutsche Bank investors conference, highlighted that King spends "on average, $100 million per quarter on paid marketing." It was also reported by venturebeat.com that from the beginning of 2014 until October that year King paid to have eleven different TV spots in the US alone that aired more than 34,000 times. This investment in TV adverts far exceeds companies such as Sony and Microsoft who had 3,000 and 7,500 ads respectively for the same period. These advertising budgets indicate the extraordinary growth in the mobile gaming market and its substantial profit margins.

Mobile gaming has also enabled the "mini game," previously the preserve of unlockable content or secret areas within console titles, i.e. games within games, to become a part of the everyday gaming diet. Mini games are now a product in their own right. The ideas are no less than their more substantial counterparts, as specific game mechanics unique to the touch-screen format functionality have also enhanced gaming concept, interaction and playability. Titles such as Imangi Studios' *Temple Run* (2011) franchise and Half Brick Studios' *Fruit Ninja* (2010) have focused on the touch gesture capability, successfully harnessing the swipe mechanic. Whilst others attempt to fit the console controller format of gameplay, using both thumbs, into a different context. Embedding a succinct gesture-based game mechanic into a game concept is harder than you might first appreciate. Many publishers large and small have suffered losses because they underestimated and misunderstood the requirements of the app gaming format and marketplace.

KEY TERMS

DOWNLOADABLE CONTENT (DLC)

Frequently this includes extra maps and levels but can be a variety of different video game elements. DLC is additional material created by a game's official publisher or a third party that extends the originally purchased game. Now common in mobile, PC and console games it is accessed via the Internet and is usually paid for but occasionally can be free.

RRP

Recommended retail price is the selling price of a product suggested by a manufacturer or producer to a retailer.

1.18–1.19
Candy Crush Soda Saga
Images of gameplay and a loading screen illustrating an extension of the Candy Crush franchise.

Esports
(or Competitive Gaming)

Gaming as a spectator sport is becoming mainstream as gamers tune into online channels to watch live gaming sessions and hear commentary. Twitch TV, one of the leaders in the new live-streaming market, saw 6 million broadcasts, 45 million unique viewers and 12 billion minutes watched in 2013! YouTube channels such as PewDiePie, hosted by the UK-based Swedish game commentator Felix Kjellberg, attracts over 34 million subscribers to his *Let's Play* screen casts. The public appetite to vicariously explore games through a "proxy player" who combines a range of skills, insightful commentary, charisma, and eccentricity seems to be growing exponentially.

Esports teams have such a significant following and level of celebrity that they are able to fill stadiums (see the *Free to Play* esports documentary). In 2011, The International Dota Championships (*Defence of the Ancients 2*) at the gamescom esport tournament in Germany had a record-breaking prize winning pot of 1.6 million dollars. The Ukrainian team, Na Vi (Natus Vincere) won the 1 million dollar prize that year. In 2014, The International attracted a staggering 11 million dollars in prize money through crowdfunding. The winning Chinese team Newbee earned an extraordinary 5 million dollars. Winnings of this magnitude are only traditionally thought of within the world of mainstream professional sports supported by major international business sponsors.

In South Korea, live televised esports is larger than traditional sporting coverage, having dedicated TV shows following the national esports league. MOBA games—Multiplayer Online Battle Arena—attract massive crowds to live events, such as the *League of Legends* series 4 world final opening ceremony in 2014, filling the 69,000 seat Olympic Stadium in Seoul.

One could speculate that these computer game leagues and tournaments could progress further into the mainstream. Esport gaming fixtures could go on to compete with the traditional weekly broadcasts of mainstream, prime time TV channels. It is closer to becoming a reality than many might

1.20
Dota 2
Defence of the Ancients 2 made by Valve is a MOBA game available on Steam. For more on esports see People Power page 176).

imagine as the next generation of smart TVs is Internet ready, which once would have only have been thought of with computers, accessed separately in a non-congregational part of the home.

Another distinct parallel with physical competitive sports is betting on the outcome of these events. Esports betting is starting to evolve in tandem to its popularity. Live betting online through gaming hubs, which utilize virtual currency, are becoming more commonplace. The more you play and achieve the more virtual rewards you receive. Some of these virtual items are rare and therein hold a value to others. These can be traded or used as currency. Virtual items can be used to bet on live gaming events online, on websites such as the CS:GO Lounge (the marketplace for trades and bets relating to *Counter-Strike: Global Offensive*). Considering how close to the mainstream esports is becoming, it may not be long before the odds are being offered in high street betting shops alongside traditional sporting fixtures. In a betting shop window, one poster would have the betting odds on a football match, and the poster next to it advertising esport odds for Invictus versus ViCi.

www.twitch.tv

1.21
Twitch logo
Twitch is an online live video-streaming channel established in 2011. Primarily focused on video games it specialises in competitive gaming and *Let's Play* formats.

INTERVIEW
STUART SAW

• •

European Regional Director, EMEA at Twitch TV and esports shout caster Stuart Saw aka The Stupot, discusses esports and the future of streaming live gameplay.

Is Twitch's aim to attract prime time audiences, who would normally watch live sporting events such as football matches, by offering viewers the opportunity to watch online games such as Invictus play NaVi?

It's been available on TV before, Sky has run content on their own channels and other channels such as Xleague have existed in the past. Ultimately though, it didn't work; TV scheduling didn't suit esports so I can't imagine it will take off on TV again any time soon. I could be wrong, and I know that a number of TV executives are looking at the numbers on Twitch with interest, but the practicalities of the content hold it back from going into TV, at least in the UK.

Our goal is to be ubiquitously available for both broadcasters and viewers across all devices, you can see that via our mobile apps and via our console integration. We've recently integrated into Amazon Fire, which is the next area of growth for us, but where that ends up is still to be decided.

Is traditional media becoming another dead technology? What does the future look like to Twitch?

There's a place for all the technologies, Twitch represents a seismic shift in consumption trends, as people engage for longer periods of time in digital native content. However, look at the rise of HBO and the concept that we're in TV's greatest era right now for content. I cannot foresee a massive convergence any time soon that renders one technology obsolete for multiple reasons, ad revenue being a key factor.

Science and Gaming

Human–computer interaction was born out of academic research in the 1950s. The practice of using computer games to define and model ideas, scientific propositions continues. The flexibility to construct and iterate within gaming environments has proven to be a useful platform for training, testing ideas and exploring theoretical discussion. This is evident in training simulations such as serious games (for more on serious games see Game Engines page 93 and Games Imitate Life page 113). Commercially, training simulations are commonly used in aviation, such as pilot training. In addition, the virtual-reality training of surgeons for medical procedures is on the increase.

The video game industry has been at the forefront of providing adaptable technology that can be molded to explore multivariate results (i.e. results involving two or more variable quantities) or initiate meaning. *Sokobond* (2013) by Draknek is an elegantly realized puzzle game, which utilizes the symbols found in chemistry, a visualization of the periodic table as the main game mechanic, the checkerboard layout resembling the grid form of many board games.

Another example of science and gaming is the MIT Media Lab's (Massachusetts Institute of Technology) use of gaming environments. It has been exploring the physics theory of relativity to conceive an open source game called *A Slower Speed of Light*, in a first person prototype.

VISUAL EFFECTS OF SPECIAL RELATIVITY GRADUALLY BECOME APPARENT TO THE PLAYER, INCREASING THE CHALLENGE OF GAMEPLAY. THESE EFFECTS, RENDERED IN REAL TIME TO VERTEX ACCURACY, INCLUDE THE DOPPLER EFFECT (RED- AND BLUE-SHIFTING OF VISIBLE LIGHT, AND THE SHIFTING OF INFRARED AND ULTRAVIOLET LIGHT INTO THE VISIBLE SPECTRUM); THE SEARCHLIGHT EFFECT (INCREASED BRIGHTNESS IN THE DIRECTION OF TRAVEL); TIME DILATION (DIFFERENCES IN THE PERCEIVED PASSAGE OF TIME FROM THE PLAYER AND THE OUTSIDE WORLD); LORENTZ TRANSFORMATION (WARPING OF SPACE AT NEAR-LIGHT SPEEDS); AND THE RUNTIME EFFECT (THE ABILITY TO SEE OBJECTS AS THEY WERE IN THE PAST, DUE TO THE TRAVEL TIME OF LIGHT).

MIT Media Lab, description of *A Slower Speed of Light*

1.22–1.23
A Slower Speed of Light
A Slower Speed of Light is a physics concept-based game, a first person prototype. It combines fantasy gameplay with theoretical computational and physics research. It was created using OpenRelativity, an open-source toolkit for the Unity game development environment.

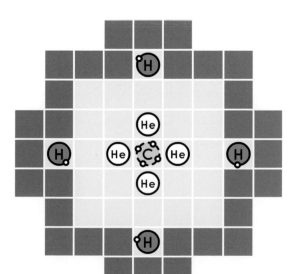

1.24
Sokobond
Sokobond has been praised for its ability to teach the player about molecule structures and is an award-winning indie puzzle game based on the laws of chemistry. The puzzle image shown in 1.24 contains the elements He: helium; H: hydrogen; C: carbon. *Sokobond* is similar to *SpaceChem*, which combines logic-driven problems found in computer programming with the science of chemistry.

GAME GENRES

Video game genres can refer to individual styles of gameplay and/or to a particular game design mechanic that is distinct from other genres. Most often game genres are not pure breeds, but are instead hybrids with many overlapping traits. This fluidity is observed in many transmedia formats, and most widely recognized in feature films, when narrative and genre styles are combined to maximize the viewer's immersion in the story and aid the suspension of disbelief. This section explores the video game genres currently dominating the gaming world. It will discuss the most commonly understood definitions but should not be considered definitive. The categorization of video games is a live subject of study and as technology develops, new genres will emerge.

1.25
Hitman: Absolution
This is the fifth title in the Hitman franchise. Produced by IO Interactive, these are third person shooter games about an elite assassin. The franchise's popularity has led to two Hollywood movies.

First Person or FPS

Denoted by a first person perspective, these games are experienced through the primary character's eyes or POV (point of view). First person is most commonly associated with shooting games, hence the term "First Person Shooter" (FPS), and routinely provides the player with a close-up view of their game character's hand or hands holding weapons and gadgets that, along with other game objects, can be utilized, collected, upgraded, and traded.

Context

Although the genre dates back thirty years to Nintendo's *Duck Hunt* (1984), it really took off during the 1990s with classic PC-based games such as *Doom, Castle Wolfenstein* and *Quake*. It then made a very successful move into the console market—exclusively on the N64—with the classic *GoldenEye 007* (1997).

CONTEMPORARY EXAMPLES: *Far Cry; Call of Duty; Battlefield; Killzone; Crysis; Counter Strike; Halo*

Third Person

The third person genre is defined by seeing the whole of the player character or avatar from a 2D (two dimensional) or 3D perspective. The game camera can follow from behind, above or the side from variable distances, allowing the player to observe the character being controlled. In some games, the external view of the avatar or vehicle can occupy around a third of the screen, but in others such as 2D platformers, the avatar may be very small. Some games allow the player to switch between various POVs of their choosing, first, third, and top down. Third-person games can cover a wide range of subgenres including shooting, fighting, adventure, maze, and platform games.

Context

The vast majority of games could be loosely classified as third person. The origin of third-person view could be linked back to *Tennis for Two* (see A Brief History of Video Games) in its simplest top down form. More familiar iterations of this concept are found in arcade classics such as *Space Invaders, Asteroids, Galaxian* and *Defender* as well as early transformat games (arcade, console, handheld) like Nintendo's *Donkey Kong*. This popular genre style continues to be explored in both 2D and 3D varieties. *Assassin's Creed* is a good contemporary example of a third-person player view that is used to negotiate the storylines.

CONTEMPORARY EXAMPLES: *The Division; Infamous: Second Son; DMC; Brothers: A Tale of Two Sons; Assassin's Creed; Hitman; Gears of War; Metal Gear Solid; L.A. Noire; God of War; Mario Kart*

Fighting Games

Fighting games are often referred to as "beat 'em ups." Usually a one- or two-player game that has arcade style action, which can be played against the computer, but also in partnership with other players, or against individual, or multiple human competitors. They are often based in an arena or single location, or alternatively force players along a fixed scrolling direction that leads the player to their next opponent(s).

Context

Beat 'em ups have been an enduring gaming genre since the 1980s. The most influential titles such as *Street Fighter 2* (1991), *Mortal Kombat* (1992), and *Soul Calibur* (1998), were all originally released on arcade machines before moving to consoles. These genre-defining titles featured distinct graphic styles, gore, and significantly the use of increasingly complex control combinations and sequences to achieve special moves. The desire for novelty titles has seen a range of new games riding the wave of interest created by blockbuster films based on graphic novels. A pre-existing lexicon of comic characters have led to games such as the DC Universe's multi-combo drenched *Injustice: Gods Among Us* (2013).

CONTEMPORARY EXAMPLES: *Mortal Kombat; Injustice: Gods Among Us; Fist of the North Star; Tekken; Street Fighter; Arcana Hearts; Soul Calibur; Marvel vs. Capcom*

Strategy: RTS/A-RTS

Defined by the point of view of a virtual god "from above," these games require players to manage the creation, collection, and allocation of resources, using them to defeat one or more opponents. Often played over long periods of game time, in-game assets such as technology, characters, units, abilities, and even buildings become available in real time, as the game progresses. These types of games can be turn-based, or played in real time—hence the acronym RTS (real-time strategy)—as the world around the player(s) evolves, or they can be a mixture of both. Thematically, players may have to build civilizations, armies, or squads that they then command in an effort to conquer lands and overthrow empires. Games such as the historical *Total War* series combine both turn-based and RTS elements to great gameplaying effect.

Action Real-time Strategy (A-RTS) games share the continuous gameplay attributes of RTS but without the resource management aspect (see the MOBA genre section, page 43).

Context

The god game definition is linked to this genre, being another form of RTS. A British video game developer, Peter Molyneux was the originator of the god game. In 1989, he created the game *Populous* with his fledgling games company Bullfrog Productions. Bullfrog was bought by EA in the mid-1990s, Molyneux went on to lead Lionhead Studios and subsequently 22Cans, where he continues to design and rethink the god game with *Godus*. (See Resurrection Mode page 177.)

CONTEMPORARY EXAMPLES: *Civilization; Command & Conquer; Total War; Crusader Kings; StarCraft; Black and White*

1.26–1.27
Monument Valley
Multidisciplinary
digital production
studio ustwo created
the impossible
geometry puzzle
game *Monument
Valley*. This BAFTA
award-winning game
is featured in season
3 of the Netflix series
House of Cards.

Puzzle

Puzzle games are identified by puzzle solving
activities that can, amongst other things, test
logic, memory, knowledge, and sensory sensitivity.
Gameplay can frequently be under time pressure
and can be experienced through many different
gaming scenarios, some bite sized and others far
more immersive. The look and game style can be
bright and colorful, with matching sound effects,
such as *Candy Crush Saga* (2012) with its sweet
shop fantasy graphic style, or woven into stories
full of ambiance and mystery where the player
needs to understand complex narrative links to
solve and conclude the game as found in *Gone
Home* (2013) or *The Witness* (2014). Sub-genres
include physics based puzzle games, often set in
cartoon landscapes, such as *World of Goo* (2008).
Brain training games and apps are another part
of the puzzle game genre.

Context

With the developments in 3D graphics in the 1990s,
landmark point and click puzzle adventure games
such as *Myst* (1993) gained prominence. *Myst* was
designed and created by brothers Robyn and Rand
Miller (now known as Cyan Inc.) who have returned
to the puzzle led narrative twenty years later with a
new mystery adventure, *Obduction*. Smart, touch-
screen devices have been important in the rise of
new types of puzzle games like quizzes, such as *2
Player Reactor*, which focus on the player's reaction
time to questions.

CONTEMPORARY EXAMPLES: *Monument Valley;
Gone Home; Machinarium and Samorost; The Witness;
The Room; Tetris; Candy Crush Saga; Eeets Munchies;
Professor Layton; Dr Kawashima's Brain Training*

Sandbox/Open World

Sandbox or open world is a non-linear, free roaming gameplay environment where the player can choose to discover and interact with any part of the whole gaming world. It references a time in childhood of free, imaginative play, and unhindered creativity. Sandbox games allow the player to experience the game and problem solving in a non-linear narrative approach.

The first game that can be defined as a sandbox game is *Elite*. This ground-breaking game was originally released in 1984 by Acornsoft for the BBC Micro. This was the first example of a sandbox game where it was possible for the player to explore the star systems of our universe, and to trade, purchase system upgrades, and fight other spacecraft to steal their cargo. This genre is closely related to the Massively Multiplayer Online (MMO) format, and more recently, an increasing number of RPGs, formerly known for their linear game structures, allow the player to define and organize their own experiences within the game. This genre

is utilized in a variety of formats from indie handheld games to blockbuster AAA titles on the main consoles.

Context

A common feature of many open world games is the development of crafting tools as a key game mechanic. Crafting allows the player to either develop new or improved tools from found objects as well as manipulate or redefine the game environment. This is not exclusively employed in the open world context as other game genres such as RPG, 2D side scrolling games have utilized this sourcing/making process to enhance gameplay.

CONTEMPORARY EXAMPLES: *GTA: Grand Theft Auto; Skyrim; Minecraft; Rust; DayZ; Terraria; Don't Starve; Project Zomboid*

MMO/MMORPG

MMO stands for massively multiplayer online. This can also be referred to as MMORPG, combining a role-playing game element. MMO is one of the great gaming phenomena of the twenty-first century, being played concurrently from PCs, consoles and smart devices by vast numbers of players from a multitude of locations and time zones. Players control a character that can be improved over time as they complete missions and quests. Worlds, levels and game data are persistent, being hosted on remote servers.

Context

Huge sandbox games such as *World of Warcraft* (WoW; 2004) or *Elder Scrolls online* (2014) can engender a significant obsessive following where players can invest months or years of their life in an attempt to build a legendary online avatar; leveling up or increasing their powers to be a dominant force in the game world. The value of these leveled up avatars can be realized in the physical world. Entrepreneurial players have sold their WOW character online identities, built up over years, for significant sums of real world currency on websites such as eBay.

CONTEMPORARY EXAMPLES: *Elder Scrolls; World of Warcraft; Diablo; Guild Wars; EVE online; Elite; Dangerous; Final Fantasy; EverQuest; Second Life*

MOBA

MOBA stands for multiplayer online battle arena. This genre traces its roots back to the late 1990s and a customized *Starcraft* map called Aeon of Strife. MOBA games such as *League of Legends* (2009) or Valve's hugely successful game *Dota*, (*Defence of the Ancients*) utilizes a specific gaming mechanic: the standard gaming map is defined by a three lane attack or defense system emanating from both ends of the level map to a central battleground. A-RTS is connected to and part of this genre.

Context

The format of this game type is popular enough to feature in huge international esport tournaments (see Twenty-First-Century Gaming: Esports page 34, Crowdfunding page 174, and People Power page 175), commanding massive stadium audiences that would normally be associated with large sporting events or concerts. The top teams enjoy a level of celebrity and notoriety that can only be compared to the status of pop stars. Top players can earn huge sums from winning video game tournaments.

CONTEMPORARY EXAMPLES: *League of Legends; Dota; Starcraft; Diablo; Heroes of the Storm; Marvel Heroes; Heroes of Newerth*

RPG—Adventure

As we've already seen, RPG stands for role-playing game, a genre where the player takes on a specific character within the game. For example, in *BioShock Infinite* (2013) the player assumes the role of the main protagonist Booker DeWitt throughout the game. Other RPGs allow the player to play more than one character i.e. the *Ratchet & Clank* series, to enable the completion of tasks by either character, may be defined by size or skills. Alternatively, titles such as the *Fable* series allow the player to make choices, which define or alter the course of the games and the character's development in the gaming world. Non-playable characters or NPCs may then treat your in game character differently because of the choices made, leading to consequences in the game world such as the decision to help an NPC, or to attack, and steal from them.

Context

The acronym RPG predates much of what we know of modern computer games, as role-playing in a fictional interactive narrative has existed for some time in tabletop forms such as *Dungeons and Dragons* or Warhammer as well as live action scenarios known as LARP since the 1970s.

CONTEMPORARY EXAMPLES: *The Last of Us; Tomb Raider: The Final Hours; Dishonored; BioShock; Tearaway; The Shadow of Colossus*

Side Scrolling/Platform

Initially defined by its flat 2D movement and appearance, side scrolling or platform is defined by the width of the screen space and platform structures (things you can jump on in the game narrative to negotiate the gaming landscape). This was one of the earliest genres to be established in the 1980s, just as the first computers and consoles began producing legendary games like *Manic Miner* and *Chucky Egg* (see also the fighting games genre on page 40).

Context

Game franchises such as Mario have embodied this game style, which has evolved to include hybrid incarnations switching between 2D and 3D realizations of the side scrolling platformer from games like *Viewtiful Joe* through to puzzle games playing with the user's expectations of space such as *Fez*.

CONTEMPORARY EXAMPLES: *Limbo; Super Meat Boy; Braid; Little Big Planet; Zombality; Sonic The Hedgehog; Donkey Kong; Under the Ocean; Super Mario Brothers*

1.29
TS 2015: Train Simulator
Developed by UK-based Dovetail Games. The New York to New Haven journey is one of the many real-world routes to be simulated.

Simulation or Sim

Simulation or sim is a prevalent gaming genre, existing largely within the PC gaming scene. Sims can focus on vehicle simulation, management and construction, and even life cycles and evolution, as typified in the game *Spore* (2008). It is based on a natural and accurate representation of the world or a specific aspect of the real world.

Context

Flight sims have been a typical and enduring part of this genre i.e. accurately flying a plane using real world information in a virtual computer generated (CG) cockpit. Many other simulated real world but more mundane subject matter (compared to the mainstream of video games) have been adopted over time. Being based on reality, they are informative in a way that games based on fantasy are not, and have a strong enthusiasts support base.

CONTEMPORARY EXAMPLES: *OMSI 2 (bus sim); Car Mechanic; TS 2015: Train Simulator (see image 1.29); Bridge Project; Professional Farmer; Ski Region Simulator; Surgeon Simulator; Euro Truck; Open Sea Fishing; Bear Simulator*

Racing

Racing games, like many other gaming genres, can cross over or combine several genres i.e. role-playing games, sim and so on. From high-octane arcade style racers, to playful character-based family multiplayers or super realistic, near-impossible to steer racing simulations, this genre has been one of the enduring game types. Vehicle customization has become a key component of many contemporary driving games.

Context

The genre stems from the 1970s ultra minimal black and white arcade classic *Death Race 2000* (1976). The vibrant full color Sega arcade favorite, *Turbo* in 1981 predates Namco's huge arcade hit *Pole Position* released in 1982, which went on to be one of the highest grossing arcade games of that time.

CONTEMPORARY EXAMPLES: *The Crew; Forza Motorsport; Gran Turismo; Mario Kart; F1; Race Driver: Grid; Sonic All Star Racing; SSX; Burnout Paradise; MotorStorm; Need For Speed; F-Zero X*

Sports Sim

Another genre with an extremely devoted following is the sports sim. Sports games are divided into two main camps. They are either a serious real world sim (football for example) where you can play your favorite team in the latest club kit or the gaming world can be one that is a playful caricature of a fantastical reality.

Context

Advances in gaming technology are enabling real-time rendering techniques of in-game content such as visibly increased amounts of polygons at sustained high frame rates, such as sixty frames per second (FPS). The sports sim is an example of this, offering stunning levels of realism which begin to produce an Uncanny Valley effect. Attention to detail, stadium atmosphere, and stylized commentary all blend to create the engaging sensation of a live sports event.

Other kinds of sports game are often visually extravagant and humorous such as the *SSX* snowboarding series. Titles such as these seek to explore a sporting fantasy, where a larger than life sports experience is more about task-based adventure, over the top sporting prowess and high scores from arcade style combos. These attributes are prized over realism.

CONTEMPORARY EXAMPLES: *FIFA; NBA 2K; Madden NFL 25; SSX; Wii Sports Resort; UFC; Table Tennis; Football Manager*

KEY TERM

UNCANNY VALLEY

Defined in 1970 by Japanese roboticist Masahiro Mori, the term "uncanny valley" can be applied to CG characters and robots that look almost but not quite human, producing an eerie, or uncanny, effect. The "valley" refers to the dip in a graph mapping viewers' responses to humanoid characters. Initially, positive responses increase as characters appear more human, but they then drop off dramatically as viewers are repulsed by an uncanny "animated corpse" effect in not-quite-human characters. As the characters get even closer to a believable human, viewer's revulsion recedes and positive responses return – forming the upward side of the "valley" in a graph.

CHAPTER REVIEW

This chapter has presented and challenged ideas about the origins of gameplay, the history of computer games and how games are made. The chapter focuses on the importance of game mechanics having an ancient past and that board game concepts are at the heart of many contemporary video game genres. The chapter also investigates the origins of modern computer games, the ascension of gaming technology and how it has transformed from niche activity to the center ground of global culture.

Key Points

THE ORIGINS OF PLAY: Examining the origins and structures of board games provides us with a deeper understanding of the origins of modern game mechanics. These mechanics have evolved, undergoing a transformation through cultural exchange. In history, we see gameplay as both a pastime and a teaching tool, sharing knowledge from one generation to another.

INDUSTRY OVERVIEW: Outlining how games are made and who makes them. Game genres and their respective game mechanics provide the game designer with a common framework to create new content. Games companies work with hierarchies and structured roles. These highlight a variety of possible career paths within the video games industry.

A BRIEF HISTORY OF VIDEO GAMES: The emergence of new electronic technology in the twentieth century saw the birth of human–computer interaction and was instrumental in laying the foundations of gaming technology. This chapter explored the unique period of innovation and imagination of the latter half of the twentieth century, when pioneers established the games industry through academic research, as well as through experiments in arcade and home entertainment. Knowing what has passed and what has been accomplished in the past provides perspective and context to the study of the contemporary games industry.

TWENTY-FIRST-CENTURY PERSPECTIVES: New directions and development cycles enable us to see and speculate about the future trends of game design. In a post-Internet culture (defined by the generations born after and growing up in an Internet saturated digital culture), transmedia franchises utilize multiple media outcomes to attract a wider audience, increase market share and maximize profits.

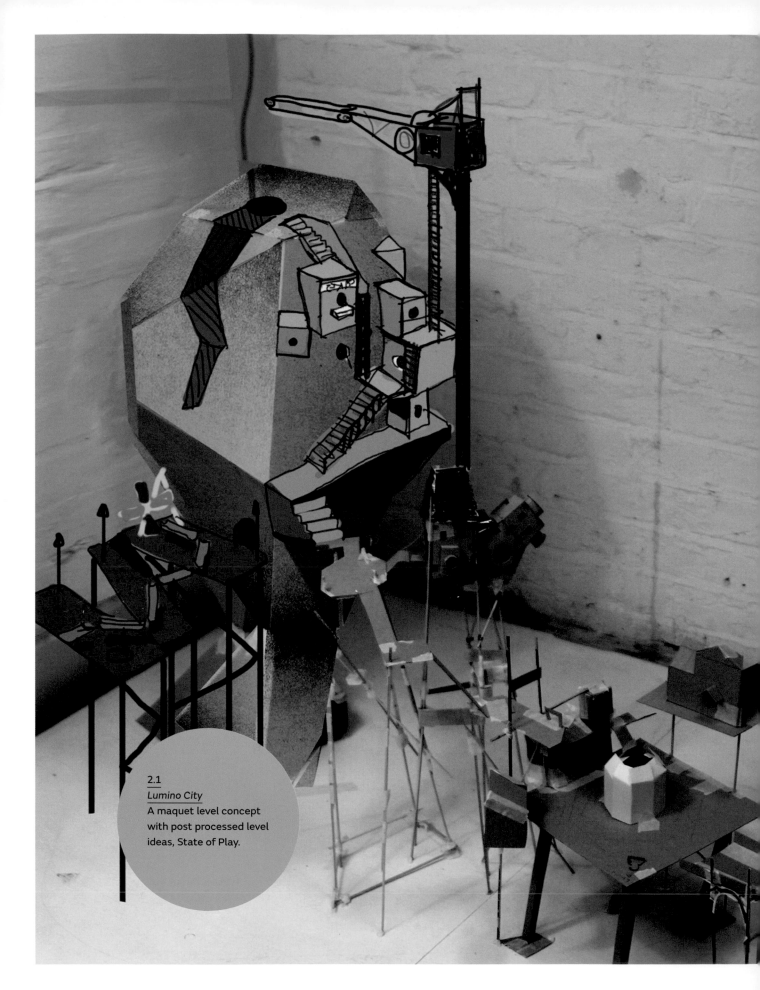

2.1
Lumino City
A maquet level concept
with post processed level
ideas, State of Play.

2

WHO MAKES GAMES?

TOPICS COVERED
Team Insight / Recruitment Agencies /
Graduate to Developer / Legal Advice

049

Whether you are working on your own, in a small indie team, or in the open-plan offices of a multinational company, a range of skills is needed to produce video games. Like any feature film, the credits of many contemporary video games can sometimes list hundreds of people who collaborated in their production. This chapter is an examination of the roles, structures, and workflows within traditional studios and the wider industry.

TEAM INSIGHT

Roles

Teamwork is a fundamental component of video game creation, and it is a vital skill to nurture and develop. Individuals who can communicate effectively, work well in teams as well as alone, and demonstrate an intrinsic motivation for creating video games, are valuable assets in any studio.

We cannot explore all the variants and multiplicities of team composition and dynamics, but in this chapter we aim to give an overview of core structures and associated roles. It is worth noting that as the scale of a company increases, there is greater capacity for niche specialist roles within project teams, as the demand for skills expands based on the technical difficulty and complexity of the title in development.

The following breakdown of roles is not exhaustive, but the explanations indicate the potential variety of roles within a games company. The list will vary depending on the size of the company. For example, in a small indie setting an individual may be required to perform several of these job functions, and, therefore, may have overall more of an influential role in a project. By comparison, if you are working on an AAA game for three or four years, for a large company of 200 employees, then you may find that you work in a very specific, highly specialized role, and are not heavily involved in other parts of the content.

GAMES COMPANY TEAM SET-UP

This simplified diagram outlines the hierarchy and pathways of a company, but any of these pathways can have many sub-specialists. For example, within a programming team you can have several sub-roles managing the various parts of development such as a software engineer; tools, software engineer; engine, software engineer; gameplay interfaces, software engineer; gameplay animation and so on. Each of these roles will have specific responsibilities for the project, reporting to their respective senior software engineer.

In addition to this, there are many roles that sit outside the core team that communicate and interact with it at specific points in the development process, such as QA testing, middleware programmers or voice artists. These roles provide specific skills that may be required and are often contract-based work rather than full-time posts. Sometimes these additional processes are essential for a game's success.

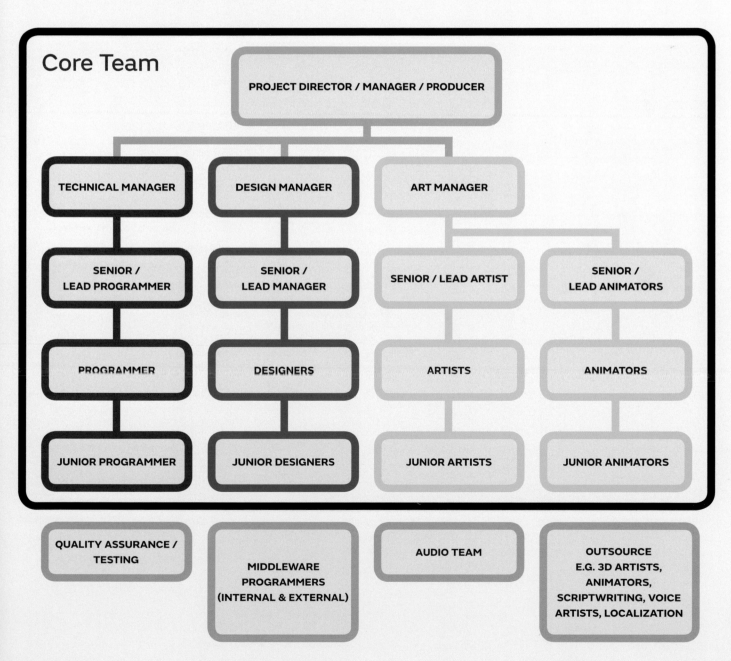

Producer

The producer sits at the head of the team and the success of the project rests on that individual's shoulders. Producers are principally concerned with process logistics: ensuring that the game is developed in the agreed timescale, managing the overall game delivery process with budget oversight, and team management. (See the interview with Dylan Beale on page 56.)

Creative Director

The creative director steers the creative vision of the project. This person oversees high-level decisions regarding the game's development as he or she has an understanding of the project as a whole. The creative director works closely with the lead designers and programmers. This role requires good communication skills with an ability to inspire excellence across the team, and possibly across multiple projects.

Writer

The role of the writer overlaps with the lead designer. This individual is responsible for the overall story, developing character arcs, dialogue, scripting cutscenes as well as any other text used throughout the game, i.e. tutorials and in-depth descriptions, UI (user interface) menus.

Game Designer

This dynamic position requires a specific focus, not unlike a conductor guiding all the parts of an orchestra, game designers must be able to understand how to lead the audience through the narrative structures. It is a challenging role full of contradictory demands; balancing game mechanics with the expectations of the game that you want to make, to the game you can make, all within the project's timescale. This role overlaps with that of the creative director, writer, and level designer.

Lead Level Designer

Once a game has an established narrative and blueprint, the lead level designer contributes throughout the iterative design process, where the game evolves and development leads to change. The design is fine-tuned. In this role, the designer must have an established technical knowledge of the whole development process, and be able to discern what is and what is not possible during production.

Level Designer

The level designer, mission designer and level editor define the architecture of the game campaign, enhance game flow, develop kill zone strategies for NPCs, object asset placement and so on. The designer will work closely with the lead designer, artificial intelligence (AI) programmers, and level artists.

Lead Programmer

The lead programmer is responsible for all aspects of programming required to create the game. This role is critical in the creation process with immense responsibility and requires specialist knowledge and skills. This person works closely with the producer and manages the specialist programming teams (tools, engine, AI and graphics). The lead is responsible for implementing the game design concept across a wide variety of elements, developing new tools for each aspect of the game. The programming tools most commonly used are C++, Python and Make. Programmers are also expected to be good at math. (See the interview with John McCarten on page 64.)

Tools Programmer

Tools programmers are responsible for developing custom software tools to make the game development easier. These may differ from project to project and will cover a range of bespoke needs, smoothing out day-to-day issues and enabling the team to produce focused work. They work with networked systems, efficient and networked data structures, and user interface (UI) design.

Engine Programmer

Engine programmers work on the core technology upon which the rest of the system depends. This deals with background file loaders, debugging menus, profiling routines, application program interface (API) design, parallel software design, and scheduling, and other duties covering critical systems.

AI Programmer

AI programmers add intelligence to the game. They ensure that the built-in opponents appear to be interacting intelligently, whilst writing efficient code that does not diminish the game frame rate and slow down the gameplay. They are responsible for routing and navigation algorithms, implementing psychology, message passing, game physics—how players interact within the game environment—and optimization strategies.

Graphics Programmer

Graphics programmers work with the hardware to add polish to the game. This role undertakes the development work for high dynamic range rendering, optimization techniques, the application of physics for particle behavior, depth of field processes, vertex and pixel shaders, floating point textures and color blending theory to create seamless visuals throughout the game.

TOP TIPS FOR BUDDING GAMES ENTREPRENEURS

Ian Livingstone CBE

Games industry veteran, co-founder of Games Workshop and Creative Industries Champion

01 Do not be afraid of failure. Failure is success work-in-progress.

02 Retain ownership of your intellectual property. Try to avoid trading it away for project finance.

03 Do what you are good at. Partner with somebody to do the stuff that you do not want to do.

04 Make yourself investor-ready by ensuring you have a well-prepared presentation before asking for investor money.

05 As people say, get some "skin in the game" [invest some of your own money] to demonstrate that you are invested in your own ideas.

06 Ideas are cheap. It's the execution of the idea that is the hard bit.

07 Be yourself and follow your heart. Try not to be a "me-too" person.

08 Hard work and sacrifice should be seen as a positive part of the journey.

09 Listen to everybody and treat people well.

10 Enjoy what you do, or do something else.

Games Artist

Games artist is a broad term covering several roles. Games artists have become more specialist as the industry has matured, each art discipline having different requirements. These are split between 3D and 2D digital outcomes; see the terms below.

3D Modeler and Texture Artist

These roles vary depending on the studio or project's needs. They can be two separate positions in a company depending on its size. The work can range from creating in-game objects, to character modeling, and 3D scenery realization. This is achieved using software packages such as 3D Studio Max, Maya, Softimage, Cinema 4D and others. Often working from concept art, the artists create the model or asset and the subsequent texture maps. (See the interview with David Bowman on page 68.)

Animator

The role of animator can be divided into several animation specialisms: character, cutscene, rigging, scenic and motion capture. Animators are constantly learning new techniques to achieve the highest quality within the game. They are responsible for visualizing convincing physical movements that convey emotion and conviction. A character animator's main duty is to create a range of in-game animations for specific characters and actions. These actions are blended and combined to create fluid movements responding to the in-game action and interaction. Tasks include run and walk cycles, character fidgets, melee and ranged attacks, defense moves, and lip-syncing animation for cutscenes. They are also responsible for animating virtual cameras with a directorial focus on storytelling. Animators also produce scene animations made up of non-character based elements. (See the interview with Will du Toit, page 62.)

Animation Rigger

Animation riggers or character riggers have a challenging role that involves problem solving. Riggers are assigned tasks based on manipulating geometry and environment interactions. A laborious process, this requires precision and an eye for detail for creating skeletal bone structures within 3D meshes to animate specific parts. This can include facial rigging. They collaborate with 3D modelers and animators to refine the animation process and outcomes.

Concept Artist

The concept artist's role is to realize the narrative concept into a visual form, creating the style of the game. It is usually a 2D role, typically working on character, or environment, or asset design. The artwork is passed on to the production team. This person needs to be a skilled artist with exceptional drawing ability, and a vivid imagination, as well as being a good communicator within an iterative design process. Rendering skills in both traditional and digital mediums are a prerequisite.

Environment Artist

Environment artists or modelers are responsible for creating scenery, vehicles, architectural and general 3D assets, as well as color, texturing, and lighting the game environment. They work closely with concept designers, level designers, and the broader design team to realize the immersive experience of the game world. (See the interview with Karen Stanley on page 74.)

Technical Artist

This role bridges the gap between the art and programming teams. It can be a role that has progressed from either discipline. And it works with both game aesthetics, and the underlying technology of the game engine. The role will vary from company to company. It will include tasks such as plug-in creation, script creation, VFX implementation, hardware shader creation, and art asset creation.

VFX Artist

VFX artists create special effects for the game. They require strengths in texture creation and an understanding of particle systems, as well as geometry effects, whilst working within the technical restrictions of the hardware. These creative specialists work closely with the programmers to achieve stunning visual effects.

GUI Artist

GUI stands for graphic user interface, pronounced "gooey." These artists often come from a background in graphic design. Their responsibilities include the menu system (front end), in-game HUD (heads up display) and elements such as score, health and ammo graphics.

Render Wrangler

Render wranglers are responsible for supervising, monitoring, and controlling the rendering process of CGI (computer generated imagery) often via a group of networked computers devoted to rendering images, known as a "render farm." They are involved at various stages of the design process, performing a variety of tests, i.e. lighting effects, pre-visualization, and final animated scenes. They work closely with animators and compositors.

Audio Designer

Audio designers are responsible for all manner of sound creation within the game. These range from voice recording and editing, musical composition for interactive scores, level soundscapes, Foley sound FX, as well as working with voice-over artists and actors for scripted cutscenes. They need good communication skills, and work closely with the other teams to ensure that the audio functions correctly within the specific aspects of the game environment. They use either in-house tools or third-party hardware and software.

QA/Testers

The Quality Assurance or QA team works closely with the development team. They are primarily responsible for testing the functionality of a game to ensure it plays and looks as intended. Through many hours of gameplay, game testers search for defects and glitches, commonly referred to as "bugs." When they find them, they must establish what steps are required to repeat the problem and document them in a detailed written report that contains all relevant information about what was happening at the time the bug manifested itself, e.g. level, playable character, NPCs, and object interaction. Game testers need to be methodical and organized, generate and implement test plans, know the game design well, and employ good communication skills whilst making constructive suggestions for improvement.

Localization

The localization process oversees and ensures the game is effectively converted and delivered for audiences and regions in a global market, i.e. language translation. This is an essential part of the process, focusing on maximizing the game product for international sales.

ON THE OTHER SIDE OF THE SCREEN, IT ALL LOOKS SO EASY.
Jeff Bridges as Kevin Flynn
Tron, 1982

INTERVIEW
DYLAN BEALE

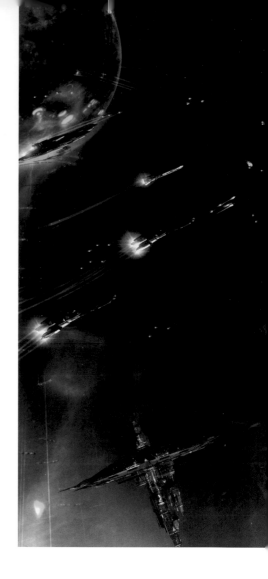

• •

Industry role: Dylan Beale is Chief Production Officer for Born Ready Games and Edge Case Games. He works on games such as *Strike Suit Zero* and *Fractured Space*. He discusses the importance of team dynamics and resource management in an independent games company.

Can you describe your role as a chief production officer and discuss some effective project management practices?

My role is to make sure everything runs smoothly, everyone's happy and no one's feeling constrained. If you're a small indie team and you've got one person who is not able to do the job, the knock on effect is bad. You need a well-oiled machine.

If someone were thinking about going into a production role in games, a multitude of skills are needed, including an overall ability to step back and assess a variety of situations. If there's a problem, how can we solve it? That's the key, knowing when there are not enough resources. Knowing when to say no to a task, preventing feature creep and knowing when feature creep is a good thing.

At the end of every cycle, such as a two-week sprint, you have time to review, see what went well and what went badly. You assess what needs to be fixed and how to continue what you are doing well. Over time you should get better and better.

The scrum concept is based on the premise that a backer is paying for the game, or that someone is in charge of the game project. They specify "I want this," and the product owner (games company) calculates what will be needed, for example: one animator, one artist, one concept artist, one designer, one programmer and a QA person to test that it all works. This unit then spends two weeks working together autonomously, which is important. The backer doesn't talk to them over the two weeks. If a team state that they can deliver, you have to trust them to complete the designated work in the two-week sprint.

At the end of the second week, the team delivers the best possible working version, which is then reviewed. The work may need some final adjustments before it can be signed off. It's a methodology; a way of working that has been taken up by most of the game studios around the world, large and small.

This differs from the old waterfall management method widely employed in the games industry,

which generated an atmosphere of persistent pressure. By contrast, an autonomous set of developers who are free from the immediate pressures of being constantly assessed, who self-manage, produce better results. It's all about ownership.

Project managers need to carefully consider the project and the team size needed. Also, who's paying, what they want and the timeline. If you're a four-man team creating an iPhone game, do you need to do a big waterfall project or a scrum project? Communication is essential as working remotely, away from a central studio, as well as working in small teams have become far more common. This can present various pitfalls concerning communication, although challenging, if you get the communication right, it can yield huge pluses as it allows people to focus without distraction.

2.2
Strike Suit Zero
Strike Suit Zero (Born Ready Games Ltd) was initially released on PC and Steam, ported to Linux, Mac, and Oculus, and then the Director's Cut was released on PS4 and Xbox One.

Has game design and project management changed over the last 20 years?

When thinking about project management, as a team, you have to think about the team size and about the project as a whole. How will it be released? Previously you had seven months to finish a game, you put it on a disk, released it and that was it, you never saw it again! It doesn't work like that anymore. You either have a game as a service, i.e. live online, which is the future, or a game is released, which then has multiple patches (download updates). The last stage of a game (tail) is much longer than it used to be. So considering the project and the team size before you start, can lead you to thinking about how you want your team to work and the processes behind it. This can change from project to project.

What scrum seeks to avoid, which is often found with work for hire projects punctuated by pre-set milestones, is that big list of things that need to be delivered by a certain date. It is a given that at every milestone it is impossible to deliver the agreed work. Inevitably things go wrong and when you get to the agreed milestone you end up negotiating with a third party whilst still hoping to get paid and promising more for the next milestone assessment.

Are sprint goals useful with small teams and does it help with the challenges of time management?

Short-term goals are much easier for people to focus on. Two weeks is the usual length of time for a sprint. If you're in a small team then weekly sprints are an option, but if you are going to do a proper scrum a lot of time is devoted to reviewing and planning, which can be problematic. We found that the optimal sprint cycle is two weeks.

Regular project review keeps everyone on track. Working with a two-week cycle is enough time to deliver something worthwhile. It allows for a day of review and a day of planning. That is two working days out of ten, leaving eight days to produce definable game content. On the Friday at the end of the two weeks, it is then presented to the team for comments. Everyone thinks about it over the weekend and on Monday, it is discussed with the group.

I try to build efficiencies into meetings, by timing them and by ensuring only the relevant people attend. I prevent unnecessary meetings. In a team design meeting, always have a chairperson, who can see that everyone is heard and has time to speak. Meeting management is critical; telling people in advance what the meeting is about enables them to think about their ideas and input beforehand.

2.3
Fractured Space
Currently in development by Edge Case Games, who are based in the gaming industry hub centered on Guildford, south east England. The game was initially released on early access via Steam.

What do you see as the main issues facing an effective team?

Email and mobile phones are very distracting in an office environment. One of my rules is that we try not to send emails at all in the studio unless it's work critical. Apparently, it takes twenty minutes for the creative mind to get back to where it was before the concentration was broken. We turn off the alerts and the sounds for text message and emails, so if you're working on a document, or a piece of animation, or code, you won't be disturbed.

KEY TERMS

BEAT
Effective rhythm of work.

BUILD
To create or compile a working version of the game or game level to be tested by the QA team.

IP
Intellectual property, referring to ownership or use of an original concept or idea.

MILESTONE
A defined period of time or point in a project often with a conditional deadline. Linked to work for hire project management.

QA TEAM
Quality assurance, this team reviews the game content stage by stage, ensuring that the game and assets work as they should.

SCRUM
A time separated out for a team meeting to discuss, assess, and set goals. Linked to sprint.

SPRINT
A defined period used to facilitate a positive cycle of focused work. These cycles are often measured in weeks to effectively manage and achieve project goals. Linked to scrum.

WATERFALL
Top-down style of project management, where the team or individuals are constantly assessed.

WORK FOR HIRE
A fixed contract style of project funding, where the milestone requirements are large and spread over longer periods of time than sprints, and have a fixed completion date.

TASK
SCRUM TEAM EXERCISES

● ●

Dylan Beale discusses the use of scrum ideology in the workplace, and how it has benefited individual and team workflows for Born Ready Games.

Scrum Lego

When initiating a scrum exercise you can see people falling into their preferred roles, working to their strengths. A creative person is going to sit at the table and build stuff. I'm not creative but I am good at design. What I do is supply them with whatever resources they want.

For the Scrum Lego we used 20 kilos (44lbs) of Lego to build a futuristic town defined by eight specific building types. We divided the group into four teams of five. We didn't think about the structure, or what the team demographic was, but we should have. Each sprint was eleven minutes long. The first sprint that we did was awful. By the fourth sprint everyone knew exactly what they had to do and deliver to complete the task.

The task starts with the product owner who commissions the project. The project manager or team leader, having listened to the product owner, then relays the details back to the team. The team then review the project plans. The project manager then supports the individual team members with resources so that they are not blocked in any way in completing their part of the task. For example, at the beginning of the task it is decided the game will be a 2D side-scrolling game and the player will be an egg. That is the criteria. It will be an iPhone game and the first playable date is set.

The ideal iterative scrum process would have milestones. A decision is made that it can be delivered. Anything else from that point is the iterative scrum process and everyone works together towards the first playable. What the first playable will look like, will be down to the team.

Team Task 1

Scrum LEGO

20 kilos (44lbs) of assorted Lego (or as much as you can get your hands on). Choose team leaders or project managers. Define teams of five: 1 x project manager, 4 x team members with varying skills. Each sprint is eleven minutes long, there will be four sprints in total.

01 Choose an individual to be the product owner i.e. the person who sets the task or theme. This could be a professor delivering the session, someone outside of the groups.

02 One member of the group of five will be designated as the project manager.

03 The product owner (or baker), sets the task, discussing it with the project managers i.e. design a small settlement on Mars, requesting some key features.

04 The project managers listen to the product owner describe their concept design. The managers then convey the task information in detail back to their respective team members.

05 The project manager guides the team: which involves allocation of tasks, resource management and overseeing the task to ensure an accurate, productive, and timely outcome is achieved within the eleven-minute sprint.

06 The product owner reviews the sprint outcomes with the individual teams, assessing what has worked and what has not for the next sprint.

Scrum Ping-Pong

This is a team working exercise designed to improve communication and efficiency. Carry out the exercise eight times, attempting to improve the technique in each attempt. At the end of the eight attempts, assess the difference between the first go and the last pass. In addition, the idea is to estimate how many Ping-Pong balls you will be able to cycle throughout the exercise. As each cycle happens, you can see how people organize and you can see people problem solving.

With each attempt, estimate how many balls can be effectively passed as the technique evolves and is enhanced. Did it work, review how it could be made better? Was the estimate accurate or did the team under or overestimate the task. Once you get to the end (of the balls) as long as you're counting and everybody has passed a ball, you can reuse the Ping-Pong ball.

By the final attempt the group should be problem solving, with strong teamwork and individual's taking their time. It should be metronomic, quiet and focused. It's about working to a beat, and doing it well. Making people think about efficiencies and processes.

> **"**
>
> **IF I WERE A TEACHER I WOULD BE REALLY KEEN TO TRY AND GET THIS INTO THE CURRICULUM.**
> Dylan Beale
>
> **"**

Team Task 2

Scrum Ping-Pong

A Ping-Pong ball passing game played amongst the entire team. Get as many Ping-Pong balls as you can while following the rules below:

01 All the balls have to be passed.

02 The player has to let go of the ball before passing it and the other person cannot touch the other team member at the same time.

03 Each ball has to go to each member of the group.

04 You are not allowed to pass to your immediate neighbor.

05 Each ball has to be returned to the person that it started with.

06 The task is to pass as many as you can in either one or two minutes.

07 Simply throw the balls to each other!

For our team it went like this:

FIRST PASS: We stood in two lines opposite each other and threw it diagonally and it was mental!

SECOND PASS: For the next round we tried having some people kneeling, i.e. can the body position be changed to improve the process.

THIRD PASS: Next we tried people picking up balls and dropping them into other people's hands, working diagonally.

FOURTH PASS: As above, up and down was tricky, so one line was standing up and the other kneeling down. And so on...

INTERVIEW
WILL DU TOIT

● ●

Industry role: Senior animator and 3D artist Will du Toit talks about flexible working practices for both AAA titles and working independently as a 3D artist.

Where are you currently working and on what kind of games?

I am currently working at IO Interactive in Copenhagen, Denmark. The company is known for producing the *Hitman* series of games as well as *Kane & Lynch*, *Mini Ninjas* amongst others. My current role is senior animator on an unannounced game title for next gen consoles. I have also held the role of principal gameplay animator on the most recent release from IO, *Hitman: Absolution*.

Working on long- and short-term projects or contracts, can you describe the benefits and pitfalls of working as a freelance digital artist?

The real benefit of working as a freelancer is that you are better paid and you get the chance to work on multiple projects over a short period. This will give you a new, fresh showreel every few months, which will greatly improve your chances of landing the next job.

As a freelancer, you will usually get paid by the hour, sometimes by the day. You can also get paid more for working extra hours at a different pay rate, usually 1.5 times your usual rate. This will depend on what was negotiated in your work contract. This means that for every hour you work over the eight-hour work day you will get 1.5 times your hourly rate for each extra hour worked. In contrast, full-time employees never get paid overtime in the games industry, despite always having to work extended periods of overtime. The full-time employees do get additional benefits, which is why better pay is usually given to freelancers to compensate them for the lack of wider benefits.

When you work on many short-term projects, shifting employers regularly does mean that you

will probably have to move around the country, or around the world to follow where the work is. If you like traveling that might be the perfect kind of job, but it's not for everyone. There is an alternative to having to move around as a freelancer. New working methods like remote working are becoming more common in the games industry, which allow you to work from your home or an office of your choosing while still contributing to a project based in another city or country.

Transferable skills: can you expand on how your career as a digital artist within the games industry has enabled you to work and create in other areas?

The real benefit of the games industry is that it takes a team of many very talented people with very different skills to make one game. This means that you have access to all kinds of specialized knowledge from experts every day you are at work. I try to take advantage of this by learning as much as I can from my colleagues who have this experience and knowledge. I do that by asking as many questions as my colleagues can endure. Since the games industry is a technology driven industry, there are always discussions going on about the latest technology and techniques, which are a great opportunity for learning new skills too.

For example, I became interested in 3D printing about two years ago and started asking the character artists how to build things in ZBrush for 3D printing. As experts, they helped me get up to speed with that skill faster than if I was just trying to learn it on my own. Later, once I had some 3D printed characters on my desk, some colleagues saw them and wanted to know more about my process and in that way I could pass on what I had learned to them. So, it can be a two-way learning experience.

What key pieces of industry advice do you have for students wanting to enter the games industry as a digital artist or animator?

Animation in the games industry is still primarily focused on action and therefore very good body mechanics is an essential skill to have to get into the industry. For the past few years, the industry has started to shift in the way that animation is delivered into the game engines. Before the PlayStation 3 generation of consoles, the animation pipeline would be like this: you created your animation in a piece of software like Maya, which was then exported to that game engine and a programmer would code it into the game. Depending on your budget, you would then get a chance to go in and polish that animation, most of the time that would mean fixing bugs.

On the current and next generation of consoles, new tools allow the animators to have more control of how animations are implemented. The new pipeline is more like this: you create an animation in Maya, that animation is then split up into smaller layers, like an upper-body and lower-body layer when it is exported to the game engine. Then in the engine, the animations are combined and additional procedural animation is applied to the combined animation. Then this whole package of animation might be handed to a programmer to connect it up to the game systems.

What this means for an animator is that while timing and spacing, posing and setting key frames are essential skills, these are only the starting point of the skills and knowledge needed, as the industry moves ahead. An important requirement now is knowing how to assemble small chunks of animation into a great looking package that can respond dynamically to the player's inputs inside the game engine. Luckily, many free tools like Unity allow you to experiment with these new techniques as a student.

2.4–2.5
Hitman: Absolution
Hitman: Absolution proves that having great hair is not everything.

INTERVIEW

JOHN McCARTEN

• •

Transferable skills: John McCarten is a visual effects (VFX) programmer at WetaFX, he discusses making the transition from games industry programmer to working in feature film FX. John worked in video games for over a decade on major titles such as Rockstars' award-winning *L.A. Noire*.

What was it like working as a programmer in the games industry? Can you describe the pros and cons?

Working as a programmer in the games industry involves a lot of focus and an extremely keen eye for quality, as it's a consumer-facing field. I got into it through a strong childhood interest in video games. I was also attracted to the glamour of the industry, and the idea of making a complete product you can see in a shop and point at, which is actually quite a rare opportunity for a programmer since most code is created to support business infrastructure.

I like to dabble in various creative fields and video games were a great combination of creativity and programming. I love being able to influence the creative process and have a large impact on the content, which is possible even as a coder. Coding games is one of a few domains that still require squeezing out every drop of performance from the machine, and it's also a rapidly developing field. This attracts people with outstanding skill and passion, which is great to be around.

The main drawbacks to working as a video game programmer are the long hours and often unpaid overtime that you are asked to work. This cannot be understated. It's generally less well paid than programming roles in other industries, such as banking or web development. It's a very volatile career with jobs often ending in redundancy. You may also need to move city or even country to find new employment. It's also a very young industry and when I left my last video game position at age 32, I was in the senior age range of the production staff. The long hours and instability are not geared to someone who wants to raise a family or buy a house. This means that every year the industry loses a number of extremely talented people, as they simply can't balance the demands with their increasing priorities outside of work. As a programmer, some of the more frustrating, but exciting, aspects are the fluid and rapidly changing requirements, which makes it difficult to plan and execute complex features. There are techniques to address this problem, such as iterative development, but even then, it's still hard to avoid uncomfortable hacks or fudges.

What do you consider the most significant skills needed to be a successful programmer in the games industry?

Having a strong personal interest in video games kept me motivated and driven to innovate. I think an extremely high personal standard of quality is very important, as video games are scrutinized intensely by the public and you won't be there next to them to explain away the deficiencies in your work.

I also believe it's vital to have the ability to communicate with people from other disciplines, since as a programmer you're generally serving someone outside the code team. They might be designers, or they might be animators, or testers, and being able to discuss technical matters with these people as well as receive suggestions or criticism, is key to producing tools that work and content that is fun.

What excites you as a programmer in games? What sort of tasks do you relish: controlling worlds, generating NPC AI, the game mechanics?

I really relish working on content systems such as puzzle mechanics, or AI scripting, as you really get involved with the content of the game. And as a coder, these systems are the closest you have to creative expression. Most of my experience has been on tool development and in that context I enjoy working with the artists as I enjoy the cross-discipline dynamic and the satisfaction of seeing them take simple tools I've made and go on to create great things with them.

How easy was the transition moving from the games industry into the film industry?

The transition was relatively easy as I had spent quite a number of years working on animation and tools for managing in-game cinematics, this field is directly transferable to the VFX industry. For those working on pipeline tools, rendering, and animation, there are also directly applicable roles within VFX. For gameplay systems, AI, there is less of an overlap, so for people with those backgrounds it might be a bit harder. Being in a location close to a major VFX studio is also beneficial.

As a programmer, do you have the same creative freedom working in film as in the games industry? What are the key differences?

The big difference between video game work and VFX work is that as games are often produced by a single studio, they make the whole widget, audio, script, design, and code, so any individual in that situation can potentially have a significant effect on any aspect of the product. For example, I've known of general office managers designing innovative menu systems. Large movies are produced by a collection of vendors and production companies and are orchestrated by the main production company and the director. Because of this arrangement, a VFX vendor is only responsible for a portion of the content, so their influence is more limited and roughly equivalent to a single department of a video game studio. As a coder at a VFX company, this effect is even more compounded, as your role is limited to working on tools and not the content at all. Compare this to actually working on content systems in games, such as AI or gameplay mechanics. Essentially my creative input is limited to how much empowerment you can offer an artist in solving their problems.

Is there a noticeable difference in the working cultures of the film and games industries?

The first thing that struck me is that games studios are engineering centric, whereas it seems to me that VFX studios are more art driven. Working practices are more organic and less formal. Programmers aren't considered as crucial in VFX studios simply because the facility is not a producer of software. Additionally, most software tools have viable off-the-shelf alternatives and so a coder's role is often to facilitate a workflow or scale a solution.

A big point of difference is the strong stratification of the hierarchy in VFX compared to games. You never meet the upper management, when working on game I would know the very top tier producers and game directors of the projects I have created, on a VFX project you are extremely unlikely to ever meet the director for example.

I've found that projects can be significantly shorter in film than games; I've worked on several games that have taken more than three years to produce. The VFX for a major movie project will take a lot less than that, making it easier for a VFX artist to build a significant portfolio more quickly than a game artist. As a coder, you have a short period in which to develop software for a show, and often what you're working on will be for the second or third show in the production queue. When working on a specific show you're often limited to just debugging tools and helping artists through problems in existing systems.

I've also found that VFX artists, commonly known as technical directors, are far more code savvy than video game industry artists. I know of a number of TDs that have developed significant pipeline tools and have even written a large number of C++ plug-ins. There appears to be a continuous spectrum of technical ability in VFX roles, rather than the sharper artist to coder transition that you might find in a games studio. This may be due to the age differences found in these two areas. VFX TDs tend to be from a wider age range from varied backgrounds, having had more time to develop a larger skill set. As a coder this changes the dynamic significantly as you find your client more able to contribute to the development of systems.

An important distinction is that visual fidelity is rarely compromised in VFX, whereas a game has to balance many competing requirements, specifically performance and visual quality. Performance is a concern in VFX but if a shot takes one minute extra to render it's not always a disaster. In contrast, an additional 1/15s in a render loop would kill the performance of a video game. This takes off some of the edge of optimization, so I've found less of a need to constantly rework systems for performance and this allows me to move on quickly to new problems.

When working on *The Hobbit* trilogy, were you responsible for overseeing specific sections or parts of the film FX. What was your technical role and can you expand on it a little?
My work was used in many places throughout *The Hobbit* trilogy, but as I am a software engineer rather than a content creator, my work is not directly on screen. In general, a VFX programmer has a more abstract contribution to the content versus say a video game gameplay programmer; it's more akin to the tool developers on the engine team.

As a programmer at Weta Digital within the creatures department, which is responsible for the rigging and simulation of characters, I developed and supported a range of systems to help with simulating muscle, skin, and cloth. These tools were used to create characters such as Gollum, the Goblin King, and many digital double shots of Gandalf and the dwarves.

What excites you as a programmer in the film industry? What sort of tasks do you relish: technical VFX, controlling worlds, generating AI?
Things that excite and interest me include working on high profile projects at the leading edge of VFX. I am also interested in migrating game concepts such as real-time rendering, GPU acceleration, and close to final visualization to help reduce the artist feedback loop.

I really enjoy working with some of the best people in the industry and meeting leading figures in VFX research. I've picked up many things from VFX that would be exciting to bring to a video game, and maybe one day I will.

A DAY IN THE LIFE OF A VIDEO GAME PROGRAMMER

John McCarten

The average day would depend on the phase of the project and can be roughly categorized into four stages; I am assuming a traditional AAA big console game project in this example.

PRE-PRODUCTION This involves exploratory prototyping, tool development and many meetings and should be the busiest phase of development for a coder. We pad out the architecture of the system with UML (Unified Modeling Language), document writing, and whiteboard diagrams. There's usually a lot of technical discussion about the platform limitations, as these often are a bottleneck for the game design and have to be considered early, especially when working on a new platform. The hours are usually standard and the workload is usually quite light. At this point, the project may not have secured funding so sometimes you need to create a number of pitch demos to rustle up publisher interest, this can often change the direction of the project quite quickly, and result in a couple of late nights. Depending on the engine you might be using, a lot of work goes into the basic tools at this point, things like the game editor, animation exporters, texture conversion tools and so on.

PRODUCTION The project has now secured funding, the basic tech is finished and in an ideal world only the content has to be created. A coder's day is filled with responding to feedback from the producers, designers, and artists, building up the features of the game and debugging tools. For programmers working on content systems such as gameplay mechanics, they often work closely with artists directly to complete specific features of the game. Work hours at this stage fluctuate, often staying within contracted time, but with the odd push to meet a milestone or trade show deliverable. This phase can last from a year to several years depending on the project.

CRUNCH At this point, the game is about three to six months from completion, but it's usually still some way off complete. All bugs need to be fixed or negotiated at this stage; it's easy to underestimate what an effort that is. The day to day during this phase is pretty formulaic and routine, but often long, as a programmer you will hopefully not be solving large technical problems. You arrive at work maybe later than you would do during production to compensate for later nights. You'd check the bug database and email for issues. As a coder, you might debug 2–4 decent problems a day. There are always a couple of persistent problems that haunt you for the duration of the project, which miraculously are fixed at the last minute. Towards the very end of the project, bugs start to thin out, at which point you test your own systems, since as the coder of the system you probably are aware of a couple of fringe cases that the testers may not be able to pick up on. You work hard to avoid the embarrassing post-release online video of a bug you overlooked. During this time, the publisher often gets more involved in the studio to offer rapid feedback. Often you're working more than twelve hours a day, six or seven days a week. Lunches are long, nights are late, and you eat every meal with your work colleagues.

POST-PRODUCTION Often a relaxed, enjoyable period, whilst you bask in the project after-glow and hopeful success. Wrap parties and launch parties are the order of the day. Lots of holiday time is taken, often more days than your allowance to compensate for overtime. Sometimes coders are allowed to undertake their own work, try out a few ideas, and learn new techniques. More recently, this time would be spent bug fixing and working on patches. I imagine as time goes on this post-production phase will be eliminated as the need to develop title updates expands, and games become more of a service than a product.

INTERVIEW
DAVID BOWMAN

● ●

Transferable skills: David Bowman is a 3D artist at Blue-Zoo Productions. He discusses making the leap from computer games to working on animated TV series. After years of working on video game console titles, David fulfilled a lifetime ambition to work on an animated children's television series.

What is your role, where are you currently working, and how long have you been at the company?

I am a 3D model supervisor and I work for Blue Zoo in London, UK. I am the head of modeling on a children's television show called *Tree Fu Tom* (see image 2.6). It is my job to lead on all modeling work and to link between all departments. I work closely with the series director providing advice and help at every stage of the production. I really enjoy my work, having a very wide rage of responsibility.

How did you get into the games industry, and how long did you work in games?

I started work as a runner in a games studio at the age of 18. I have always been a practical worker, rather than an academic. Whilst working as a runner I would stay after hours at the studio learning how to use the software. When I started there, I had never used any 3D software.

I have never been afraid to ask for advice, and the staff at the company helped me to learn all that I needed to know. I was promoted to work on a team after nine months. My career has gone on from there. Many of the people that helped me in the beginning are still friends.

What are the things you most enjoyed about working in the games industry?

The atmosphere differs from company to company. I loved being part of a small company that was struggling to survive. Working until 3 am night after night is a lot easier to do if you are doing it with your best friends.

How has your career as a digital artist in the games industry enabled you to work in other digital creative areas?

A good artist pulls on experiences and things that they have seen on a day-to-day basis. I find that everything that you do in life will help you down the line. A good example was when I once sat in a small hut on a frozen lake, ice fishing for eight hours, and I didn't catch anything. Years later, I was asked to model an icy environment. I remembered staring out of the door of the fishing hut and noticing the way that the ice had formed interesting patterns on the surface of the ice sheet. As an artist, if you are open and observant nothing is wasted.

Making the transition from computer games to animated children's television was always my aim. The move from games isn't an easy one to make, but having a good understanding of low poly modeling and efficient texturing gave me a good base to expand my artwork into higher resolution work.

What are the best ways for prospective CG artists to show their work when seeking employment? What do you look for when hiring? What do you personally focus on?

Enthusiasm is key. Only show your best work. I'd rather see fewer examples of high quality work, than sit through a 20-minute showreel containing everything that you have ever modeled. That said; avoid endless rotations of the same model. Maintaining a good showreel should be a continual process. Don't spend five weeks editing it when you could put a version out there and focus on adding new work. Remove your photo and any other pictures from your CV. Also, make sure that your CV is one or two pages long at most, succinct and easy to read.

2.6

Tree Fu Tom

A children's animated series made by the London-based studio Blue-Zoo Productions. It is an example of how creative technical skills can be used across a range of digital media productions. Transferable skills lead to increased employment opportunities.

INTERVIEW
MALSARA THORNE

• •

Industry role: Malsara Thorne is the director of Datascope, a games industry recruitment agency. She discusses what employers are looking for, what makes a good showreel, the fundamentals of an outstanding resume, digital portfolios, and websites.

Can you explain the role of the employment agency as a gatekeeper to games companies? What bespoke services do they offer to either party?

One of the main reasons why clients come to us is to help them track down "hard to find" candidates who are specialists in their field quickly and effectively. These candidates are generally not always actively searching for jobs. We recruit people from the industry and in some cases have to go outside the industry. This is a time-consuming operation, and most clients do not have the workforce or the time to carry out this task effectively.

In some cases clients do not always want their jobs advertised; some roles are highly confidential and require a careful search and selection process. We are able to do this very effectively and will search worldwide to find the right candidate with the specific skills and experience our clients generally call for.

It may feel like we are "gatekeepers" but we are giving our clients what they want. The games industry is a sector where there is a high level of interest from people wanting to enter it and we handle a large volume of resumes/CVs on a daily basis but unfortunately, they are not all qualified or are poorly qualified for the roles we have on offer. However, we do provide career advice and tips on how to get into the industry for those candidates who we feel have a real interest and potential. We also have a graduate page on our website, which offers tips and advice on starting a career in the games industry. www.datascope.co.uk/graduates

We have been working in the games industry for nearly twenty-five years and in that time have built up a comprehensive database and network of contacts. We use this as our main source of candidates when a client asks for our help. Having worked for the games industry for so long we have an in-depth understanding for the industry, the people in it and what the clients want.

What do you offer candidates?

We work with companies around the world across all continents. There are very few clients in the games/mobile industry we do not work with, so we are able to offer our candidates a wide choice of companies and locations to choose from when they come to us. We don't just offer them the available roles on our books. We approach companies on our candidate's behalf even if there is no obvious vacancy.

Some vacancies are confidential and are not advertised. Candidates only hear about these if they are registered with us. We offer our candidates a confidential, one-to-one service and work with them throughout the hiring process from giving advice to interview techniques to helping with presentations and showreels, we guide them all the way through until they secure the role they want.

What is a key piece of advice you would offer to students/graduates when preparing to apply for a job?

I think the single most important piece of advice I would offer students is to do the right course that is recognized in the industry for what they want to do. Secondly, it is important to be aware of what is happening in the industry. Speak to people in the industry, join a games-specific forum, read the industry press, and keep in touch with what is going on, so when you do apply for a role, you can say something relevant in the cover letter that will make you stand out from the rest. Thirdly, make sure your skills are up to date and relevant

Can you share with us some showreel dos and don'ts? For example, do you advise graduates to send links of websites by email or a DVD in the post? Is there a preferred medium?

These days a portfolio link is the way forward and is the preferred medium. It must be easy to access and download. For artists the competition is fierce. One way of gaining exposure is to post your work on various sites such as Cgsociety, Carbonmade, Wix, Behance, Artstation etc. Our consultants generally look for a range of skills that highlight the artist's commercial and personal work and demonstrate their artistic flexibility.

Are internships a way into the video games industry?

Yes, definitely but very few companies in the games industry offer internships unless you are a maths or computer science graduate looking to do programming. Alternatively, you could start at the very bottom and become a games tester. But it is hard to move up or anywhere else from there unless you want to go into QA.

What important things are employers asking for when seeking a junior or graduate to join a team?

We are now actively courting graduate programmers from the top universities in the country and encouraging them to consider jobs in the games industry. Not only do employers want to see an excellent academic record but they also want to see a demonstration of skills that graduates have put into practice outside college work. For example, coding work or games projects they have done as a hobby goes a long way in getting noticed. It's also really important to show an interest in the games industry, although having a passion for games alone is not going to secure anyone a job without relevant knowledge or skills in some area.

What are your top tips for writing a CV/resume for the games industry and are there any specific differences to that of a standard resume?

This is the same for any sector, we all like to see a well-written resume that is free from spelling and grammatical errors and one that is easy to read and not too long. A resume that stands out from the rest needs to show extracurricular activities relevant to that job and industry. For example, if a candidate is applying for a programming role, they are better off writing about the four months coding experience they've gained whilst developing a game in their spare time than their work experience at H&M as a sales assistant during their summer holidays.

A top tip is to put yourself in the employer's shoes and think about what they might want to see in a resume for a particular role. A cover letter explaining why they should consider you for the role will always get you noticed. Ask yourself, what is the company looking for from the person for this role and what can I offer that is relevant that will add value to them?

LEGAL ADVICE FOR INDIE DEVELOPERS

JAS PUREWAL, PUREWAL & PARTNERS

• •

Jas Purewal is one of the leading European lawyers in digital entertainment, video games, and technology. Jas has advised independent games studios including 22Cans (*Godus*), CD Projekt (*The Witcher*), Facepunch Studios (*Garry's Mod and Rust*) and Ndemic Creations (*Plague Inc.*). In addition, he has also advised a number of global games publishers and media organizations including EA, Nintendo and Koch Media regarding their EU games, film and entertainment businesses. Here Jas outlines some key points to consider when setting up as an indie developer.

TEN TOP LEGAL TIPS FOR STARTING A GAMES STUDIO

01 **SET UP A COMPANY.** It is nearly always a good idea to set up a company to run your games business. It shields you from personal liability against business issues and debts. It's often more tax efficient. It permits you to bring other people on board easily. Plus, it looks more professional. Your accountant or lawyer can advise you on the right type of company to use in your country of operation.

02 **GET ON THE SAME PAGE WITH YOUR CO-FOUNDERS.** If you are starting a company with other co-founders, then agree upfront what your interests in it will be, who will fund its early steps, and how you will run the company day to day. Well-advised companies will set up a "shareholders' agreement" to govern this. These steps can reduce or avoid a great deal of problems down the line if founders disagree with each other or even part ways.

03 **TAKE EMPLOYMENT LAW SERIOUSLY.** Employment law has a big impact on all businesses: it governs when you can hire people, how you have to treat them, and what happens if they leave. It also often requires you to pay employment taxes. Having a good standard employment agreement (and often an employee handbook too) is necessary. Human resources services can help with many of your practical needs.

04 USE CONTRACTORS SENSIBLY. In the early days, many small studios don't need many full-time employees. Part-time staff could be brought on as contractors for specific tasks, which gives you wider access to expertise but without the overheads associated with employees. A good contractor agreement will delineate their responsibilities. Remember though that whether a person is classed as an employee or a contractor is ultimately a question of what they do, not what they're called.

05 INTELLECTUAL PROPERTY LAW IS YOUR LIFEBLOOD. Legally, a game is literally a bundle of intellectual property rights, so to have a successful games business you must have at least a basic understanding of "IP" law. This means knowing the fundamentals of copyright law (the branch of IP law that protects creative works), trademark law (which protects a name/brand/logo), and patent law (which protects inventions). Depending on your business, other IP rights may be relevant too. An industry lawyer can advise you on when you should spend money on IP protection and—just as importantly—when you don't need to.

06 CONTRACTS CAN BE YOUR BEST FRIEND AND WORST ENEMY. A contract is a legally binding document that explains what two or more people will do for each other and in exchange for what. A successful games business will use a wide range of contracts a lot, including: development/publishing, distribution, licensing, merchandising, financing, and other contracts. Contracts can be used to your advantage but also to your disadvantage. Therefore, it will repay you significant dividends if you take the time to understand basic contract law principles, how contracts work in practice, and if you collect some standards that you can use and reuse.

07 KEEP AN EYE ON REGULATION. The games industry is becoming more regulated over time. Be aware that there are laws in different countries about things like how you can interact with consumers, how you can use data, what you are allowed to say in marketing materials, what content you can have in a game, what age rating it can get, even (in some countries) how its business model operates.

08 KNOW ABOUT INCENTIVES AND RELIEFS. Different countries are beginning to make different financial incentives available to games companies. You may be able to benefit from local, regional, or even international funding schemes. Some countries, such as the UK, France, and Canada, offer tax breaks for video games production. These kinds of incentives can help give your business a leg-up.

09 SPECIAL LEGAL CASES. Some legal situations are particularly complicated, including financing your business, mergers and acquisitions (i.e. buying and selling businesses), and legal disputes. These are all areas where it's particularly important to get things right legally, because they can have a significant impact on your business. Take specialist legal and accountancy advice where necessary.

10 BUILD A RELATIONSHIP WITH AN INDUSTRY LAWYER. Finding and building a long-term relationship with a games industry lawyer should help you a lot over time; he or she will be able to advise you on all the above areas, this should be more cost efficient and hopefully be more aligned with your business. In addition, good lawyers often have good networks and their contact list can be valuable. Good lawyers are more than just legal professionals—they are trusted and impartial advisors too.

INTERVIEW

KAREN STANLEY

● ●

Industry role: Upon graduating from the University of Hertfordshire, UK, Karen landed her dream job at Sony Entertainment as an environment artist. Here she discusses the transition from student to industry junior.

What awards did you win as a student, and did this help at interviews?

I entered the CG Student Awards for 2013 and was placed second. I was also a finalist in 2014. It was a nice talking point, not only for interviews, but also with other students from other universities across the world as so many entered.

What do you advise game design students to focus on in their studies?

Find what you love doing in the industry and focus on it, whether it be environment art, character art, design, tools, graphics coding or AI. With many options to choose from, you're bound to fall into something you love!

As a student, what were the key things that you learned and found helpful?

Personally, I'm an environment artist, but I found learning multiple engine pipelines helped me pick up new tools easier as I'm not stuck in one workflow. A lot of companies have their own production pipelines tools, so it's good to be open to learning new tech. Also the industry is moving towards a physically based pipeline so as an artist it's important to understand this. Networking and people skills are also important, its one of the major things university helped me with. Not only was I surrounded by people who I was and still am constantly learning from, they also became important connections into the industry.

Was there a defining game that inspired you towards your specialist route in the games industry?

The *Killzone* series has always been a favorite as I love the art direction. But the game that made me want to become an environment artist was *Unreal Tournament* (1999) and the SDK (software development kit) that came with it. Although I wasn't big into the Mods (modification) for it, it was my first glimpse into how games are created and my first experience with a games engine.

What have been your most effective study tools?

Other people—polycount forums, my lecturers, and classmates—just listening to them and getting feedback. I don't believe there is such a thing as

2.7
The Shadowed Crow
This award-winning environment is part of the student showreel, which enabled Karen Stanley to gain employment at Sony Entertainment after completing her undergraduate studies at the University of Hertfordshire, UK.

self-taught in our industry, as making games in a studio is a team effort. This doesn't mean you have to go to university, but you need to show other people your work on forums and learn from them. As an artist you need to learn the tools, but it's what you do with them that matters. A real benefit is to pick up tips and tricks from other people to help you to speed up your workflow, and spot errors that you can't see when you are too close to the work.

Portfolio advice: dos and don'ts?

In general for environment art, a good website portfolio of still images showing wires, texture maps, and so on seems to be preferred and should be your first priority over a showreel. I like showreels as I like environments to have subtle movements and effects, they can be fun to make!

- In general keep them short, no more than 90 seconds.
- Only show your best work, this goes for the portfolio too—if you question it, remove it.
- Keep the music calm and edit to the beat.
- If you worked on group projects be clear about what you did.
- Don't forget to put your contact information at the start or end!
- Also, add your contact details in the video descriptions if your reel is uploaded to YouTube or Vimeo.

CHAPTER REVIEW

This chapter has focused on who makes video games, highlighting possible routes into the video games industry. It has also covered a range of industry roles and necessary skillsets. In addition, it has focused on the flexibility and transferable nature of industry skills. We've also seen that a career in the games industry can lead to exciting parallel career opportunities in areas such as film and TV production.

Key Points

INDUSTRY ROLES: Games companies are made up of many important and overlapping roles, each focusing on specific core skills and the combined expertise needed to successfully create a game. Teamwork is an integral part of the industry, for both large AAA studios and small indie development teams alike.

TEAM STRUCTURES: The video game production pipeline is made up of many interconnected parts. To function effectively, clear team hierarchies and communication structures are vital components when working in a proactive and reactive design environment. Fluid iterative design cycles are key to creating a successful game.

TRANSFERABLE SKILLS: Digital creatives and designers can employ specialist 2D and 3D skillsets in parallel digital creative industries. An ongoing approach to learning, beyond education in the workplace from peers, is an important and exciting aspect of teamwork. Within the workplace, new ways of working can be acquired and these can provide new creative opportunities to alternate routes to employment.

RECRUITMENT: Recruitment agencies are a key part of finding out about jobs and entering into the video games industry. As gatekeepers, they provide a service, advising both employer and job seekers on matters such as portfolios, websites, and showreels, and many other factors vital to gaining employment.

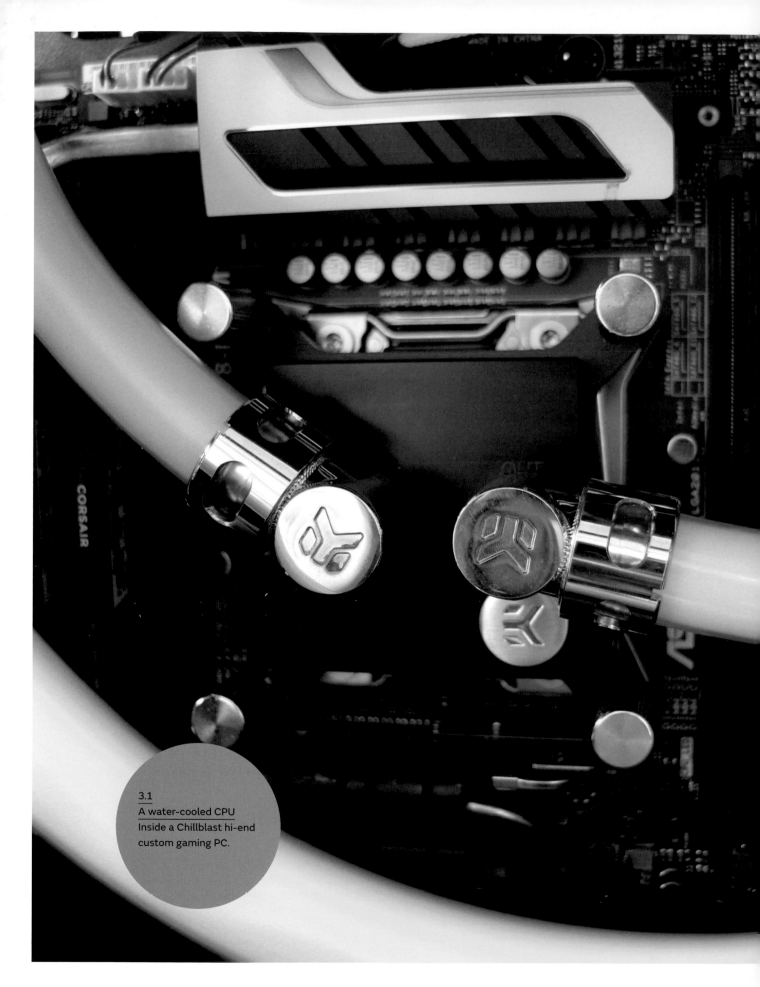

3.1
A water-cooled CPU
Inside a Chillblast hi-end
custom gaming PC.

3
GAME TECH

TOPICS COVERED
Key Technologies / Gaming Platforms /
The Internet / Game Engines / User Interface

Powered by Moore's Law and fueled by consumer desire, the battle to be the ascendant gaming technology, software, and hardware is ceaseless. Players crave the latest hardware, hyperrealistic graphics, and more visceral interaction. This, combined with the unstoppable momentum of technological development, drives the games industry forward.

KEY TECHNOLOGIES

Humankind has a habit of producing ever more complex technology, which is one of the reasons why video games exist at all. Since its early days as a product of academic curiosity, video gaming has advanced symbiotically with other evolutions in technology. Many of the methods by which we interact and experience video games were developed for purposes other than gaming. For example, the joystick had half a century of development in aviation before it was brought into our homes in the 1970s. In turn, games helped drive the boom in early home computing, as the early buyers were attracted to the idea of programming them to play video games.

While technological progress has undoubtedly brought desirable benefits, such as greater realism and new ways to play, technology has improved at such exponential rates that obsolescence is a problem. This means the cutting edge can often be outdated as it hits the shelves, because technology companies are already planning for the next generation of products. This is arguably good for the video game industry's profits, as we all rush to buy the latest kit, but it makes it difficult to identify which technologies will power the video game industry with any medium or long-term certainty. Frequently, the pioneers of new ways of playing or using the most up-to-date tech have not been the beneficiaries of the new markets they have helped create. On occasion doing it best is better than doing it first.

What follows is a discussion of the current technological landscape, its context and influence.

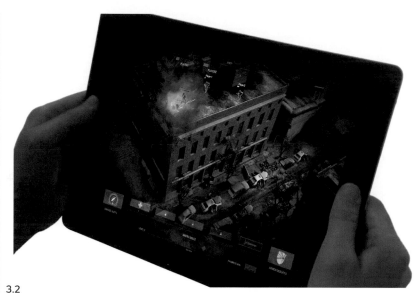

3.2
Second screen
Console gaming offers new options
in gameplay through companion apps.
Tom Clancy's *The Division*, by Ubisoft
will employ second screen gameplay
options and is due for release in
early 2016.

MOORE'S LAW

Moore's Law is a prediction in computing
from 1965 when Gordon E. Moore published
a paper entitled *Cramming More Components
onto Integrated Circuits*. Moore observed that
the number of transistors within a chip had
doubled approximately every two years and
speculated that this trend would continue,
leading to a doubling of processing power
and advances in miniaturization that
would profoundly impact business and
consumer technology.

In 1968, Moore co-founded Intel with
Robert Noyce and together they produced
the first commercial processor, the Intel
4004. Released in 1971, the 4004 contained
approximately 2,300 transistors. Since then,
the generational improvements foreseen by
Moore have led to the central SoC (system on
a chip) in the Xbox One, containing around 5
billion transistors.

Moore's work has proven to be incredibly
accurate and only recently, as the limits set by
the physical world begin to be reached, is the
rate of improvement predicted to slow.

Displays

Since the Magnavox Odyssey pioneered playing
games on television sets, TV technology has been
key in their development. Televisions, along with
computer monitors, have displayed most of the
video games that have ever been played. However,
the small screens of mobile and handheld devices,
whose market is expanding exponentially, are rapidly
catching up.

Originally, monitors and TVs used CRT (cathode
ray tubes) to display pictures. This technology was
bulky, not very portable and took up significant
space in the home and office. Thankfully, it is now
obsolete. Instead TVs and monitors using LCD (liquid
crystal displays) screens have become the default,
due in part to how thin and light they are compared
to CRT. Despite being around for many decades—
LCD was used in early portable games—it is only

recently that this versatile display method has
matured and become economic enough to dominate
the TV and monitor markets.

While LCD might continue to be the tech
powering our gaming screens for the near-term, it is
already common to find LED (light emitting diode)
and OLED (organic light emitting diode) powered
displays in mobile devices, TVs and monitors,
sometimes in combination with LCD. While these
technologies offer further improvements, greater
efficiency and the possibility of flexible screens,
they are still relatively expensive and still have many
technical hurdles to overcome before becoming the
new default. Some key considerations and features
of screens follow.

Aspect Ratio

This is the relationship between the width and height of a screen. Since the millennium, the trend is for monitors and TVs in the home to become more like cinema screens where the viewport is noticeably wider than it is tall, hence the term "widescreen." The aspect ratio of TVs and monitors have moved in recent years from a ratio of 4:3 to 16:9 with some displays available today with a ratio of 21:9. Much of the change in aspect ratio has been due to demand for a widescreen cinematic experience at home amongst film lovers and game players.

Resolution

As screens have got wider, the resolutions have also improved. The density of pixels present defines the resolution of a screen. The more pixels the sharper and more defined a picture can be displayed. Until recently, TVs and monitors displayed graphics in SD (standard definition) such as PAL 720x576 at 25fps or NTSC 640x480 at 30fps), and HD (full high definition 1920x1080 or HDTV 1280x720 pixels) is rapidly becoming the norm.

Dual Screens and Second Screens

Dual screens were first seen in Nintendo's Game & Watch series and were later revived for the Nintendo DS. These devices feature two linked screens, positioned side by side, that offered new ways of playing games. A contemporary development of the dual screen approach is called a "second screen." This is where devices with screens, such as a TV and a tablet, run complementary services and interact in real time. The Nintendo Wii U has attempted to normalize this approach in video games by bringing second screens to the home console.

Developed by Ubisoft, Tom Clancy's *The Division* (2015) is one of many new games that seek to exploit this technology (see image 3.2 previous page), as players can use tablets and mobile devices to interact with the game world, while other players are simultaneously using consoles and PCs. Although related, the play mode and features are different between the two screen types.

Touch Screens

Touch screens are the basic screen type for tablets, and are standard on new smartphones. They are also becoming more common on PCs and laptops. Screens of this type offer different interaction possibilities. This type of physical interface can't give the same physical feedback offered by controllers with D-pads (directional pads) or joysticks.

Head Mounted Displays and Virtual Reality

A head mounted display (HMD) is a small screen worn on the head that displays an image in front of one or both eyes. These devices can either fill the wearer's vision or allow them to see through it like a HUD (heads-up display). One of the most famous HMDs in recent years is Google's Glass.

In gaming, the HMD is mostly associated with virtual reality (VR). In the 1990s, there was great excitement around VR, but the fad fizzled quickly because of the technology's limitations. In recent years, the Oculus Rift has revived the buzz. VR involves wearing a HMD that fills the wearer's field of vision with a computer-generated display that gives the wearer the impression of being in an alternate reality, as all other visual stimuli has been removed. As wearers move their heads, the headset detects the movements and gives a continuous graphic impression of the environment. Other HMD devices are being developed for market, such as the Sony Project Morpheus or the astonishingly low cost Google Cardboard, designed to work with existing smartphone technology.

3.3

Oculus Rift

Oculus Rift began life as a Kickstarter project, which was successfully funded in September 2012. Less than two years later, it was sold to Facebook for $2 billion (£1.4 billion). Other VR kits are in development, such as Project Morpheus by Sony.

3.4

Nintendo NES Gamepad

The legendary Nintendo designer Gunpei Yokoi created the D-pad; he applied it to his Game & Watch series. His innovation removed the need for a protruding joystick that would have reduced the device's portability. The design first seen on Game & Watch has defined a signature style for Nintendo on both its consoles and portable technology ever since.

Controllers

Gamepad

The gamepad is the primary control device used by consoles since 1983, when it was introduced for the NES (Nintendo Entertainment System). The NES gamepad took its design cues from the Game & Watch handhelds, the first gaming machines to include a D-pad. This innovation greatly influenced the evolution of the gamepad and has since become the default directional device for handheld controllers with variations of the concept featuring on devices of Nintendo's rivals to this day. Gamepads also incorporate a range of buttons, sometimes used in combination, that activate different game features, and small analogue joysticks.

3.5
Atari 2600 joystick
An icon of the birth of the video game industry and a visual shorthand for retro gaming.

Joysticks

A joystick or control stick is a device used to move graphic elements on a screen. As stand-alone devices, they usually incorporate one or more push buttons to allow for extra gameplay options. Control sticks had been used in the arcades for some years; the Magnavox Odyssey (1972) was the first console to bring the joystick into the home. The Sega electro-mechanical arcade machine is believed to be the earliest instance of a joystick used in the arcade, but it was the Atari 2600 that went on to define it.

3.6
A Mad Catz joystick
Set-up for flight sims and space combat, i.e. *Elite Dangerous* (2014) with Oculus Rift.

3.8
Rock Band special edition
More than your typical game controller, *Rock Band* (2007) was designed for collaborative play.

3.7
Kinect
The Kinect has moved beyond being simply a device to play video games with, and has now been adopted by artists to create interactive and digital pieces away from the video gaming universe, see Kinect.justthebestparts.com for an introduction.

Motion Sensing

Motor sensing detects the movement of either a device or the person or persons playing a game. They provide new gameplay and interactivity options for video games. It is only recently that these peripherals have reached a level of sophistication and precision for a consistent and satisfying playing experience.

Nintendo and Sega were both early pioneers of sensing devices. In 1989, the Mattel Power Glove sold over 100,000 units in the US. Licensed exclusively to Nintendo it was a novel experience but difficult to use. It took nearly two decades for Nintendo to return to the concept with the Wiimote for the Wii.

In 1993, Sega launched the Activator for the Mega Drive/Genesis. The Activator was an octagonal-shaped, full body motion controller that was placed on the floor, plugging directly into the console. Players stood in the middle of the pad and their body movements intersected with infrared light beams projected upwards towards the ceiling. Unfortunately, the Activator was to be both a technical and commercial flop. Nintendo revisited the floor controller with the Wii Fit Balance Board in 2007.

Sony also have a long history in trying to crack this kind of interaction, starting with the EyeToy released for the PlayStation 2 in 2003, which combined motion, color, and sound detection in one piece of kit. However, the Nintendo Wii was the first console to include motion sensing as standard when it was included in the Wii remote. These were wireless controllers that used accelerometers to detect their orientation and acceleration. They brought motion sensing into the mainstream and familiarized a new generation of gamers with the concept. Since then, the Xbox Kinect, first seen in 2010, uses computer vision through infrared structured light to accurately sense sequences of gestures and actions.

Games utilizing motion-sensing devices entice players to forgo their sedentary positions and jump around the room providing an experience completely unlike the traditional idea of what it is to play a video game. Titles such as *EyeToy: Play* (2003), *Wii Sports* (2006), *Guitar Hero* (2005), *Rock Band* (2007) and *Dance Dance Revolution* (2010) have transformed gameplay; physicality is the key to their success.

3.9
Dance Central and *Just Dance*
The BAFTA-winning games such as *Dance Central* and *Just Dance*, utilize the Kinect. (For other insights into physical games, see Lateral Thinking, page 101)

3.10

Elite Dangerous

This revival of the original sandbox classic is a good example of a first person HUD interface, where the in-game graphics illustrate geometric and diegetic elements. For a full description of these terms see page 86.

The Interface

The controller technology discussed previously is employed to interact with video game players doing something in the physical world to elicit a response in the virtual one. When we click, touch, press, and swipe, we expect feedback and cues as to what effect our actions are having. We want to know what is going on, what we need to do next, and what we can use to do it. Although tied up in the overall design of a game, one vital part of the feedback process is a game's visual interface. These are usually supported by sound, and occasionally physical feedback, for example vibrating controllers. An interface's design is crucial in immersing and engaging players in a game; just as importantly, they are key to retaining our interest in the game mechanic by aiding gameplay.

An interface is formed from many components and draws upon a variety of design theory and research for inspiration. However, interface design for video games is not dominated by inflexible objective criteria, if it was, all games might look and play more or less the same. This is due in part to the aesthetic and subjective design considerations that make games fun and make one title stand out against another. However, in recent years there have been efforts by both studios and academics to try to classify and analyze the common interface types found in some video games. The ideas now emerging tie the world of video games closer to that of the movies, as concepts used to analyze films are also applied to games. Opposite is a description of some elements and considerations common to visual gaming interfaces.

COMMON INTERFACE TERMS

AVATAR: In games, "avatar" refers to the graphical representation of the player on screen. A player may have a single avatar or many depending on the type of game.

CHI: Computer–human interaction is a cross-disciplinary part of computer science concerned with psychology, and design anthropology. It goes beyond controllers, graphics, and audio of video games. Academic research in this field led to the development of graphical user interfaces. Video games offer a distinct area of study, in that we play games rather than use them for a practical purpose.

DIEGESIS: This term describes how narrative is used to describe the details of a virtual world and tell its story through the experiences of its characters. It is well established in analysis of movies and literature. Although the concept of diagesis has been present in video games for sometime, it is only recently that it has been used to describe them. With diegesis game designers and observers are able to define what is and what is not part of the game world, and what the characters inhabiting it can and cannot see.

GUI: A graphic user interface is a screen-based interface that enables users to interact with technology, for example, computers, and smartphones. They employ a system of icons, symbols, and other graphical cues that are designed to work together in order for users to manipulate, organize, and retrieve information from their devices or software (including games). They are a mixture of functional and aesthetic considerations that help to reinforce and aid the UX. The nature of the icons can be adopted from other sources or use widely accepted symbols, for example, arrows for directions, disks for saving, cogs for settings. The Apple Macintosh successfully introduced the GUI to home computing in 1984.

HUD: A heads-up display is a graphical device in a game presented on a transparent layer that enables data and information to be shown to the player, for example health status, or remaining ammunition, so they don't need to look away from the screen during gameplay. HUDs were first used in military aircraft, but are now frequently seen in cars and other transport.

OVERLAY: Related to a HUD in that it can be transparent, an overlay is an element of a game that is superimposed on top of another element. A shift from having overt controls in the viewport to the controls appearing when needed and being pared back, therefore creating more immersion. The FPS *GoldenEye 007* (1997) was a key game in this switch.

TYPE AND TYPOGRAPHY: This is concerned with the choice of typefaces and fonts and their suitability for the game or section of the game in which they feature. Fonts can help express the mood and setting of the game, and also need to be clear and easy to read when providing instructions or feedback to the user. The choice of in-game fonts might differ between those used on menus and those seen in the game world. They may also differ from those used on packaging, cutscenes, or advertising, however, the overall effect should be complementary.

UX: User experience is concerned with the complete interaction a player has with a game. It is the coming together of the many elements that combine to make an interface; and it must meet the functional requirements of a game to be considered successful. The UX should also help enforce the game world, setting, or type of game, by feeling appropriate and considered. It should enhance the gameplay experience and not hinder it.

A VISUAL BREAKDOWN OF FPS INTERFACE TYPES

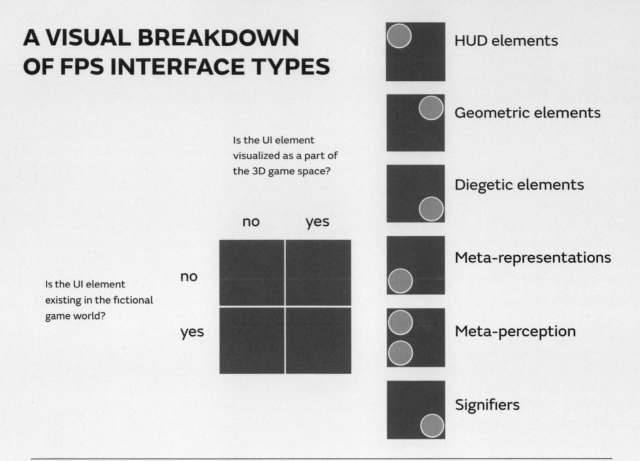

Is the UI element visualized as a part of the 3D game space?

no   yes

Is the UI element existing in the fictional game world?

no

yes

HUD elements

Geometric elements

Diegetic elements

Meta-representations

Meta-perception

Signifiers

A NEW WAY TO DESCRIBE GAME INTERFACES

"Beyond the HUD" is a 2009 thesis written by Swedish academics Erik Fagerholt and Magnus Lorentzon. It focuses on user interfaces in FPS games and was produced with the assistance of the Swedish studio DICE. Fagerholt and Lorentzon propose a system of four different combinational terms that can help describe the design elements of an FPS game. These are outlined below:

DIEGETIC ELEMENTS Diegetic user interface elements exist within the game world and both the player and the avatar can see and interact with them visually, audibly, or through touch.

META ELEMENTS Elements that don't fit within the game world, but still act to maintain the fiction are called "meta elements." These are meta-representations of information that provide information and have a plausible reason to be

there. In Tom Clancy's *The Division*, these might be the information displayed by gadgets possessed by the avatars.

SPATIAL Spatial UI elements are used to break the narrative, so that more game information can be provided to the player than the on-screen avatar is aware of. They still sit within the game world to aid the immersive experience and prevent breaks in play by switching to menus. For designers, keeping these elements as close to the game's fiction as possible helps avoid breaking the spell of the game.

NON-DIEGETIC ELEMENTS These UI elements are visibly removed from the game world, usually superimposed in an overlay style. This means UI designers have the freedom to add a different visual style to them, but usually they are influenced by the game's overall art direction.

INTERVIEW
RICARDO SERRAZINA

● ●

Industry role: Ricardo Serrazina is creative lead/UI designer at Miniclip, he is based in its Lisbon Studio, in Portugal.

What are the key aspects of user interfaces designed for games?

Game interfaces should inform the player of specific things built into the game or gained via gameplay, which allow the player to enhance or customize the experience, for example, score, lives, armor, shop, high scores, and tournaments. These things are essential to the gameplay, but they don't usually need to be present in the core visual experience, so they are treated as something separate and complementary. If done correctly, the interface never affects the user experience in a negative way, in fact it helps to focus players' attention on the important elements of the game, so they interact with it effortlessly and intuitively, but it depends on the objective. Some interface elements become almost "invisible." This means the player doesn't notice them until they actually need to use the specific functionality; only then do they become apparent and easy to use.

How does the GUI designer integrate with the rest of the development team? At what stage do they become involved?

This also depends on the process and company, but ideally the interface designer should start planning the flow and wireframes immediately after the design of the game is feature complete. Once this is done, then the graphic designers and interface programmers can start developing in parallel to the core gameplay team.

Does the interface designer play a role in creating graphical assets, or do they focus on the schematics and strategy?

Many interface designers are the actual graphical designer in charge of creating both the assets and the artwork. However, this mostly happens in smaller companies, or with extremely senior professionals in both areas. It is very important that the people involved with this process have a keen understanding of how users perceive the information given to them, and how to make it visually attractive and complementary to the core gameplay. Because both aspects are very important, ideally one dedicated person with lots of expertise and experience would be allocated to each respective area. Game designers usually take on the role of defining the user interface initially, and then tweak it with the input of the graphic designer.

Do designers rely on players' familiarity with pictographic icon conventions, for example spanners or cogs for settings, to accelerate their ability to get to grips with game functions?

Yes, more players are familiar with previously used industry standards created to facilitate the development. This has a side effect though, as more games adhere to these standards the more players expect it, so creating things in fresh original ways can be detrimental to the game simply because players are so used to the standard, they don't have the will to learn anything new. This limits creativity somewhat and you rarely get new and better solutions, as designers tend to go with "what works" and what is expected, even if there could be a better solution out there.

GAMING PLATFORMS

PCs

The PC platform appeals to a highly dedicated portion of the gaming market, which demand the highest quality hardware on which to play their games. This, combined with the versatility of the PC—they have other uses after all—supports a sustained demand for this platform. The IBM PC (personal computer) was released in 1981. It differed from its contemporaries as it was largely built using off-the-shelf components. This cost effective approach meant that similar machines, produced by rival manufacturers, were rapidly on the market. Sensing a mutually beneficial business opportunity IBM's competitors soon adopted the same standard architecture as IBM, and their PCs were henceforth known as IBM compatible PCs, as

> "
> **IT TURNS OUT THAT EARLY HOME COMPUTERS WOULD BE USED ALMOST EXCLUSIVELY FOR ONE PURPOSE ALONE: PLAYING VIDEO GAMES**
> Tristan Donovan, *The History of Videogames*
> "

they could all use the same software and hardware. Together with IBM, they succeeded in creating the mass-market in business and home PCs that has endured to the present. Their success was also instrumental in making Microsoft the corporate behemoth it is today. IBM however, has since stopped making PCs.

In the early days of video gaming the PC made very little mark, but by 1987 with the arrival of VGA graphic cards, followed swiftly by dedicated sound cards, things changed rapidly. In 1991, several leading PC manufacturers agreed a new set of multimedia standards, which gave certainty to games developers about what they could expect

all new PC hardware to achieve. Now, in the new millennium, PCs are currently the technology platform with the largest share of the video game market.

One of the PC's advantages over rival architectures is that it can be customized, allowing better or new graphic and sound cards to be added to existing PCs, or whole computers to be built from scratch from the best components geared for gaming. These high-end custom-built PCs are now significantly more powerful than consoles.

Consoles

According to the Entertainment Software Association (ESA), 51 percent of American households own a console. A similar market penetration exists across Europe. Today, the primary console manufacturers are Nintendo, Sony, and Microsoft who produce the Wii U, PS4, and Xbox One respectively.

Consoles are computers that are dedicated to the activity of playing video games. The term "video game" itself is derived from the video output of consoles plugging into the TV sets. As hardware, they have evolved in parallel with home computers. Their most recent incarnations are getting close to a complete convergence of all home media as they

3.11
Ouya
A low cost crowdfunded console, open to developers and built with Android OS.

3.12
Gaming PC
Several specialist companies such as Chillblast in the UK focus on high-end PCs and laptops designed and assembled specifically for gaming.

THE 4004 AND THE 6502

The Intel 4004 and the MOS Technology 6502 were both types of microprocessor. A microprocessor is a type of integrated circuit made out of a small piece of semiconducting material such as silicon. It contains all the functions necessary for a computer to do all its required tasks. Released in 1968 the Intel 4004 was the first commercially available microprocessor.

Before the 4004 arrived, the circuits of video games were hard-wired and each one was different. The microprocessor allowed programmers to take over the creation of games for the first time, as they could write software for the chip. This meant the same hardware set-up could run a variety of games.

The Midway arcade game *Gun Fight* (see image 3.13), released in 1975, is a US version of Taito's *Western Gun* and is widely believed to be the first video game to employ the Intel 4004 microprocessor. 1975 was also when MOS Technology introduced the 6502. Like the 4004, this microprocessor is noteworthy in video game development because it helped usher in the home computing and console boom. Its low cost, significantly below that of its Intel and Motorola rivals, meant that it featured in some of the most significant machines of the late 1970s and early 1980s including the Apple II, Commodore PET and BBC Micro.

3.13
Gun Fight
Midway's 1975 arcade classic.

can be used to access the World Wide Web, on demand services, as well as play movies and music via the Internet, or via physical media such as CDs, DVDs, and Blu-ray.

A new trend of smaller consoles focusing on the mobile, web-based indie development, and gaming scene is emerging. November 2015 sees the release of the Steam Box from the Valve Corporation. Unlike other consoles, the Steam Box, an extension of the Steam gaming hub brand, will be supported by a plethora of significant game titles, from AAA console hits to smaller niche indie dev games, whilst others like Ouya, Mad Catz Mojo, and the Game Stick seek to tap into the substantial Android market.

Handheld

A hardware platform dominated by Nintendo and Sony, handheld devices are essentially portable consoles. They can provide a gaming experience that rivals that of standard consoles despite having much smaller screens. The current generation of devices can download games, play movies, and cross over into other technological formats. (See Chapter 1, page 27 for more on the history of handhelds.)

Mobile

Mobile smart devices are the home of casual gaming providing accessible, quick, and bite-sized snackable content. Improvements in wireless networking and mobile communications across larger geographic areas, coupled with increasing affordability, have altered our understanding of gaming, locality, and connectivity. Our work, social, and family lives have been transformed by mobile technologies, and mobile gaming in particular has opened the door to new gaming demographics.

Smart Device

An electronic device that can either be used autonomously, or interact in a collective way with other devices via networks, i.e. WiFi, Bluetooth, 4G. Games companies who design specifically for mobile smart devices such as King, the creators of *Candy Crush Saga* and *Bubble Witch Saga*, can generate profits of over $2 billion a year (£1.4 billion). The extraordinary market shift to mobile can be seen in the value placed on individual games that access demographics that other formats do not. Neopets, a virtual pet website founded in 2000, is known for its sticky content or stickiness, meaning that users of the site play for a sustained period of time and are likely to come back repeatedly.

3.14

Nvidia Shield

The Shield Portable is a dedicated gaming controller with integrated screen and the Shield Tablet is an 8"/20cm screen with separate controller, which uses a Nvidia Tegra K1 mobile processor. These are examples of how tablets are redefining mobile gaming.

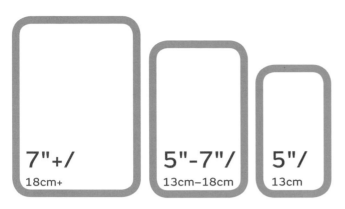

7"+/
18cm+

5"-7"/
13cm–18cm

5"/
13cm

3.15
Tablets, phablets and mobile size comparison
Smartphone screens are up to 5"/13cm, while
tablet screens are 7"/18cm and upwards.
Phablet screens are typically somewhere
between smartphones and tablets in size.
Phablets combine the functionality of the
smartphone and the tablet, and their larger
screens are easy to interact with, they
sometimes have a touch-screen stylus.
The Samsung Galaxy Note, now in its third
generation, is a prime example of this hybrid
device.

The Neopets website was sold to Viacom in
2014 for £100 million ($149 million). A desirable
business asset largely due to its millions of users, its
merchandising, and progressive advertising business
models, as well as the companies' ability to deliver
brand-focused mini game cross-promotions for high
street chains such as McDonald's.

The latest generation of tablets has a
processing capability which rivals seventh
generation consoles. Aiming to be more than just
a platform for addictive micro games and social
networking, bar the odd sandbox exception, the
latest models are placed to join the mainstream
gaming title hardware market.

On tablets, phablets, and mobile phones,
gaming applications range from the traditional
genres and titles to new social games that exploit
the range of technologies featured in these devices.
Amongst these, GPS location services have provided
opportunities for new gaming mechanics beyond the
obvious graphical content. Other mobile-focused
app games are utilizing the GPS functionality of
smart devices to connect with other gamers.

BLU-RAY, DVD, AND CD-ROM

The CD-ROM was another revolution for video
games. These cheap to manufacture optical disks,
and their successors the DVD and Blu-ray disks,
are able to store vastly more information than the
floppy disks that preceded them. They could also
store more information than the cartridges that
were used by consoles at the time of their original
introduction, as well as provide audio and video
outputs at much higher quality. Although the latest
generation of consoles continue to have drives that
can read these disks, it is likely that downloading
and cloud-based services will dominate the
distribution of games in future.

DRM

Digital rights management (DRM) is a systematic
approach to copyright protection, which is
intended to stop piracy, and the illegal copying
and distribution of video games. Broadly defined,
it involves limiting the use of games to registered
accounts and hardware, and usually requires
authentication over the Internet. In some cases,
games need persistent access to a license server
to allow them to run correctly or run at all. DRM
is a controversial practice, due to debates about
its efficacy as well as how it places limits on what
purchasers of content can do with their possessions.

The Internet

The origins of the Internet lie in early computer networks established by, amongst others, the US military and academic institutions in the latter half of the twentieth century. Today, it is a vast, computer-controlled web of servers and connections that spans the globe and drives modern civilization. Most people experience the Internet through the World Wide Web (the web) or email. The web was born in 1991 through the work of Tim Berners-Lee, a British scientist working at the European CERN research laboratory. It is the web that has enabled the rise of casual gaming and provided the opportunity for us to play video games away from the traditional platforms. It has also been instrumental in opening up the distribution of video games and loosening the grip of the publishing giants.

STEAM, a gaming hub established in 2002, has nurtured and valued the indie game scene, and other similar online portals have transformed video game publishing by establishing mainstream platforms for small developers. This shift in distribution enabled by the Internet has empowered game designers to create the game they longed to make, potentially allowing them to reap any rewards themselves (see Chapter 1, Indie Publishing and Online Hubs page 31) rather than see profits creamed off by the publishers.

However, the streets of indie publishing are not always paved with gold. The Internet is a big place and a game's success depends on not only it being well designed and fun to play, but also whether the title is visible in an increasingly crowded market. Many developers have underestimated this effect, especially mobile app games where many have not performed as well as expected (see Chapter 6: The Business of Games page 155).

The major console brands have harnessed the Internet and the web by creating their own online stores (PlayStation Minis, Xbox Live and Wii online) to entice consumers back, and maintain, and grow their user base. These portals regularly include indie titles next to their AAA mainstream titles, thereby sharing the online store exposure. This helps lure developers into the indie game market as they now have a variety of pathways to publishing and substantial market visibility.

Xbox have put forward plans to reconnect with indie developers with ID@Xbox. A self-publishing strategy for developers on Xbox One, attracting developers back with XBLIG & XBLA (Xbox Live Indie Games, Xbox Live Arcade) and allowing them full access to what can be done with an Xbox, such as Kinect functionality, achievements and gamerscore tools.

The Internet's other major contribution to gaming is to allow players to engage with opponents and collaborators around the world 24/7; many games are now designed solely for multiplay and always online.

GAME ENGINES

A game engine is a piece of software used by developers in the creation of video games. It speeds up and simplifies the process by providing a development framework, tools, and reusable assets. Their design can be limited to an individual gaming platform or operating system; alternatively, they may work across several.

The engine is usually responsible for the implementation of the game mechanics and performing common game-centered tasks, such as providing first and third person character controllers. Additionally, many make the task of making a game available on different platforms easier to achieve. All these functions provide the developer with a foundation to build upon, and allow designers to focus on the unique components of the game they are working on. Of the hundreds of different engines available, some have broad application across several game types, while others are focused on specific effects, such as modeling vegetation. Many game developers license their engines to other developers, both large and small, as a means to generate additional revenue.

AAA Engines

AAA engines are at the cutting edge of game development. They are specifically designed for big budget productions, where only the speediest and visceral graphical experiences will do. One of the most significant engines in this category is the Unreal Engine. Now in its fourth stable release, it is notable for its many applications in other fields, such as the military training sim *America's Army*, creating virtual sets for children's TV show *Lazy Town* (UE3), powering architectural visualizations, and it has also been used in medical training.

Mobile and Web Engines

Some game engines are designed to be multi-platform and work across both mobile and web applications made for smart devices. This includes games published through social networks, an area that has seen phenomenal growth. To illustrate this, *FarmVille* (2009) —made by Zynga, played on Facebook—has more players than there are Twitter accounts, having 645 million active users (July 2014, statista.com) whilst Facebook has 1.25 billion active users. *FarmVille* was created using the Flare3d engine, which along with engines like Construct 2 is used for training and education due to their ease of use.

Working with Game Engines

There are many significant acronyms and a great deal of jargon employed when discussing developing games with game engines. Many of these terms are common in the wider world of computer programming and software developers in other fields would find them familiar. The key element when working with an engine is the SDK (software development kit) sometimes referred to as a "devkit." The SDK is a collection of interfaces, libraries, tools, and code snippets that can be employed by developers and designers to create a game. The SDK is usually accessed via an IDE (integrated development environment), which serves as the principal programming interface. An essential part of any SDK is the API (application programming interface) as it allows access to the operating system and its libraries, enabling the developer team to utilize its available features.

The Unreal Engine is one of the most established game engines available, having been first released in the late 1990s. Its most recent iteration, UE4, marks a change in how game designers and coders work collaboratively to create games. Unlike its predecessor, which used UnrealScript, a proprietary programming language, UE4 utilizes C++, a common programming language that employs object-oriented programming (OOP) principles. For a subscription fee, developers can access the full source code of the engine and, using online resources and communities like GitHub, build public and private projects around it.

3.16

Crysis 3: Jungle Patrol
An example of the CryEngine graphic capability.

GAME ENGINES

AAA Engines

Listed below are notable examples of AAA engines, along with some of the games built using each engine.

UNREAL ENGINE: *Unreal Tournament, Injustice: Gods Among Us*, the *Gears of War* franchise, the *Fable* franchise, *Mortal Kombat X, Mirrors Edge, Silent Hill: Downpour, Goat Simulator*

FROSTBITE: *Battlefield, Medal of Honor, Mass Effect*

CRYENGINE: *Ryse, Crysis* and *Far Cry*

SOURCE: *Counter Strike: Source, Team Fortress 2, Half Life 2, Portal*

ID TECH: *The Evil Within, Rage, Doom, Quake*

SNOWDROP: *The Division*

DUNIA: *Far Cry 2 & 3*

ANVIL / ANVILNEXT: *Assassin's Creed II, III, IV* and *Unity*

Mobile and Web Game Engines

Listed below are notable examples of mobile and web game engines, along with some of the games built using each engine.

UNITY 3D: The market leader, in 2014 it had 45 percent of the global market share (unity3d.com), with 3.3m registered developers, 630K active developers per month, 400m web player installs, 10.7m editor sessions in June 2014, and 600m gamers. As a comparison, Facebook has around 829 million daily users. Used on games such as *Ori and the Blind Forest, Bad Piggies* and *The Forest*.

Other notable mobile web engines are:

TORQUE 3D: *Penny Arcade Adventures: Precipice of Darkness, Rocketment, Protothea, And Yet It Moves*

CORONA SDK: *Fun Run, Major Magnet, The Lost City*

FLARE3D: *FarmVille 2, Evil Genius Online, Play Fast or Fail, LightStorm*

MARMALADE: *Plants vs. Zombies, Beyond Space, Earn to Die, Stars*

GAMESALAD: *Milo and Me, Get Fiquette, Little Saw, Super Spin Tanks*

MONOGAME: *Fez, Transistor, Tower Fall Ascension*

GAMEBRYO: *Power Up Heroes, Trion Worlds, Catherine*

INTERVIEW
CHRIS BRUNNING

• •

Industry role: Chris Brunning is Crytek's Technical Manager, based in Frankfurt, Germany. Crytek has been at the forefront of software development in video games for many years. It is probably best known for the sensational graphics in titles like *Ryse: Son of Rome* (2013), *Crysis* (2007) and *Far Cry* (2004). Chris Brunning discusses the company's success and CryEngine, its titular game engine.

Can you give a brief description of the CryEngine and its functions, and why you think CryEngine has been so successful?

Initially the CryEngine was built as a technical showcase, and it has continued that way over the years. It was built around the game in the first place, but it's always been about technical excellence, particularly on the rendering side. The earlier games, *Far Cry* and *Crysis 1*, were a "smack in the face" in regard to the quality of the game, and that's very much the case now. The game *Ryse* was released at the launch for the Xbox One, and one of the biggest things about *Ryse*, in keeping with other games we have made, it is a graphical showcase.

What does a technical manager do, what do you oversee?

My role is to license the engine and work on internal projects. I also work with the team that licenses the games. I talk to the internal teams and the external people, trying to keep everybody in line so that we are all doing the same thing. I ensure that our licensees are getting the added features that they need for their games.

3.17–3.18
Ryse: Son of Rome
Point cloud data—data
represented by a set of points
within a coordinated system i.e. a
3D environment—can be utilized
in real-time animation effects.
Here the data from the ship's sail
is used to viscerally realize its
destruction mid-combat.

How would you describe the relationship between the games and the engine? What comes first, the technological breakthrough, or the implementation, or is it driven by a new narrative seeking to do something innovative?

The relationship between game and engine can work in two ways. Firstly, developments in the engine are often driven by the needs of a particular project. This means you would usually see things developed in our internal games before anybody else gets hold of them. Secondly, we also have quite a few people who are on pure research (R&D— research and development), looking at issues like how we can better develop a shelling solution or an anti-aliasing solution.

Also, we look at the technical rendering side, as we work quite closely with the leading hardware manufacturers; Microsoft on the DirectX side and also on the Sony panels. To some degree we can drive what the need is, and also try to be there when it's available.

How many people do you have in that continuous role of R&D? Is it always in flux, what size is the team?

It is in constant flux. I would say that the average team has eight people, but it depends to some extent on what stage a project is at. When we come to the end of a project, as almost every developer does, we'll redeploy people and put them onto other projects for those final tweaks or optimizations. So, it can change at that point.

We have seen the release of the Xbox One and PS4. The PC market is always pushing forward and its technical development is far more fluid than the consoles and the hardware within them. How easy is it to work across platforms and what are the challenges or issues you face?

The way our engine is designed, especially with regard to the current generational requirements, there is not that much difference. The changes that were necessary have actually improved the PC version. By the time you have a powerful graphics card, you also have a powerful CPU (central processing unit). On the new consoles, the balance is

OBJECT ORIENTED PROGRAMMING (OOP)

OOP is a method of computer programming that employs code and "objects" of data that interact with each other to achieve the aim of the program. There are four principles to OOP:

DATA ABSTRACTION. Any representation of data in which the implementation details are hidden (abstracted). Abstract data types and objects are the two primary forms of data abstraction.

ENCAPSULATION. Provides the user with a set of functions, allowing the internal workings to be hidden.

INHERITANCE. The ability in programming to derive an object or class from an existing class, whilst maintaining the same behavior.

POLYMORPHISM. Meaning one name, many forms, this refers to the ability to define multiple classes differently. This allows identically named methods or properties to be used interchangeably by the client code at run time.

rather different. It has driven many improvements on the PC side for optimization.

As the new APIs are coming along, Mantle DX12 and Metal on the iOS, they are changing things a bit. We are trying to get ahead of the game and get on that. Our engine is being written to work across all platforms. There is a level of abstraction work involved in trying to maintain as much compatibility as we can. There is an almost daily dialog between the major graphics card manufacturers and us. As computer power increases this allows us to consider what else we can do. With regard to the Xbox One and the PS4, we've done a lot more than on the PC but of course, it carries over. Due to the issues that arise with CPUs, we can now sensibly utilize the graphics card to take up the slack.

On the Xbox, the limitations are on the CPU rather than on the GPU (graphics processing unit), sometimes called the VPU (visual processing unit), a processor on the graphics card, which in some cases can be on the motherboard. Once we had the GPU optimized, there was a certain amount of spare time that could be specifically allocated to VFX. It is becoming more of a wide system, rather

than the graphics card that purely puts triangles on the screen. We are using much more of the GPU's computational power because that is where the big steps in computational power are happening. The memory tends to be very fast there. That is also becoming a limitation on the PCs, where the memory is now one of the slower parts of the system. This is also changing the way we look at content; we have to consider data throughput as much more of a problem than we did previously. Now we work towards a data design system rather than an object-orientated one; it's more data oriented. The delays you get with cache misses are significant.

Can you explain the CryEngine real-time rendering used in the environment realization of *Ryse*, *Crysis*, and *Far Cry*?
This has a lot to do with the passion of the graphics guys. We've got to be the best. Their research papers are exceptionally in-depth, and written by very academically gifted people. These papers are regularly presented at SIGGRAPH (an international community of researchers, artists, developers,

filmmakers, scientists, and business professionals who share an interest in computer graphics and interactive techniques, established 1974) and FMX conferences (the Film Media Exchange is a conference in Germany for animation, effects, games, and transmedia, established 1994). In 2015 Crytek are giving seven presentations, which is a significant number of papers. It's rare when we are not presenting something and more often than not, they are about computer graphics. This year we have two people presenting about point cloud.

Can you tell me a bit more about streaming point cloud data, which you implemented in *Ryse*?
We used it for things like the sails on the warships, which are ragged and moving in the breeze. Large-scale destruction could be attempted with traditional animation techniques but it would be far too complex to build with bones. The point cloud effectively plays back anything if you have the disk bandwidth. It also makes it easier for the animators to do things with. Code can be attached to it; it

lives more within the physical world, rather than as a playback of a series of pictures. We are looking at the continued improvement of the compression point cloud data, particularly for consoles as they have slower hard drives than the PCs. *HUNT: Horrors of the Gilded Age* (2015) is based on our latest version. All of the stuff is made with it: character and weapon customization is a part of that system.

How is CryEngine utilized in other lateral capacities outside of games?
Military sims with RT Immersive but also in feature film FX with Cinebox. Cinebox is a movie production tool based around CryEngine, two different branches of the game engine (Cinebox is part and parcel of Crytek and RT Immersive is a sister company, all using the same engine). If you can program or author content in CryEngine then you can do it in Cinebox as well. There is an awful lot of crossover, they have slightly different feature sets but very similar. I think gaming technology pushes this area far more than the film industry these days.

3.19
Real Time Immersive
The CryEngine is used to create realistic virtual simulated training environments for the military. These simulations are known as Serious Games. *Virtual Attain®*, the serious game built by RealTime Immersive, is used by the US Army to train advanced situational awareness to soldiers as part of their core training.

CHAPTER REVIEW

This chapter has presented an overview of the technology involved in video games, its impact, and origins, as well as introducing some of the thinking and software involved in making games. It has addressed the technological overlap between video game peripherals and other areas of life as technology is repurposed to create new interaction methods. It has also made the link to how we receive feedback from our games and the impact this feedback has on gameplay.

Key points

GAMING PLATFORMS: There are four technology platforms on which most video games are played: PCs, home consoles, handheld consoles, and mobile smart devices, i.e. phones and tablets.

TECHNOLOGICAL EVOLUTION: The progress of technology is constant and rapid, with the next generation of platforms already being planned as the current generation is launched. Obsolescence is assured. But being first to market with a new technology platform is not always a guarantee of long-term success.

WHERE PEOPLE PLAY GAMES: The biggest slice of the game market is moving away from home consoles and PCs to networked mobile and portable platforms. The shift to mobile and portable platforms as the primary way people interact with computer technology is not limited to video games.

CROSS-POLLINATION: The continual interchange of technological innovation between different fields and industries has altered the way we play and interact with video games. The smartphone and its related technologies in particular have led games to be played in different ways and contexts.

THE IMPACT OF THE INTERNET: The Internet and the web are the key drivers of the modern video game distribution model. They have allowed small developers access to new markets, which were previously dominated by a few large companies. They have also helped introduce a new social era of gaming, where individuals play games over networks across the globe.

SKILLS CROSSOVER: When making games there is a large crossover of skills between video games production and other industries that require strong programming and design skills to create CGI and interactive content.

USER INTERFACE: The primary method of providing feedback and in-game information; a user interface can serve both aesthetic and gameplay purposes, which when done well aids gameplay. Academic research has provided new ways to discuss user interfaces by introducing the term diegesis, which refers to how the interface relates to narrative and storytelling within a game. Diegesis is already used in the analysis of movies and literature.

4.1
___
A Light in Chorus
Due in 2016, this is an exploration
game set in a world made entirely of
particles. You move around the world
as a reconfigurable swarm of points;
adopting the shapes of things around
you, illuminating hidden landscapes
and revealing shadowy fragments of
a much larger mystery.

4

LATERAL THINKING

Topics Covered
Physical Gaming Environments / Online
Communities and Alter Egos / Games as Art

For many, video games are now part of day-to-day life, but the contexts in which they are found are changing. Video games are again moving on, their boundaries only constrained by data connection or battery life. Gaming is becoming a far more collective experience, not only found online or in MMO, but one which inhabits the world around us, equal to our virtual connected lives.

PHYSICAL GAMING ENVIRONMENTS

Real world, adventure-based gaming began to emerge in mid-nineteenth-century England with the birth of letterboxing. This is a form of treasure hunt where weatherproof boxes are hidden in the countryside and hikers (players), guided by written coordinates and instructions, embark on an orienteering exercise cross country, using a map and a compass. Hikers would leave a postcard addressed to themselves or to a friend, in the box, and take one that had been left by a prior visitor. They would then post it onto the unknown recipient, hence "Letterboxing." The pursuit continues with thousands of hidden boxes on Dartmoor, Devon (UK), alone.

Real World Applications

As we grow older, opportunities to express youthful behavior through collective play become fewer. Common amongst many communities since the birth of civilization, people have sought to engage each other in unifying gaming events. The catalytic effect of mobile technology is presenting new opportunities for collective experiences through games.

The revolution in mobile technology, and the subsequent app explosion, have seen the desire to be outward-bound rekindled. Some of the main proponents of this physical and digital culture have been geocaching, munzee, and dead drops, which

4.2
Original Letterbox
The original Letterbox site was sited near Cranmere Pool in 1854, Dartmoor National Park, England.

4.3
Open box
The open box with a visitor notebook to sign and date as proof of the find and an ink stamp kit. The goal is to collect as many individual letterbox site stamps as possible.

KEY TERMS

ALTER EGO
A second or alternate identity or personality.

DEAD DROP OR DEAD LETTERBOX
Historically associated with espionage and used to disseminate anonymous information or data in a secret location. Its contemporary reinvention by digital artist Aram Bartholl in 2010, the Dead Drop network, utilizes USB drives cemented into walls. The drops are used to manually share file information in a physical location, i.e. sharing peer-to-peer un-clouded files.

GEOCACHE
A container used to house a number of items in a hidden location. The GPS coordinate location of the cache is listed on the Internet and mobile app. Caches are found using mobile GPS location devices, known as geocaching.

GPS
Global Positioning System, a way of navigating by using connected orbiting satellites that create a network of position information providing precise time and location data.

MUNZEE
Freemium or free treasure hunt game, similar to geocaching using QR (quick response) code technology, in addition to GPS location devices, to prove the find instead of a logbook.

4.4
Parallel Kingdom: Age of Ascension (2013)
A multiplayer location-based game that uses Google Maps. It reveals a hidden world to players through their smart devices, populated with strange and fantastical structures, creatures and characters as well as collectible resources, that is ready to be explored and conquered.

are forms of location-specific digital adventures. These have been used to create sequential storytelling, and land art, as well as the traditional treasure hunt.

The catalyst came in May 2000 when the GPS3 standard (Global Positioning System) opened up a new standard of satellite tracking precision, which previously had been ring-fenced for military applications. This provided a far more detailed global grid in GPS coordinate communication. Early indications of this new trend in location-based gaming became manifest in Stockholm, Sweden in 2002, with a game called *BotFighters*, made by It's Alive. Played on far more primitive cell phones than used currently, the gameplay was text-based using SMS messaging. Players chose a robot from the community website, stockpiled ordnance, i.e. rockets, lasers, and guns, and headed out for battles in the city. At the time, it was seen by the mobile companies as another lucrative opportunity to increase user spending, as each text in a battle cost 20 cents. Some mobile phone bills amounted to $4,000 (£2,712).

Since February 2011, the newer GLONASS-K Russian standard has been accessible to a range of mobile devices. The indie app market has focused on locality as a leading game mechanic to drive a new wave of MMORPGs. Android games like *Zombies, Run!* (2012) and *Claim Your Area (CYA)* (2012) as well as iPhone game *Own This World*, a bit like the board game Risk but in your neighborhood, *Turf Wars* and *Zombies, Run!* embody this idea of geographically engaging the player through localized gameplay, to stand or fall in the well-trodden roads of their own neighborhood.

In 2009 *Monopoly City Streets* redefined the classic titular board game by creating a Massively Multiplayer Online Real Time Strategy (MMORTS) game, reworking the concept into real physical locations by utilizing Google Maps and OpenStreetMap digital mapping apps.

The GPS game may have come of age when Google launched *Ingress* in 2013. An augmented reality MMORPG created with Niantic Labs, *Ingress* began life as a closed Beta (limited invitation only) in October 2012. Since then, the game has grown to engaging over 500 million players in a worldwide gaming network.

Ingress is built on Google Maps and accessed via smartphones. Digital possession of real,

4.5–4.6

Ingress

Meaning to "see with new eyes" Google's *Ingress*, developed by Niantic labs, is an example of social, location-based gaming in cities and towns. These screen grabs show aspects of the gameplay: Portal keys containing an image of real local landmarks can be collected while portals represented on the intel map can be attacked when a player is within a specific distance of its real-world location.

4.7

Ingress intel map

Shows portal locations, the color represents which of two factions is dominating each neighborhood. This map illustrates faction activity across the globe. The Resistance, in blue, seek to defend humanity from the influence of a new and potentially extraterrestrial energy source called "Exotic Matter/XM". The Enlightenment in green wish to embrace the energy and evolve humanity.

identifiable locations of interest are the key game driver, for example, public art, pubs, and plaques become strategically important territory markers, or "portals," for a faction (Resistance or Enlightenment) to claim or defend using their smart devices. These battle territories are in a constant state of flux, as the sides battle to create "control fields" across towns, regions, and across the sea. The gameplay is defined by a sense of ownership of local territory and collaborative play.

In *Ingress*, players (agents) can partake as individuals, but many organize into teams or clans, who work together to link geographically far-flung portals. Mostly this is done on foot, but occasionally, in an attempt to capture extremely remote portals, some players have flown to isolated locations, which are inaccessible for parts of the year due to adverse seasonal conditions to link up territory. The popularity of *Ingress* means that thousands of players can be mobilized to a single Anomaly event. These timed meetings take place globally in different countries and cities across all seven continents.

Ingress is similar to a former MMORPG, *Shadow Cities* released in 2011, which ceased operation after three years. It is *Ingress'* connection to the real world, and the blurring between reality and the game, that has helped it to succeed where *Shadow Cities* failed.

Another dominant figure in the location-based gaming scene has been the award-winning *Parallel Kingdom* (2008), which has over 2 million users. It is a territory-based MMORPG, where players battle unusual creatures, build, protect, and discover new territories worldwide. This game is designed to connect with other users for collaborative play with an emphasis on social gaming.

Pervasive Media Studio is a UK studio with links to education; it commissions interactive games in an urban setting. Through an initiative called the Playable City, it commissions digital artists and designers to create unique, fun, and engaging games, or digital narrative adventures in public spaces, such as *Hello Lamp Post*, *These Pages Fall Like Ash* and *2.8 Hours Later*.

Similar city wide game experiences such as the prototype *BikeTAG Play Test: Colour Keepers* (2012), are game and art experiences designed to encourage players to explore cities. *Colour Keepers* took place in Bristol in the UK using pedal bikes and smart devices in combination with other technology. It involved collaboration and battle elements linked to different team colors. The convergence of various technologies made the play visible in the physical world, creating a dynamic player experience through social interaction and discovery.

4.8

BikeTAG Play Test: Colour Keepers (2012)
BikeTAG uses LEDs, proximity sensors, and smartphone technology. Participants kit out their bikes, and choose one of three colors. The rider's route is recorded by GPS and uploaded live to an online map in his or her chosen color.

4.9
PulzAR™ on the Sony PS VITA
This puzzle game uses augmented reality to add a new dimension to mundane locations like a canteen table. In this example players employing AR Play cards (see 4.10) redirect lasers to destroy earth threatening asteriods.

Augmented Reality (AR)

Augmented reality is a technology that overlays visual interventions on top of the real world through a smart device, by using location data gathered by phones and tablets. Apps and games utilize the camera on smart devices to combine what is seen with the computer-generated layer of graphic content.

Augmented reality games tend to use a gameplay mechanic based on the immediate surroundings of the player, blurring the line between what is real and what is digital; a superimposition upon what we see or hear. It is different from virtual reality, where the user experiences immersion into a virtual environment.

Both smart devices and the traditional gaming handhelds have explored this medium. The Sony PS VITA: AR Play uses the real world area of the player as the game arena to play in, similar to the Sony Eye Toy: Play range.

4.10
AR Play cards
Designed for use with the Sony PS VITA the AR card symbols and markers (similar to a black and white QR code) are placed on a surface by a player or players. The software recognizes the symbol allowing it to assign a graphic outcome to a physical space providing a composite view through the handheld device (see 4.9).

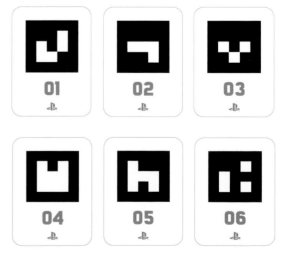

ONLINE COMMUNITIES AND ALTER EGOS

Sub-cultures offer a sense of belonging. We often recognize like-minded people through tribal motifs, communicated as outward expressions. These identifiers can be presented as forms of personal adornment, uniforms, sporting club colors, or distinctive fashion trends, reflecting a cultural movement, such as cosplay or fursuiting. Social activities that united the cultural sub-groups of the twentieth century have been enhanced and transformed by the Internet, connecting like-minded people in a new way.

How we express social belonging has developed with the growth of online communities. The known but often obscured digital world of avatars allows those who enter it a veil of anonymity, as well as the possibility of reimagining themselves to others. These personas or virtual exoskeletons, are often inhabited as virtual lives manifested through social networks and gaming hubs, which greatly differ from daily existence. In extreme cases, an individual's virtual life as an avatar can become more significant than their life in the physical world. (For more on virtual lives see the *Second Skin* documentary, dir. Amy Talkington, 1998. Also see The Cost of Progress page 135).

The online world is a place of the imagination, a platform to assert control over the projection of who we are and how we want to be perceived by others in name, purpose, and form. These new digital faces—avatars, personas, alter egos—allow us freedom of expression to pursue our alternate selves. Through these projected lives, people vicariously negotiate inner dreams to be the hero or antihero; to be more handsome, or beautiful, or to conquer fantastical foes against outrageous odds.

From sports grounds, to places of worship to gaming hubs, it is in human nature to gather

---

4.11

Cosplay

Cosplay (costume play); devoted fans dress up as characters from a video game or animated series. Below, Teraana performs as Ziggs—explosive expert—from the MOBA game *League of Legends*.

4.12

Second Life

Players' online personas may differ from reality. *Second Life* is a 3D virtual world that offers customizable avatars to players.

THE MOMA 14

PAC-MAN (1980)
TETRIS (1984)
ANOTHER WORLD (1991)
MYST (1993)
SIMCITY 2000 (1994)
VIB-RIBBON (1999)
THE SIMS (2000)
EVE ONLINE (2003)
KATAMARI DAMACY (2004)
DWARF FORTRESS (2006)
FLOW (2006)
PORTAL (2007)
PASSAGE (2008)
CANABALT (2009)

and focus our collective purpose and energy to achieve a desired outcome. We define "territorial uniqueness" (coined by Desmond Morris in his book *Manwatching: A Field Guide to Human Behaviour*, 1978) individually and collectively to defend a definable territory as ours. For many people, of varying ages, it is a part of daily routine to be a person of an enlarged identity, sharing experience and histories in a hidden virtual world.

GAMES AS ART

We should consider how the medium is being transformed as video games enter a period of cultural maturity. Away from the gilded halls of the big business that dominate the industry and their AAA titles, indie games have become a thriving playground for fresh ideas, uniquely styled outcomes and laid bare game mechanics. Industry cycles, disseminated technology and code, have allowed creative individuals the freedom to express via a game engine what other media fail to provide. A thinking play space offering the possibility of making ideas visible, and bringing them to life through movement and interaction for both maker and player. Artists and designers are exploring this new canvas with impressive and sometimes surprising results.

Traditional artists have often gravitated to more commercial income streams and forms of creativity to earn a living. Since the beginning of the games industry, artists have found a home in game design. Not merely for the financial rewards and the opportunity to bring stories to life, but also to combine career aspirations with the youthful dreams of living a creative life into adulthood. The rediscovered freedoms of indie development are

yielding some wonderful outcomes.

Video games can be recognized by their multi-faceted transcultural identity. They are now widely accepted as a major part of consumer entertainment, equal to TV and film, but it has only been in recent years that they have—controversially many would say—been regarded as an art form in their own right. Games as art redefine what is considered high culture, and challenge our understanding of this contentious digital aspirant.

A turning point in the validation and acknowledgement of video games as being culturally significant and worthy of greater recognition was reached in 2009 when MOMA (Museum of Modern Art) in New York bought fourteen computer games to establish their collection of games as an art form including *Pac-Man*, *Tetris*, *The Sims*, *EVE Online* and *Canabalt*. Since this watershed, MOMA has continued to expand its collection with new acquisitions including *Pong* (1972), *Space Invaders* (1978), *Asteroids* (1979), *Tempest* (1981), *Yar's Revenge* (1982) and *Minecraft* (2011). In addition, Ralph Baer's Magnavox Odyssey became the first console to be included.

INTERVIEW
ARAM BARTHOLL

4.13

1H (2008)

1H stands for "one handed weapon". These cardboard model replicas of weapons from *World of Warcraft* come from ready-made templates downloadable from Bartholl's website. These replicas of virtual items are meant to be carried around In everyday life without being used.

4.14

Dust (2011)

A 3D-printed, reduced scale concept model of the FPS *Counter-Strike* (1999) Dust map (de_dust), a virtual gaming environment. This map is one of the most popular in the game with a high frequency of shared experience and familiarity amongst gamers. This has led to a place that does not exist being discussed as if it were real. Bartholl's intention is to tap into this idea by making the virtual, physical.

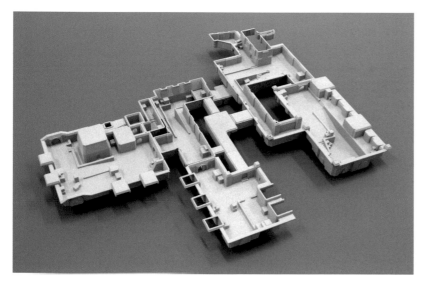

Berlin-based digital artist Aram Bartholl talks about gaming, virtual identities, and his artwork, which reflects on our digital lives. His work examines the blurred lines between our virtual existence and our tangible physical existence; indicating a shared history and memory of places that do not exist.

Can you talk about a few pieces of your work: 1H, Dust and First Person Shooter and focus on your fascination with digital narratives?

I've been doing these translations—virtual to physical—and rebuilding these objects for ten years. To put it in context with my other work, I think it's interesting how the gaming community were the first to know, to have that awareness, that the digital has become everyday life.

Regarding *Counter-Strike* and the Dust map, I have these pictures and examples of how some kids can rebuild the map in the sand on the beach, because they know it by heart. They re-enact the game by making poses. We are in a significant questioning stage in society, wondering what is going on and how far things will go. I believe, back when I started these pieces, there was an early awareness of the big impact these digital environments have on our lives. Gamers were the first ones, in a playful way, to deal with this and take these elements and re-enact stuff. I, of course, do it the same way.

The underlying question is: "I have played these games so many times and I remember the space but where is this space?" All these projects are based upon the *Counter-Strike* Dust map, as it is one of the game's levels I played intensely ten years ago.

Do you have a background in playing games?

I grew up with game consoles and computer games; it's a genuine part of my life. You play these games and wonder where is this space and wonder what would it be like to have this 3D crate (see image 4.15) now in the city. Blurring the different spaces, breaking the boundaries, and making you think about how much reality is happening for yourself, online, or in games. How does it relate or measure up to everyday life? It's interesting today as to how differently I see it. In the beginning, there were only a few people making pictures for the web and I was developing these projects. Now it has become a cultural phenomenon in society.

When I started using the Internet in 1995, people said "what do you want this for?" Then there were all the different steps in between; all these questions and copyright discussions, in many ways it has become more mainstream. As a big picture, it is interesting.

What is the rationale behind exposing the digital through public interventions such as 1H (one handed weapon)? Do they help externalize society's connections with simulated life?
It is always interesting to create work in public spaces. The axe in 1H works in that sense but there are other pieces where it works also, like the big project Map—a pubic installation begun in 2006

of a scaled-up Google red map marker placed in real locations highlighting how technology and innovation shapes our age; our social networks and culture. When you encounter these projects, people ask "why is it here?" They have this moment of irritation, something is going on, but they are not sure what. Also walking in public with the axe, it is a lot about how you try to explain *World of Warcraft* (*WoW*) to a curious public; how closely people work together, its social friendships. It's hard to give someone an idea what this is like, compared to social life in families or society.

I like to take these objects as symbols of what happens in virtual spaces. *WoW* is extreme in terms of friendship, friendships broken and how individuals play on and on. The moment you take these things to a public space, it poses a bunch of questions. What's your reality? What rules apply, in this digital

4.15
Dust: Crate installation (2013)
Comprised of a set of remade 3D assets from *Counter-Strike: Global Offensive (CS:GO, 2012)* that are printed to replicate the wood texture from the video game. Here they are positioned in a disused prison yard in Sherbrooke, Canada.

4.16
First Person Shooter (2006)
A do-it-yourself cut out project
that can be created from a
postcard downloadable from
Aram Bartholl's website. Wearers
of the glasses take part in a
provocative and comical comment
on the blurring of lines between
everyday life and violence in
video games.

space and what rules apply here on the street? People strip naked on *Chatroulette* but not in public. What would you do in *WoW* that you wouldn't in public?

Is there an aspect of addiction to these things, where we want to lose ourselves in alter egos, in other worlds?
What's interesting is that these 3D spaces, especially games, represent cyberspace, the old idea of virtual reality in a 3D space. I remember when I first played *Doom* (1993), that was something new, in the computer. I see it in a different light today.

Like the 2013 Snowden leaks from the NSA, and information sharing by Google and Facebook, which happened before, our whole lives are digital already (our digital alter egos). Although many people may not notice, it's still affecting everybody. It's like an iceberg, there's the peak, but then there is so much that is unseen, but which is already in place. It's not polygons and 3D cyberspace, it's us! All the data from us, the data we leave, we create the metadata.

These video game focused projects leads us to consider how digital space bleeds into physical space, forming a new reality. We are already living digital lives in the Matrix. But it is something we cannot see and are unaware of.

How do you plan to get the Dust level map (image 4.14) physically made?
In 2013 I was at a festival in Sherbrooke, Canada and I built all these crates in a prison yard (Dust excerpt 1, Quebec—see image 4.15). I approach large-scale projects from different angles. I did this with the scaled-up textures printed on the crates. The prison yard itself was very much like a computer game map because it had these enclosing walls. You then have the "skydome" above.

For another part of the show, we were creating an entrance scenario with a big gate, made only from cardboard with no textures on it. The entrance is one of the gates from the Dust map. In this way, I am testing the map, the scale, different locations, and ways to build it. A big concrete version of the Dust map as a gallery based sculpture is a long-term goal. There is no planning for that right now. It will be big and expensive (3D printing aside)!

People who know the Dust map will have many memories of it, but do you think they are looking at your work and notice the textures?
It's more about the space. With the crates, it's more about the picture, but with the architecture, it's about the space. We have evolved to remember space. Of course, playing repeatedly you know the space much better than a lot of other spaces in real life! This is why it is unbalanced; this is a virtual world on a server. How many people have actually been there? How many people have been to Mecca, or Times Square compared to how many people have been in that game? It's really interesting, a lot of people, many more people than some of the most famous places on Earth! That is why I like to play with cultural heritage, exploring what needs to be built to exist.

112

4.17
Video still from *Serious Games I
—Watson is Down*

4.18
Video still from *Immersion*
A soldier wears a VR headset
during a conflict reconstruction
in California.

Games Imitate Life

Another artist to examine the use of games is Professor Harun Farocki. His work addresses the uses of media in an age where war is televised instantly. The lines between what is real and imagined are increasingly blurred as the connections between war game environments, live televised conflicts, and the footage of drone strikes become ever closer.

In his short film, *Serious Games I–IV* (2009–10) Farocki examines the re-appropriated uses of sandbox war simulated game arenas, such as *America's Army*. The uses and application of virtual environments by the military are varied. Works

such as *Serious Games I—Watson is Down, II—Three Dead, IV—A Sun with No Shadow* were filmed at the Twentynine Palms military training facility in California. The films explore alternate uses of gaming technologies to train recruits for war in a classroom setting. Whilst *Serious Games III: Immersion* conveys a scene where American war veterans are led through the processes of "exposure therapy," using a VR set-up utilized by Air Force psychologists attempting to treat post-traumatic stress disorder (PTSD). The soldiers encounter a virtual recreation of the traumatic events that took place on a recon mission.

INTERVIEW

MIKE BITHELL

• •

Industry role: Mike Bithell is an indie developer who created *Thomas Was Alone* (2010). He talks about defining an individual direction as a games designer, and working within your means to create stunning and celebrated games.

How long have you been making games and how did you get to where you are now?
I started playing on my dad's old computers. I started at about 13, fiddling with QBasic and making tiny little text games. My hobby growing up was making things on a computer, interactive CD-ROM stuff.

I went to university to study computer game design, on one of the first three game design degrees in the UK, which was at Newport University in Wales. I was in the first year of it. Afterwards I got a job at Blitz Games, working on Nickelodeon games, doing third-person shooters and kung fu side scrollers, and worked my way up from being a junior designer.

Then a friend of mine moved to London to start Bossa Studios. In 2010 they brought me down as

their lead designer and I made a bunch of Facebook games. Bossa are probably best known for the game *Surgeon Simulator* (2013), but I had nothing to do with that. In my last years at Bossa, I was working on *Thomas Was Alone* (*TWA*) in my spare time. It was a hobby game, because I wanted to make something and release it on my own.

The first prototype for *TWA* was in Flash, but in the first few weeks of moving to London I went to an indie game event; the first ever UK meet up of developers that used an engine called "Unity." No one was using Unity at the time as it was new. I went along and listened politely. Afterwards we went to the pub to socialize and I was cornered by two of the ten people that worked at Unity at the time. They said "You've got to make your game in Unity, every indie game is going to be made in Unity" and gave me a copy. I started playing with it. I got really into it and it took over whilst I was making *TWA*. I never expected *TWA* to do well, but it went massive. I quit my day job and started making *Volume* [Mike's new game in development] on my own, and then slowly a team has built up.

4.19
Thomas Was Alone
The minimalist design was significantly influenced by the early-twentieth-century art and design style characterized by The Bauhaus school.

Your games are thoughtful, witty and elegant. What are your influences and inspiration from outside the world of video games?

For *Thomas Was Alone* it was the Bauhaus, colliding with Swiss typography and a lot of *The Hitch Hiker's Guide to the Galaxy*. A slight interest in AI and sci-fi narratives, with too much interest in drama and melodrama; a love of platformers and an interest in slightly savvy music.

For *Volume*: too many Marvel movies, far too much interest in Robin Hood and history in general. I like contextualizing legends and storytelling through the ages. I love Shakespeare, we take a few patterns from his stuff. I'm really obsessing about how YouTube is emerging as a form of communication. The whole thing is about a YouTuber and features a bunch of YouTubers. The idea of fame. Everything that happens to me ends up in a game. This is how it works.

I worked as a graphic designer for a year, early on in my career; I'm a hack but I love it and it's affected my taste. I like the ornate but I tend to gravitate towards simple shapes, forms and colors. Two fonts are too many fonts. We all have our own

4.20

Volume

Volume is Mike Bithell's stealth puzzle game. The follow up to *Thomas Was Alone*, is another interesting example of reduced game design, working within limited means. The main level mechanic is based in a room, each iteration of the room takes on a different puzzle layout.

tastes, it's not that one's better or worse, and my tastes affect the games I make. Anyone who says it doesn't affect their games is a liar.

My art direction decisions are also based on the resources available to me. *TWA* basically cost my time and about £5,000 ($7,500). *Volume* is probably going to come in around £250,000 ($373,000). It means that when making a game, the normal way you might think through your environments wasn't going to happen. So, you work out a way to make one nice room and fill it with low poly art. Why is it low poly art? You find the narrative reason why. What works with low poly? Well a minimalist UI and you build from there. In the indie world, so many projects run into trouble because they don't think about the money side. I always try to make games that realistically use the resources available.

Do you think there is a reaction in indie games to reject the hyperreal aesthetic of AAA?
Absolutely. It's not my style though. If I had £20 million ($30 million), I would make a game that looked like *Watch Dogs* (2014). Or I would make ten games that would look like *Volume* but much better. I do what I want to do. What I do is not a reaction and I produce what I want to produce.

I have five games in my head that I have always wanted to make as a jobbing designer. It occurred to me, that if I win the lottery, it's these five games that I would make. I still have that list and I won the lottery with *Thomas Was Alone*. *Volume* is the second game on that list and it is also the second cheapest. Everything needs to be conscious.

4.21
Lumino City
Hand-crafted maquettes and
delicately considered level designs
set the scene for the game *Lumino
City* by London-based indie studio
State of Play.

INTERVIEW
LUKE WHITTAKER

● ●

Industry role: Luke Whittaker is
co-founder of games company State of
Play, based in London, UK. He discusses
the design processes involved in making
the game *Lumino City* (2014).

**What did you study and in what
medium did you specialize?**

Katherine Bidwell (State of Play co-founder) and
I met when we were studying on the New Media
Production course at Bournemouth University.
Dan Fountain, our coder, studied there too a few
years later. The course allowed you to use a wide
variety of digital processes, including film, game
design and animation, and towards the end we were
encouraged to specialize and work together with
people from different specialisms. Both Katherine
and I specialized in the art side, and Dan specialized
in coding.

Detailed thorough pre-production is a vital
element for any project. Proper planning can save
time and money when considering the production
costs of 2D and 3D asset creation, modeling,
texturing, animation, and rendering. All of this before
the work is realized in a games engine.

**Why have you explored video games through
traditional art and design techniques? What
is it that you find compelling as a medium?**

After you've started making games, where
filmmaking, storytelling, illustration, animation,
interaction, and sound design all come together to
produce the finished result, every other medium
seems somehow dull and lifeless by comparison.
Gaming has another advantage in that it demands
activity from the audience. That comes with its own
challenges, of course; for a start the game has to be
comprehensible and free from technical issues in the
way that, for example, a painting doesn't. However,
they are interesting problems to grapple with.

Lumino City is completely self-funded, and I
would recommend it as a way to work if you have
something you're passionate about. There are other
pressures though, in that you need to be able to
support yourself. We have done that by staying

4.22
Lumino City
"The model is nearly finished, the signage lights are wired. The game has taken three years. In fact, we thought it would be out a year ago but we were intentionally flexible. If something needed more time, we gave it more time."

4.23
Lumino City
Laser cutting was used to create very intricate cardboard structures.

4.24–4.25
Lumino City
Development sketches and digital concepts.

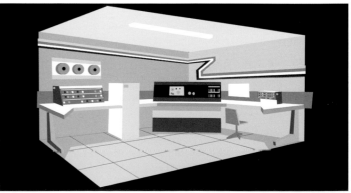

small, and doing animation work and smaller games like *KAMI* (2013) for iOS, which have helped fund the work on *Lumino City*.

At first, we began a process of sketching, and simultaneously working on a very rough 2D version of the game. We needed that process to be absolutely sure our game design mechanics worked, because once we'd built and filmed a physical model, there was no going back. No moving doorways or buttons if the design wasn't right.

The game was filmed with a motion control camera, which is often used for high-end film and TV jobs, so it's extremely expensive to hire. We could only afford it for a day, but it was the only way we would get the shots from up high on an eight-foot (2.5m) tall model. So, after a year's build, we had to film the entire game in a day, and had a complicated multi-layered script to do so.

TASK

Desk Game

Sitting at the desk where you normally work, look at what's in front of you. Think what you could do to it to turn it into a game. Take a camera and photograph your space, then using whatever software you find the easiest to use, find a way of making it work. You might use stop-frame, 2D Flash animation, or map the space in 3D, meaning you can bounce a ball around it. At this stage a certain amount of improvisation and hacking is fine; there's no right way to make a game, use the tools in ways which suit you rather than what you're supposed to do. The idea is the important thing, as is the ingenuity you use getting it to work.

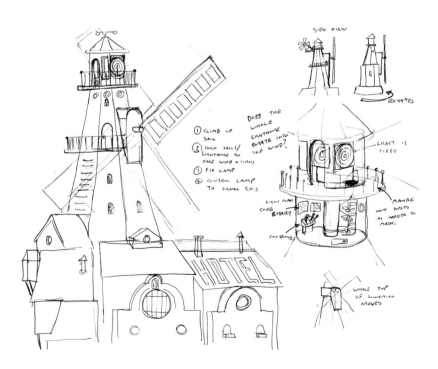

4.26
Lumino City
Early development sketch of the gatehouse building interior.

TOP SIX PIECES OF ADVICE FOR AN INDIE DEVELOPER

JOSEPH RYAN

At university, Joseph Ryan was the project lead and game designer for Sony's PSP Minis "PlayStation First" competition, in which he won a commission to develop a game for release on the PlayStation Network. Now an indie developer, he outlines key advice for working as an indie developer.

01 **STAY IN CONTACT.** When you're working with people remotely and not in a physical space, it can be hard to feel like you're actually collaboratively working with someone. Communication is key. Daily or weekly conference calls are essential.

02 **DON'T LET THINGS LINGER TOO LONG.** If you decide in one meeting that you're going to do something, crack on with it. During the time before you speak again, you may forget how you were going to achieve this goal and begin to lose your way. Pick up the phone and have a conversation with someone. Otherwise, a week or two will have passed until the next scheduled meeting and you will have meandered around having achieved very little. That's a week lost and squandered energy.

03 **BE OPEN.** If something is bothering you, don't let it eat away inside you. Don't play the blame game; you're working as a team. If something doesn't work right don't point the finger but find a way to progress.

04 **KEEP MOTIVATED.** When you've been working on a project for a long time, it can be hard to see the light at the end of the tunnel. Negativity can creep in and those uneasy questions of doubt. Try to stamp out negativity within the group when you see it. Set milestones, not as something to beat people with if they don't achieve them, but as something to spur on the group to guide them. Checkpoints or milestones can help the team feel good when they are reached. Keep old builds and assets around, to remind you of the progress you have made. Having something to look back on, as a measure of progress, is good for morale.

05 **PLAY TO YOUR STRENGTHS.** As a small team, you might not have the workforce to get a job done quickly, but the advantage of a small team is that you're not a hulking colossus with a multi-tiered system that can't make decisions quickly. You can sign off on decisions quicker and review them just as quickly. There is a flat balance of power, so everyone has a voice. People doing their jobs can feel better about what they're making, as they have a direct say in how they deliver and interpret the task. Thus, they become the master of their own domain and feel ownership over the project.

06 **YOU CAN'T DO EVERYTHING.** If you're straight out of university, you may be used to being the sole decision maker. But, in the long term, you can't do everything. You have to let go of the project control that you once had. Allow other people to do their jobs; that's what they're there for, and they don't need you behind them second-guessing every decision they make. The same is true of the project. Don't try to cram every idea you've ever had into one game. With the freedom you have as an indie developer, it may be exciting at first when you think that you can do all the things you've been dying to do. In reality, you can't be all things to all people and you can't execute each idea efficiently. The old adage "jack of all trades, master of none" is true. Budget, time, and planning are important and one of those is bound to give. Do a few things very well, not many things badly. There will always be other games you can put your ideas into.

4.27
A Light in Chorus
Championing beautiful aesthetics with puzzle solving gameplay. The meandering environment of *A Light in Chorus* is brought to life through point cloud data, engendering an ethereal ghostly aspect to the digital world.

INTERVIEW
ELIOTT JOHNSON AND MATTHEW WARSHAW

• •

Games as art: Two fine art graduates, Eliott Johnson and Matthew Warshaw, coded their own engine to explore their beautifully translucent 3D-gaming vision, *A Light in Chorus* (*ALIC*).

Why use game design to explore art practice?
(EJ) I've always made work that either describes or uses contemporary technology. This medium can express ideas, which would be difficult to articulate in other media. In this respect, working within games is a perfect fit for me, both the players and (especially) other developers already have the right vocabulary and are able to have a conversation that is both highly technical and conceptual. It's immensely fulfilling.

> ❝
> **AS ARTISTS WE'RE PERHAPS MORE PRIMED TO LOOK FOR INFLUENCES IN STRANGE OR UNUSUAL PLACES.**
> *Eliott Johnson*
> ❞

I find my relationship with images and other traditional media increasingly passive. There's something inherently exciting about the directly participatory/experiential aspect of games. I think a lot of performance and conceptual art shares similar ideas, which the industry is only just beginning to explore within gameplay. Games are able to do this within play space, rather than the silent reverence of galleries. Ideas can be far more accessible and open for discussion. Many of the really interesting ideas found in the history of art have been buried, obfuscated or confined to academia. They deserve a bigger audience, one which is able to engage with people in a very direct, participatory and more relatable way.

How did you realize your vision of a world defined by point cloud data?
(MW) The game engine originated as a collage of various old projects: half-baked rendering engines, input consoles and shaders. The first ALIC-specific step was creating a set of renderable points that could morph between various file-defined states, working within the confines of what I know

121

4.29
A Light in Chorus
The ferris wheel looms above
and the forest beyond.

about OpenGL [Open Graphics Library—a multi-platform application programming interface (API) for rendering graphics]. The code has come a long way. It's a collaborative process of conversations, new ideas and tools, along with the occasional blog post. I owe a huge amount to programmers who create open source online tutorials.

(EJ) For the artwork I am using a combination of off-the-shelf software and my own tools. I take normal polygonal objects and "light" them with points. It's like an entirely virtualized LiDAR or SONAR process, and it's the distribution of these points that I spend most of my time refining, rather than on specific modeling tasks.

One of the advantages of the art style is that it allows us to generate far more content than would normally be possible in a game art pipeline. This is important, as we are a small team tackling an ambitious project. Whilst there's still some overhead in traditional asset creation (modeling, texturing), once I ray cast the points onto the objects, we delete the geometry and the viewer's mind does an astonishing job of filling in the blanks.

It's a style with a very unique set of design problems, which both of us work hard to address. One example of this is draw distance. Everything is additively blended as we are limited in how much can be on screen at any one time. We have to try and lead the player in the game environment, without relying on distant landmarks. It's much harder than you'd think. The immediate environment needs to be filled with a distinctive arrangement of objects or you just end up lost.

TASK

Situationist Theory

This task will be familiar if you're aware of situationist theory, a theory that indicates an individual primary response to immediate situations or surroundings. This works best for when you are stuck on a problem, in need of new input or a catalyst to progress:

GO ON A LONG AIMLESS WALK. Explore little alleys and streets that you may have passed before but never ventured down. When you return, write down what you thought about on the walk, or just describe the things you saw. Taking in lots of new and varied visual information can be a very useful way to generate ideas, sometimes a small thing can come back to you weeks later and make all the difference to your work.

CHAPTER REVIEW

This chapter has presented and challenged the perception of how games are accessed experientially. It has also shown that within the industry aesthetic considerations and narrative exploration are broadening. Games can be utilized to convey important ideas, they can be influential and cross international and cultural borders as never before. As a creative medium, artists are exploring virtual worlds, through avatars, cultural symbols, and environments, as society continues to embrace digital culture. What a video game should be, or can be, is continually challenged.

Key Points

LATERAL COLLECTIVE PLAY: As access to mobile GPS technology has taken off in the last ten years, games design has re-appropriated this new location-based mechanic. Multiple forms of individual and collective gameplay have changed the way we play digital games, as well as where we encounter game narrative structures.

GAMES AS ART: For decades, video games were made for a niche market. Video games are now not only part of mainstream culture, but also accepted and defined as an art form by leading international art institutions. This step recognizes their contribution and social significance as a transcultural visual language. This visual language is evolving in its subject matter and influences, purpose, and production; it is no longer defined by its former narrow processes and outcomes.

SOCIAL POLITICAL COMMENT: Existing in a connected digital culture and acknowledged as a visual language and art form, video game narratives provide a rich platform to address other wider societal issues. Alongside other mediums, such as graphic novels, TV and film, artists and commentators utilize video game ideas and settings to investigate and discuss leading societal questions.

RUGS

DISCRIMINATION

BLING

VIOLENCE

5.1
PEGI icons
Visual descriptors to illustrate game content used by Pan European Game Information (PEGI).

5

GAMES AND SOCIETY

Do video games have boundaries? The arts and popular media have always challenged the status quo and video games are no exception. Partly driven by fear of the new, video games have been accused of many things: dumbing down, being a corrupting influence, and deliberately courting controversy. The result is that societies have sought to regulate and control gaming content. This chapter examines the background, considerations, and social responsibility that video game makers need to reflect on.

A SOCIAL RESPONSIBILITY

Game designers can sometimes take their perception of the world around them for granted, forgetting that others may see it in a different way. Game content can fall foul of misunderstanding the context it is used in, by either the relevance or importance of cultural, religious, and political differences.

For example, in 2012, the *Call of Duty* franchise caused a stir when the Favela multiplayer map in *Modern Warfare 2* had a picture frame adorned with sacred text on a bathroom wall. This caused offence to some as, under Islam, the text could be anywhere in a home except in a bathroom. The position of

the frame was therefore considered offensive and unacceptable in the game. Once this problem was flagged, Activision Publishing removed the map until the release of a game update. In a statement Activision said that "… our development studios are respectful of diverse cultures and religious beliefs, and sensitive to concerns raised by its loyal game players." To avoid these kinds of controversies, many games are designed to be obviously distanced from everyday life: using frog avatars rather than humans, lasers not bullets, green goo not blood, therein potentially making them universally acceptable.

Video games are regulated in a similar fashion to other forms of media and, like other media, the type, and effect of regulation varies between countries. Existing law, such as the Obscene Publications Act in the UK, combined with established conventions on defamation or copyright has always been applied to video games, but

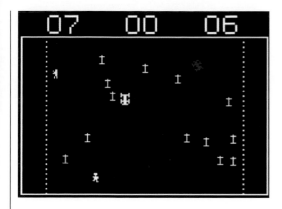

5.2

Death Race
A screen shot from the
arcade game which caused
public outrage for its "Hit
and Run" gameplay despite
a lack of graphical realism.

5.3

Death Race, arcade poster
Features a picture of the two-player arcade
cabinet. The game's theme was based on the
1975 dystopian sci-fi film of the same name.

in many areas it has taken some time for the law
to catch up.

In the 1970s, video games were taking
their first steps into becoming mass-market
entertainment. What was produced by early
game makers and sold to a relatively small number
of consumers was largely unrestricted; this is
unsurprising, given that the unrealistic graphics
offered by the available technology meant there
was no blood, guts or nudity to cause offense.
Equally, the popularity of the arcade and the new
home computers and consoles led the media to
eulogize about the potential of these novel products
(e.g. the Magnavox console, see The Age of the
Console page 23), rarely did they discuss the
game's content. However, it was not long before
controversy hit with the media and legislators alike
taking a more critical stance.

The first video game to cause a media storm
for controversial content was the 1976 arcade
game *Death Race* (see images 5.2 and 5.3). Created
by Exidy and based on the film *Death Race 2000*,
it caused upset long before *Grand Theft Auto*
was imagined. The graphically primitive *Death
Race* was criticized for its hit and run theme, as
players were required to run down human-like
gremlin characters that when struck would emit
a scream and turn into a tombstone. This marked

the beginning of the debate on whether video
games, like other media before them, were to
blame for society's psychological ills. For many, the
debate still rages. A discussion about the way we
interact with video games and the subject matter
they tackle forms part of a much larger and more
complex philosophical discussion concerned with
censorship, psychology and society. Our aim here is
to introduce the subject area, providing a pause for
thought, reflection, and debate.

There is a robust debate in industry, society,
and academia about acceptable themes for
video games and what the long- and short-term
effects of playing a variety of game types might

IN APRIL 2009, *HALO 3* PLAYERS CELEBRATED A COLLECTIVE SPINE-TINGLING MILESTONE: 10 BILLION KILLS AGAINST THEIR VIRTUAL ENEMY, THE COVENANT. THAT'S ROUGHLY ONE AND A HALF TIMES THE TOTAL NUMBER OF EVERY MAN, WOMAN, AND CHILD ON EARTH.

Jane McGonigal,
*Reality Is Broken: Why Games Make Us
Better and How They Can Change the World*

be. No definitive answers have been reached, but there's yet to be a proven link between undesirable behavior and playing video games. Yet, there is broad agreement that not all content is suitable for everyone. It's accepted that young children should not be exposed to the extremely realistic graphical representations of violence available in some titles. This acceptance has led to video game age-rating systems such as the ESRB (Entertainment Software Rating Board) in America and PEGI (Pan European Game Information) in Europe. The question remains though: what, if any, limit is there to the subject matters covered by video games? As the video game industry is still in its formative years there seems to be plenty of time for game makers and companies to explore these boundaries.

It is the case, however, that many game producers are more likely to be compelled to set content boundaries for commercial reasons, rather than be coerced by law or conscience to create content which is uniquely suitable for certain markets (see the interview with Alex Williams of Miniclip on page 162). Commercial pressures mean that it has become more important for producers to show they take the appropriateness and safety of their content seriously. For example, those companies whose products appeal largely to children need to prove to parents and society that their content is suitable for consumption; if they don't, their profits will suffer.

Other game makers, however, have a different agenda. There are creators of video games, like those in other artistic and popular media, who deliberately set out to be controversial. Occasionally they might promote alternative or extreme ideological perspectives. This is often to court publicity; to give themselves a marketing edge over their commercial rivals. The larger publishers and studios are ultimately commercial organizations. Their focus is to sell as many games as possible to recoup costs, and make a profit from their considerable investment.

As the game industry has evolved, the nature of video games have followed the paths set by the established media formats into areas that raise controversy (video nasties/pornography), inevitably leading to questions about the nature of the games we play, and their sociological and psychological effect. These days, graphic deaths are commonplace in film and video games, but nudity and sex are rare in games. So, are there qualitative differences between watching one medium and playing another? As consumers, how do we decide what is OK for ourselves? In simple terms, it is purely a matter of taste. We want to be entertained and if we want to play or watch and it is available, why not? If it looks too scary, gruesome, or dull, choose something else.

In the game *Syndicate* (1993) players were able to kill civilians with no penalty for enacting

KEY TERM

ETHICS

A system of moral principles or a philosophical standpoint relating to conduct, motives of right and wrong, which can encompass politics and law. The *Oxford English Dictionary* defines ethics as:

1. Moral principles that govern a person's behaviour or the conducting of an activity.
2. The branch of knowledge that deals with moral principles.

5.4
Mortal Kombat (1992)
Pressure from politicians and the media, over what was considered *Mortal Kombat's* unacceptable use of violence and gore, led to rating systems being introduced.

in-game sociopathic actions. The *Grand Theft Auto* franchise has equally allowed players to be merciless to the innocent citizens of its universe, although this isn't encouraged as a route to success. It is widely acknowledged that the *GTA* franchise has deliberately courted controversy as a marketing and brand strategy.

The Birth of Regulation

In 1994, at a time when most console players were less than 16 years old, there was significant controversy in the US regarding the content of video games. Although it was not the only title involved, the fighting game *Mortal Kombat* (1992) gained notoriety after its violent scenes led to US Senate hearings that pushed the industry towards recognizing its content needed to be age sensitive. When *Mortal Kombat* moved from the arcade to the home console in 1993 parents, politicians, and the media became aware of the "fatalities," a special move performed by the characters in the game whereby on beating an opponent the winner could add insult to injury by killing them in a brutal and bloody way. The furore caused by these visceral in-game actions ushered in age classifications for video games.

The established media, for example, literature, TV, and film, have long been affected by national laws designed to limit what can be consumed in their territory. In the EU, with its common market, supranational organizations can have influence over these regulations. In general, countries worldwide are free to place limitations on what can be produced by creative industries, but these limits can be of varying degrees of severity. These regulations can be employed to ban material after it has been created, or request changes to the content (i.e. censor) or apply restrictions, usually based on age considerations, as to who can legally purchase certain types of content. Limitations to access are usually concentrated around issues of decency and violence, but often can be politically motivated.

Most consumers are familiar with the concept of ratings due to their use in cinema, but in the case of video games it is a recent phenomenon. More recent still is their legally enforceable nature. There is a link between brands and the ratings systems, as game manufacturers wish to be seen as responsible developers.

129

What are Ratings?

According to PEGI: "Age ratings are systems used to ensure that entertainment content such as films and computer games, are clearly labeled by age according to the content they contain. Age ratings provide guidance to consumers (particularly parents) to help them decide whether or not to buy a particular product."

PEGI was a voluntary system in the UK until 2012, when it became legally enforceable to restrict the sale of games to those underage. The attribution of age ratings was previously handled by the BBFC (British Board of Film Classification) but the responsibility has now been passed to the Video Standards Council (VSC)—part of PEGI— that also has a section called the GRA (Games Rating Authority).

Developed by the Interactive Software Federation of Europe (ISFE) the pan European system PEGI utilizes a thirty-seven-point questionnaire to define the age rating of a video game title. "The questionnaire is designed to meet varying cultural standards in all the member states," of the European Union. "For example, mild violence may not be a very shocking element in your country, but the swearwords in some games may be. And the same goes for gambling. If a game features gambling, it therefore automatically receives a 12-rating according to the PEGI questionnaire." It goes on to state that, "The PEGI system has been designed to advise parents and educators about possible harmful elements in a game for children under the advised age. With help of the age rating symbols and content indicators on the packaging of games, PEGI is aiming to assist parents/educators in making sensible buying decisions."

The aim of the classification board is to define what is acceptable and to protect the vulnerable and the underage through the use of certification, but this can lead to differences of opinions between the ratings systems and developers.

Ian Rice of the VSC points out that the US "ESRB [the North American classification body] ratings do not always fit with the PEGI system. For example, ESRB have a ten-age rating and the PEGI system has a seven and twelve rating. Designing a game for a specific rating system will mean that it does not always fit a global market, as there are variants in the ratings systems. A game may be rated up or down, attaining an unintended age rating in an overseas market." He goes on to state that the questionnaire has had to evolve over time to reflect changes in developer content. "With blood, in the PEGI criteria, there are only a few questions that refer to it. It does not matter whether there is blood or not. We are looking at how the character is reacting to the violence. If they react realistically, then it will get a higher rating than if they react non-realistically. The blood part was taken out of that deliberately because developers were making blood green goo instead of blood."

The VSC is kept at arms length from the games companies and the government. "Part of

5.5
PEGI rating icons
Ratings bodies such as PEGI (Pan European Game Information, not including Germany), use classification icons or the ESRB (Entertainment Software Rating Board) in America, have developed a visual identity enabling the public to further understand the suitability of the game content.

the original set-up was that they wanted to have clear blue water between the rating body and the developers." Gianni Zamo, VSC. In Europe, all games must be rated, and to do so they need to pay a fee to PEGI (made up of two bodies, the VSC and NICAM: Netherlands Institute for the Classification of Audiovisual Media). Essentially, games rating systems are funded by the games companies themselves. This fee pays for the Pan European Game Information system.

Other professional bodies that work alongside PEGI, which consumers may not be so familiar with, are UKie (UK Interactive Entertainment) and its US equivalent the ESA (The Entertainment Software Association). UKie and ESA work closely with politicians and policy makers to encourage government support, deal with intellectual property crime as well as offering advice on IP to developers and sellers of video games. UKie describes itself as "the only trade body for the UK's wider interactive entertainment industry. We exist to champion the interests, needs and positive image of the video games and interactive entertainment industry whose companies make up our membership." The ESA has a similar mission statement, focused on the US industry, but is also famous for organizing the annual industry-only E3 Expo event. Other trade bodies include ESAC in Canada and SELL in France.

DISCUSSION POINTS

01 Do video games creators have a responsibility to consider the impacts of their work?

02 Are video games the right medium to challenge orthodoxies?

03 In what ways do video games differ from more established media formats? How might these differences make video games better or worse at challenging orthodoxies?

04 Why do societies ban video games?

05 How does society decide who can play a certain game?

06 What systems, if any, should be in place to ensure that games are only consumed by suitable age groups?

IT MIGHT BE A VIDEO GAME BUT IT'S RATED PEGI 18. WE STILL ENCOUNTER ISSUES WHERE PARENTS ARE NOT MAKING THE CONNECTION BETWEEN GENRE, FORMAT AND RATING. THEY STILL SEE THEM AS A GAME FOR THEIR CHILD. IT'S AN 18 AND SUITABLE FOR ADULTS ONLY.

Ian Rice VSC
(Video Standards Council, PEGI)

Censorship and Video Games

In many countries, rating systems are now enforced and it is unusual for games to be banned outright. As discussed above the ratings are based on age, with the most violent or sexual themes only found in games rated for adults (usually 18+).

Despite this a gap remains between many parents' perception of what video games are and the reality. It is essential that those buying video games for children are better informed about their content. This desire for better information for parents and carers is a significant driver of ratings systems across the world. It would help, however, if parents took these ratings seriously.

In the EU and the US a video game in theory could be considered "banned" if it fails to adhere to any of the rating criteria, but as the big producers wish to sell their games, this scenario is highly unlikely. In the UK, if a game is refused classification or does not seek one, it cannot be sold legally in retail outlets, but may be available online. The Internet's role in providing access to content that national governments wish to censor is a controversial and global issue not limited to the UK. Some good resources on censorship and video games can be found on the NCAC (National Coalition Against Censorship), an organization based in the US.

In the UK and US, no games have been banned permanently but some have adjusted their content

5.6

Manhunt
Still unavailable in Australia. The Rockstar game was initially rated MA15+ but the Australian Federal Attorney-General Philip Ruddock appealed the age rating. Its ban is due to its use of violence, which also included forms of torture.

to ensure classification. In comparison, Germany and Australia (not being part of PEGI or the ESRB rating bodies) have refused classification for some games and, despite changes by their publishers, they remain unavailable through retail outlets.

Violent movies can be seen as analogous to violent video game titles. The body count in a range of popular movie franchises makes interesting reading, for example in the *Die Hard* films there are 377 deaths, *Rambo* and its sequels have 441 deaths and in *The Return of the King*, the last film in the *Lord of the Rings* trilogy, there are 836 deaths. Death, or imminent threat to survival, is a uniquely engaging narrative driver; its normalization and frequency mean we rarely acknowledge the quantities involved.

In 2003, Rockstar North introduced the video game *Manhunt*. The game courted controversy for its level of graphic violence. In one of the first set pieces, kills in the game see the player stealthily execute a gang member. The only possible weapon available is a plastic bag. Having selected the bag, the player approaches the NPC (non-playable character), a button click triggers a cutscene video of the murder, and then control is returned to the player. Due to its violent content *Manhunt* remains unclassified in Australia. Germany and Australia are two countries where there are many games being restricted due to content. If we compare the same

specific violent narrative driver within TV shows, the audience/censors' reaction is markedly different or absent. For example in the *Constantine* episode "A Whole World Out There" (season 2, episode 11, 2015) a character is shown being suffocated with a plastic bag. Similarly, in the science fiction TV show *Fringe*, in the episode "A Short Story About Love" (season 4, episode 15, 2012), a woman is suffocated by having cling film wrapped around her face by the assailant. Both shows aired without controversy.

The use of cling film, cellophane, or plastic bags, as a cinematic killing device is an almost regular occurrence in screen-based entertainment aimed at adults. Multiple murders are a norm at 18, or M and A (mature, adult) certificated blockbusters, but when similar things happen in video games, the game risks having its certification refused. Within the cross-section of media certification, it would appear that in the light of subjective opinion it is not a level playing field.

Why is this, what is the perceived difference to society? Is it that by clicking a button players are asked to make a choice, rather than the perception of passively watching entertainment? Can the demarcation then be defined by choice, repetition, and particularly interaction? This may be the key difference: some games are more controversial than film, and video game content is treated differently.

Simulation and Interaction

In the earliest days of the video game, the limitations of the technology meant that subject matter was rarely an issue. Contemporary technology allows for unprecedented levels of realism, as the graphics bring gamers closer to the subject matter than ever before.

The number of people now playing video games suggests that the link between violent games and violence in the real world is tenuous. However, judgments are made that take an alternate view regarding the influence of video games compared to their peers. Buttons, joysticks, and joypads are used to highlight a perceived difference from other populist media types that engage in comparable narratives. Their use is assumed to require a deeper intention and behavior—maybe indicating a level of dissoluteness—beyond a simple desire to be entertained, as players combine interaction with voyeurism.

It is unclear how choosing to watch two hours of oversized graphic violence in the cinema, in movies like the *Saw* franchise, and choosing to be entertained by two hours of graphically violent gameplay are so different. Both engender a level of morbid fascination and an interest in death, conflict, or violent retribution, as titillating entertainment. The consumer pays for both in anticipation of the next deadly thrill, a desire to be shocked whilst exploring their accepted populist (and virtual) fascination with death and corpses.

The same is true of novels, where the graphically analyzed details of death can be far more vivid and intense in their description. A substantial number of lauded gruesome films started their existence as books, capturing the reader's imagination. It is more likely that video games have become the latest in a long line of recreational pariah. (For further insights see Amor Mortis—Love of Death in this chapter on page 144.)

DISCUSSION POINTS

01 What is "fair game" as a form of entertainment? Is it a matter of everything's OK as long as it is not happening to me?

02 Should some subject matter be considered differently, depending on the delivery format? If so, why?

03 Is it a fair comparison to judge one form of adult entertainment against another?

04 Are video gaming VR simulations a stepping-stone substitute to the real world? What do they represent?

05 Are there real links between playing video games and social breakdown and unrest (high profile news items)? Alternatively, is this concept the latest populist scapegoat, or public pariah? (For further insight see Amor Mortis—Love of Death on page 144.)

06 Who should be held responsible, if anyone at all, in the event of controversy: Publishers, designers or regulators?

The Cost of Progress

Technological evolution (see Moore's Law on page 79) has brought with it a rapid and irrevocable period of change whose effects have altered our understanding of the world: enhancing economies, increasing productivity, and redefining communities in ways not seen since the Industrial Revolution. The rate of change has continued without affording society the opportunity to intellectually digest the varied meanings of this pervasive and immersive digital culture.

At the forefront of this digital revolution, the video games industry, whose identity is defined through the media, is in part in crisis. Whether it is recognized as a desirable commodity of home entertainment, or the latest in a long line of media that is considered to be at the forefront of a social degradation and decline, its reputation divides opinion.

WHETHER RECOGNIZED AS A DESIRABLE COMMODITY OF HOME ENTERTAINMENT, OR THE LATEST IN A LONG LINE OF MEDIA THAT IS CONSIDERED TO BE AT THE FOREFRONT OF A SOCIAL DEGRADATION AND DECLINE, ITS REPUTATION DIVIDES OPINION.

Alongside books, plays, film and TV, video games are no different in exploring or exploiting our desire to live a life less ordinary. Can this lead the user to being uniquely detached from reality? Particularly when the importance of purpose, meaning, or a shared history are not physically defined by the real world. Lives can be lived out in a virtual space where it is possible to take all the risks but without a cost.

One area to be considered by a twenty-first-century post-Internet generation, is computer game addiction and Internet dependency. It is not officially recognized or included in the DSM—Diagnostic and Statistical Manual of Mental Disorders (DSM-5)—as a form of addiction, but further research may change this. It points to the excessive use of computers, consoles, wearable computers, and mobile devices. Behaviors that may indicate a level of addiction are levels of a compulsive need to play games, and binge gaming leading to personal neglect.

The MMO, MMORPG, MOBAs game genres are often attributed to obsessive online gaming practices (see Game Genres on page 38). These types of immersive games present the player with challenging gameplay, campaigns, and environments, which can be accessed online all day every day. Games companies, and therefore game designers, play a part as game mechanics are designed to keep gamers coming back and to sustain players' attention over long periods of gameplay. Compulsion loops are often employed within collaborative play, the pursuit of rewards, which commonly are unobtainable in single player modes. (As a starting point for further research into behavior look at *About Behaviorism* by B. F. Skinner.)

MMO, MMORPG, and MOBAs games have been at the center of several news stories regarding gamer deaths. In 2012, a Taiwanese gamer died at an Internet cafe computer desk after a 40-hour session playing *Diablo III*, and in a similar tragedy the same year another Taiwanese gamer died playing *League of Legends* in another protracted Internet cafe gaming session. In 2008, China declared Internet addiction to be a clinical disorder, seeing it as a threat to the health of its teenagers. More recently, both China and South Korea have set up military style boot camps in an attempt to deal with what it considers its most severe cases. Addiction clinics have begun to offer treatment to individuals and families affected by obsessive gaming. (See *Web Junkies*, 2013, dir: Shosh Shlam and Hilla Medalia webjunkiemovie.com.)

THE CULTURAL LENS

The term "cultural lens" refers to the viewer's locality and their worldview. What impact or causality is there on economic, cultural, political, or religious culture in which the individual resides? And how does this view affect his or her position? Societal attitudes can account for the representation or misrepresentation, of race, color, and creed. When making games for a global marketplace, it's important to know what the story is, who is telling it, and to whom it is being told.

The contemporary video game industry was largely defined and nurtured in the Western Hemisphere (See What are Video Games? on page 20) along with significant influences from Japan. As a result, a substantial proportion of games designed and created in the twentieth and twenty-first centuries are based on real and contemporary experiences with a largely Western point of view. Where we live acts as a center, with the world spreading beyond its immediate borders, rendering a predominantly localized view of global cultural and history.

This has led to many computer games not reflecting wider cultural demographics, despite the industry becoming increasingly global. A notable exception to this globalization has been Japan where countless game titles are produced that are primarily aimed at the domestic Japanese market only. Most of these will never be localized for Western audiences or any other cultures.

Historical and Contemporary Inspiration

Gamers spend many hours transported to other worlds and exploring virtual lives, and during those experiences it is sometimes easy to not question the content. In one of the most popular video game genres, FPS, a significant number of franchises such as *Battlefield*, *Call of Duty*, *SOCOM*, *Ghost Recon*, *Medal of Honor* and *Brothers in Arms* allude to, or set themselves directly in, real-world war scenarios both contemporary and within living memory; basing their narrative structures on real events. Their choice of subject matter is unsurprising, as a large enough segment of video game buyers would agree with the statement: war games are exciting. However, there is sometimes delicate politics surrounding many of the conflicts and this coupled with the real, sometimes ongoing, trauma inflicted upon participants and populations should give pause for reflection as to their appropriateness for video games.

However, similar considerations have clearly been ignored, rightly or wrongly, by the movie

KEY TERM

WESTERN HEMISPHERE

A geographical term relating to the half of Earth that lies west of the prime meridian. In 1884, the prime meridian was established at the Royal Observatory in Greenwich, London (UK) and endorsed by international agreement at the height of Britain's imperial power. Although it is more than 120 years since it was established, the prime meridian referencing coordinates of longitude and latitude are used by smart GPS location devices.

industry, which is still obsessed with making films about the Second World War and terrorist attacks both real and imagined. To this list, we can now also add the wars in Iraq and Afghanistan.

Is the regular portrayal of these very traumatic events, in interactive play and other media, part of a cathartic process that helps society process and cope with them? Consider the highly controversial 2003 *9-11 Survivor* game, which was a mod (modification) for *Unreal Tournament* and conceived as an art project by students at the University of California. The artists' rationale for the game was that online games and mods like it are a legitimate method for people like themselves—those who are immmersed in gaming—to explore and come to terms with harrowing occasions like these. By virtually navigating around these locations the events became more "real" to them. But this method of coming to terms with trauma is not shared by all.

Matt Scheiner, a survivor of the 9/11 attack who was working on the 81st floor, Tower 1 of the World Trade Center, commented on the online survival game and considered it tasteless. "My brother (Scott) found the game and called me. I frequently play video games and do a lot of online gaming, so I normally have a thick skin, but this game really struck a nerve. To hear planes hit, the crunching noise when the buildings fall. It's just tasteless." He went on to say: "With something of that magnitude, you have to take into account what your game does to people who were there."

Despite their sensitive nature, these kinds of profoundly traumatic and violent historical events have inspired and formed the basis of a huge amount of popular entertainment across media formats, and this trend shows no signs of abating. It's therefore worth asking whether this indicates a lack of original ideas being explored or, now that commercial production costs are so high, an unwillingness by the larger media corporations to fund untested ideas? (See everythingisaremix.info, a four-part documentary by Kirby Ferguson.)

Seeing the Other Side

Some games companies in the West pursue narrative structures external to standard Western ideologies, seeking to incorporate diversity found in concurrent global histories, focusing on parallel or coexisting cultures.

Paradox Interactive based in Stockholm, Sweden, design games exploring this diversity in concurrent historical perspectives. These are based upon history, culture, religious and political affiliations. All have their own versions of storytelling and particular insight into historical events.

The *Crusader Kings II* (2012) series (Paradox Interactive), is now in its sixth expansion. It offers players the choice of playing the game through a variety of religious and cultural narrative strands. The *Sword of Islam* or *Sons of Abraham* expansions allow the player to progress through the campaign from the viewpoints of Christianity, Islam, or Judaism. This allows players to experience the story through the eyes of other cultures with different hierarchies, laws, and social structures.

5.7
Crusader Kings logo

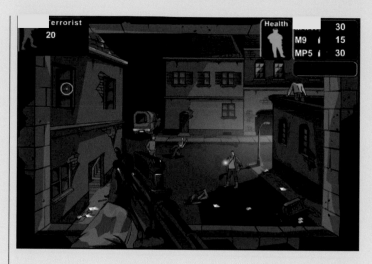

5.8
Spec Ops: War on Terrorism (2001)
The game's Belfast level incited an unintended reaction in Northern Ireland as the first person shooter narrative implied that the city was a terrorist hot spot.

A CULTURAL LENS STORY

Miniclip's Head of Web, Alex Williams, discusses the early days of the gaming hub and a game called *Spec Ops: War on Terrorism* that caused an unintentional international reaction.

In the early days, we created a series called *War on Terrorism* with an external developer, but after the first game the developer moved in-house and came to work with us. Before this, *Dancing Bush*, a political satire had been a very popular game, and it received a lot of press coverage. Many people said it was rude and wrong of us to insult the president. We insisted it wasn't insulting. Some of the voiceover and splits weren't particularly flattering, but it wasn't done to try to denigrate President Bush, it was just making fun of a popular cultural character who had opened himself up to a level of ridicule.

The *War on Terrorism* games became very popular and then we had some bad feedback. The first one was a simple point and click shooter (2D animation). It included Afghanistan, Pakistan, Belfast, and Washington, and there were masked terrorists. The terrorists wore balaclavas, so we deliberately didn't make them ethnically identifiable. Unfortunately, the Mayor of Belfast took issue with this and so the Belfast evening press ran an article stating that Miniclip was saying that Belfast is a terrorist hot spot.

There was a similar reaction on the second version of that game, there were newspapers in Saudi saying that Miniclip, the American company (Miniclip is a British company), were taking pot shots at Saudi. Even though, with the best will in the world it was just a shoot-em-up game. We didn't have a political agenda, generally kids quite like shooting games. So, we put them into that terrorist environment.

Since then, we have adapted to be less offensive; even though I don't believe it was offensive, it just raised the hackles of a few people. Rather than run the risk of advertisers thinking the content is controversial and not a good place in which to advertise, our subsequent shooting games feature aliens or zombies instead of killing people, terrorists, or making a political statement.

DISCUSSION POINTS

01 Where are the boundaries in game narratives based on historical events within living memory, and those that allude to current events elsewhere in the world?

02 Can game designers be accused of being insensitive by using potentially sensitive or inappropriate subject material that is based on or hints at, current cultural and historical events within games?

03 What role, if any, do real events have on originality in game design? Do re-hashes of real world events serve as a safe source of subject matter, compared to creative thinking? Are there any differences between major and indie publishers in this regard?

04 Are regionally focused game designers—either deliberately or unwittingly—applying a cultural lens (ideological bias), which then affects a game's narrative outcome?

5.9
Artwork from *Crusader Kings II: Sword of Islam*
One of several expansion packs available for *Crusader Kings II*. Many more computer games are offering cultural and historical alternatives that allow players to explore stories from various cultural perspectives.

INTERVIEW

HENRIK FAHRAEUS

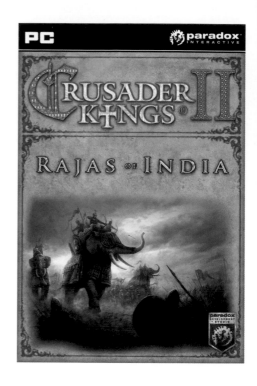

● ●

Industry role: Henrik Fahraeus is the lead game designer at Paradox Interactive, in Sweden. Many creative processes start from a position of what we know, and what is immediate. Henrik, who worked on *Crusader Kings II*, talks about designing computer games that span cultural, political, and religious divides.

Why has Paradox Interactive pursued a strand of video game development that explores historical storytelling beyond the traditional Western cultural viewpoint?

The original *Europa Universalis* (2000) game was quite eurocentric (unsurprisingly, since it was based on a board game set in Europe), but over the years, with expansions and sequels, we have constantly fleshed out the "rest of the world" content in that series. We wanted players to be free to select any country in the world, not just the European powers. This meant, of course, that we needed narrative (what we call "events") and appropriate game mechanics for these areas. So, *EU4* (2013), is much less eurocentric and filled with interesting gameplay for most cultural spheres, including the American native tribes.

What has been the response to tailoring gameplay from different cultural and religious viewpoints?

The response has generally been very good. For example, the review of the *Sword of Islam* expansion over at Muslim Gamer website was almost glowing. That is not to say we [don't] sometimes get things wrong. It is harder to portray a different religion or culture from the outside. Religion, especially, can be a minefield.

Has there been any resistance to any narratives you have explored in the *Crusader Kings* series?

Inevitably, yes. For example, in the game, we regard the Ash'ari and Mutazilite movements within Islam as schools of theology, whereas many modern Muslims simply view them as heresies. The important point in these situations is that we portray religion mostly from a political standpoint; how the policies of rulers are affected by religion. We are neither qualified nor interested in taking sides in theological disputes. Sometimes, we also use religious and cultural content just to give players some extra immersion, and to make it feel distinctly different playing in Arabia compared to Wales, etc. In those cases, we try to be extra careful to avoid giving inadvertent offense.

What kind of research document do you put together before embarking upon historical lines that could be contentious to one party or another?

There is no research document as such. The lead game designer (me, in the case of *CK2*) is in charge

5.10–5.11
The Rajas of India expansion pack
The most recent *Crusader Kings* expansion offers gameplay options via India's diverse religions: Hinduism, Buddhism, and Jainism. This broadening of horizons is a small but significant piece of evidence supporting the notion that video games are maturing, and that both game players and industry are seeking greater diversity in narrative content in the global marketplace.

of the design document, which is kept up-to-date during the development cycle. It's largely the designer's responsibility to avoid pitfalls of a controversial nature. When something is deemed borderline, we usually discuss it at higher levels as well. Now, since our games are mostly political and military in nature, we are more willing to brave contentious territory, if it is hard to avoid without compromising the accuracy of the political/military simulation.

For example, the Byzantines frequently had pretenders castrated and/or blinded to disqualify them from succession. This is a horrible practice, obviously, but it has great bearing on a game where inheritance is so central to gameplay. In order to allow other rulers in the region to use the same method, we made it available to all Greeks, Armenians, and Georgians, i.e. it's treated as a cultural phenomenon, which could be controversial. However, it's not something players have complained about much, since it's obviously not denigratory.

Now, if something similar would crop up in our pure "flavor narrative," we would be more willing to sanitize it.

Can you tell us a bit more about the sixth expansion *Rajas of India*?
Rajas of India is a huge expansion in that it extends the map by 50 percent and adds the three big Indian religions to the game: Jainism, Buddhism and Hinduism. Actually, everyone gets the map extension free, but they cannot play as rulers of the Indian religions without buying the expansion. These religions, and the new cultures of India, come with a lot of custom mechanics and narrative, featuring everything from reincarnation to the extraordinary pluralism of the Indian religions (less internal religious strife, etc.). Characters of Indian descent feature their own set of portraits with clothes and the same goes for their military units. Oh, and there are war elephants!

INTERVIEW
ANNA MARSH

5.12
Tickity Boom logo

"

GAMES ARE AS VARIED AS ANY OTHER ENTERTAINMENT MEDIUM... WHAT TYPE OF A GAMER YOU ARE DICTATES WHAT CONTENT YOU MIGHT CONSIDER WATCHING.
Julia Hardy,
Games Journalist and Presenter

"

Industry role: Anna Marsh has sixteen years of video games experience and has worked with the likes of Sony, Creative Assembly/Sega and Eidos as well as with developers such as Crystal Dynamics, Rebellion and iO. She has more recently turned her skills to setting up two indie games companies, Tickity Boom and Lady Shotgun. She discusses being a successful games designer in a predominantly male-orientated industry.

As a woman in a predominantly male-orientated industry, despite common gamer stereotypes, do you find the video game industry to be relaxed about gender?
I have never had any issues with being female in the industry, outside a few daft comments that never stood in the way of my career.

It's been estimated that worldwide there are approximately an equal number of women and men playing games, does this surprise you considering most of the content available? Why is society still surprised that women play video games?
No, it doesn't surprise me. When I was a girl, I and all my girl friends played games on our ZX Spectrums and BBC Micros. I think marketing has a lot to do with it. As games got bigger and bigger business, the marketers decided that the target audience was going to be male, and that's the way it headed.

Has access to mobile smart devices and the introduction of new video game formats led to greater diversity in those who participate in games as entertainment?
Touch screens are awesome. They have totally democratized the game landscape because there's no learning barrier to controlling the game any more. If you're used to game controllers, you lose sight of how much of a barrier they are to people who don't play games generally. As a designer, I love working with touch screens, I think for everything you lose in terms of tactical and specific response from a game controller you get back 100 fold from the fact that you can just TOUCH the stuff in the game! This, and digital delivery through the app store, has massively opened up the potential audience for games.

Despite the continued lack of women working in the games industry, are we going to see more games such as *The Last of Us* and *Gone Home* where the central character and story arc is from a female perspective?

I personally don't care much if the central character is male or female. Although generally not only in games, but also in much cinema and to a lesser extent TV, it's telling that the majority of characters are male. In real life, the world is pretty much 50/50 male female, so our entertainment is holding up a very warped mirror that shows women as a minority. Even if something isn't overtly sexist, this marginalizing of female characters does create the impression that male is the default, the "normal." Now, I get the feeling that companies are using "female lead" as a kind of marketing ploy. I hope we get over this to a point where the character's gender is the least important thing about them. I play more mobile than console/PC games these days due to time constraints. It's much less of a "thing" here, particularly as the mobile format includes game types like puzzles, where there is no character anyway.

In recent years, we have seen less young women applying for jobs in sciences and other technical sectors in the UK. How can women be encouraged to see the video games industry as one that offers great rewards and routes to a serious global career?

Well, I'd temper that sentence about great rewards and a serious global career. If you have the brains to be in games, then almost undoubtedly you have the brains to have a much better paid career with better promotion prospects in technology, science, or engineering. Games are not that well paid and if you decide to go it alone as an indie that gets even more precarious! Many young people looking to work

in games, are seduced by the fact that it's "cool." My feeling is that we need to make sure that girls aren't gender-tracked by peer pressure and ingrained ideology too early because it does start early. My 5-year-old daughter recently got told at school that her red "Angry Birds" bag is "for boys," how can a bag even have a gender? Kids of both genders get these ideas very deeply embedded, just like all of us, because that's how ideology works. I'd like to eradicate the "girls" and "boys" aisles in toyshops for example. I know its impossible to live outside of ideology, but it would be nice to try for one in which kids are free to play with what they like, and wear what they like, without being dictated to by silly social ideas.

ANDROID PHONE GAMERS ARE ON AVERAGE 41 YEARS OLD AND 53 PERCENT ARE FEMALE, WHILE THE AVERAGE IPAD GAMER IS 42 YEARS OLD, 54 PERCENT ARE FEMALE.
tabtimes.com, Dec 4, 2014

5.13
Buddha Finger (2012)
Made by Lady Shotgun, *Buddha Finger* is a casual game with a touch-screen swipe mechanic and frenetic gameplay. It was featured on the Apple's iTunes Incredible Indie Games list and in Microsoft's Next Big Thing indie collection.

AMOR MORTIS—— LOVE OF DEATH

Video games have continued to expose our fascination with death and rebirth. This medium, like others before it, has brought to light the vicarious desire to experience heroic existences. The plurality of digital daydreams, triumphant fantasies of adventure through adversity, often against incredible odds, are reincarnated and replayed ad infinitum. Never before have we chosen to experience or enact death with such frequency. Whilst broadly accepted as entertainment, sections of society have blamed video games for inspiring individuals to commit domestic atrocities.

Violent News

The pursuit of power and control is evident across human history. Our fascination with death, survival stories surrounding great triumphs, the telling and retelling of trials against adversity and ensuing tragedies date back to the most ancient of stories.

Revisited as an allegory, *Beowulf*, the sixth-century poem set in Scandinavia, recounts a great evil that haunted the Danes. A subverted progeny, partly hailing from the Danes' own ranks, and a hero who vanquishes a terrifying foe only to repeat the mistakes of those before him. As with most heroic stories, further complexities lie beneath the surface, imperfections appear, and the unforeseen generational cost is paid by those involved.

Are there any unforeseen consequences when visceral content combines with interaction? Can it precipitate a reaction in game players and is it a consideration for publishers when they produce extraordinarily realistic content? Do these new levels of realism play a part in linking video games to recent terrible events?

Alfred Bandura's Bobo doll experiment (1961–3) involved studies of human interaction and group behaviors. His studies show that children observing adult behavior are influenced to think that those types of behavior are acceptable. Therefore, in some

THIS IS A WAR UNIVERSE. WAR ALL THE TIME. THAT IS ITS NATURE. THERE MAY BE OTHER UNIVERSES BASED ON ALL SORTS OF OTHER PRINCIPLES, BUT OURS SEEMS TO BE BASED ON WAR AND GAMES.
William S. Burroughs,
writer and poet

instances, their aggressive inhibitions are weakened, suggesting they themselves may be more likely to respond aggressively in future situations.

Certain news stories have captured the public imagination far more than others. Shocking unexpected events such as the fatal stabbing of school teacher Ann Maguire by one of her teenage pupils (UK, 2014) and acts of gun violence against communities often perpetrated by lone individuals, have ignited the debate around the role of violent entertainment, gun ownership, and the psychological make-up and lifestyle of those responsible. Both video games and movies have often been cited as contributory factors in these devastating events. Ultra-violent massacres are scrutinized in depth, the assailant's lives are laid bare in the ensuing media frenzy over minutiae, in an attempt to understand and qualify what has taken place.

In the UK in 1993, the murder of 2-year-old James Bulger by two 10-year-old boys was linked to *Child's Play 3*. The 2007 Virginia Tech massacre (US) where 32 people were killed, and 17 injured was linked to the Japanese film *Oldboy* (2003). More recently, the film trailer of *Gangster Squad* (2013) set in 1940s America, featured a shooting in a packed cinema. It drew parallels to the Aurora Colorado Multiplex theater shooting of June 2012 at a screening of *The Dark Knight Returns*. Twelve people were killed and 58 injured in this event. This prompted calls for the pivotal scene to be cut from the final film release.

Professor Jonathan Freedman, who has written a report for the Motion Picture Association of America, writes, ". . . since 1992 there has been a dramatic drop in violent crime, including violent crime committed by young males, to the point that it is now below what it was when television was introduced many decades ago. It seems obvious that media violence did not cause the earlier increase just as it did not cause the more recent decrease." This statement indicates that there is no link between media violence and violent behavior in society. Professor Freedman points out that public opinion highlights media content to be a causal factor of a significant event, which can easily be based on personal belief rather than on the outcomes of thorough scientific research.

Video games have been placed at the center of this debate and named as a critical influence in other domestic gun crime massacres. In July 2011 the Utoya Island massacre took place in Norway,

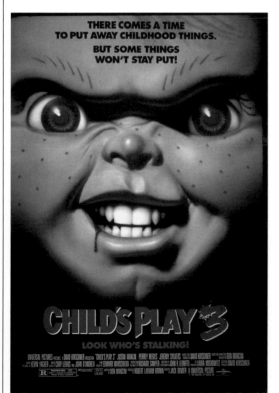

5.14
Child's Play 3
Violent movies, such as *Child's Play 3*, and video games, such as *Grand Theft Auto*, have been cited as causes for real-world violence. The debate as to their influence on viewers and players has been ongoing for decades and shows no sign of resolution.

145

VIOLENT CRIME TRENDS, ENGLAND AND WALES
Annual violent incidents per 100 population

SOURCE: CARDIFF UNIVERSITY

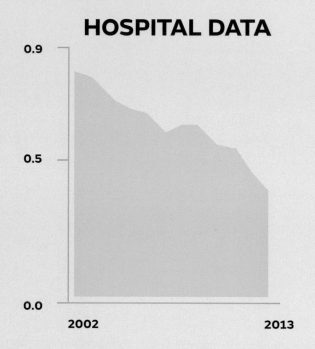

HOSPITAL DATA

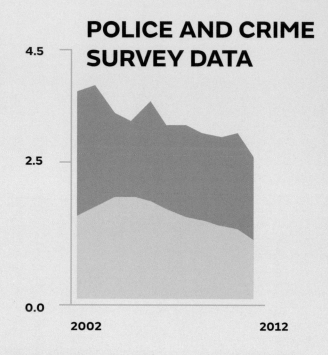

POLICE AND CRIME SURVEY DATA

● OFFICAL CRIME SURVEY OF ENGLAND AND WALES
● RECORDED CRIME

77 died. The perpetrator, a 33-year-old militant nationalist called Andrej Breivik was jailed for 21 years. Breivik planned, and virtually trained for the event, utilizing computer games such as *Call of Duty: Modern Warfare*. He spent months training with simulations of a whole array of real-world weaponry, including holographic scopes, and developing his sense of target acquisition.

During his trial Breivik stated, "It consists of many hundreds of different tasks and some of these tasks can be compared with an attack, for real. That's why it's used by many armies throughout the world. It's very good for acquiring experience related to sights systems." He went on to add, "If you are familiar with a holographic sight, it's built up in such a way that you could have given it to your grandmother and she would have been a super marksman. It's designed to be used by anyone. In reality, it requires very little training to use it in an optimal way. But, of course, it does help if you've

practiced using a simulator."

Since then, British MPs (Members of Parliament) have attempted to pass new legislation about video game content. In 2012, Keith Vaz, Chair of the Home Select Committee, called for a ban of violent video games after the Breivik massacre. He devised a bill seeking new powers to ban certain material in video games, and adding to the existing powers of age certification: "to provide for closer scrutiny of aggressive first-person shooter video games . . . is concerned that PEGI as a classification system can only provide an age-rating and not restrict ultra-violent content." The proposal did not engender much support (eight out of 650 MPs voted for it) and it was not passed.

A recent statistical study by the University of Cardiff, Wales may indicate one of the key reasons so few signatories supported the 2012 bill. Their study demonstrates that from 2002 to 2013 there was a year on year fall in violent crime, in spite of the

DISCUSSION POINTS

01 Can entertainment influence an individual's mental health or actions?

02 What scientific evidence exists to suggest that video games are to blame for inciting violence?

03 Does the media create a culture of blame or incite a level of hysteria, rather than report the facts?

04 Should computer games exactly replicate and simulate contemporary military weaponry?

05 Are viewers passive recipients of mass media or do they seek out sources of pleasure, i.e. forms of entertainment? (For further research look at Hypodermic Needle Model theory and Uses and Gratification theory.)

06 Can the digital age engender a skewed understanding of everyday life?

07 Can levels of gaming realism challenge our understanding of right and wrong?

08 Does the instantaneous nature of digital media, live news feeds (connected to small town incidents across the world), engender a sense of societal fear rather than one of growing stability?

continued rise in digital entertainment. The collated data was provided by both the police and hospitals in England and Wales. In 2013, the data showed a 12 percent fall in victims of violent attack needing to be treated in hospital, a drop of 32,800 cases on the previous year.

Similarly in the United States, some senators have sought to focus public outrage towards violent video games, following the civilian shootings such as at Sandy Hook Elementary School (December, 2012, Newtown, Connecticut), rather than numerous societal factors and the evident ease of access to high-powered firearms in the US.

THE RECRUITMENT GAME

It is not uncommon for big business to utilize the latest in technological advances, gadgetry, and visuals, to entice consumers to their brand. It should then be no surprise that in the United States the army has created its own war sim called *America's Army*, also known as *AA*. One of the most popular of digital entertainment genres, the FPS genre, is utilized to attract young people into a career in the army.

In 2008, the US Army sponsored a FPS tournament using *America's Army* as their game of choice. The tournament was held at the army training center in Rancho Cordova, California, attracting teenage participants. This enraged some war veterans, who took to the streets in protest. The veterans held up placards, which stated that "Real War is Hell." Protester John C. Reiger, president of the Sacramento chapter of Veterans for Peace said "It's like giving candy to kids," and "It's sort of like military pedophilia in a way, preying on our young people."

The implementation of successive technologies leads us to consider our position beyond many notional twenty-first-century norms. Some of the most interesting, innovative, and lateral uses of simulated virtual environments are combat zones, also known as "serious games." One example is *VI* (*Virtual Iraq*), it includes real topographical data and is used therapeutically as a rehabilitation tool by the US Army. Having returned from the theater of war, soldiers engage in virtual scenarios in a 3D game environment, enacting conflict simulations to evoke memories and engage traumatic events. (Also see Games Imitate Life on page 113.)

5.15
America's Army logo
Released in 2002 as *Recon*, there have been more than forty release updates to the current version called *Proving Grounds*.

5.16
America's Army
This AA level illustrates building structures, possible routes, and tertiary in-game structures.

DISCUSSION POINTS

01 Is it acceptable for a military body to utilize contemporary entertainment mediums, such as a video game? Does it cross a moral or ethical line?

02 Is it important to consider what war veterans think of contemporary conflicts becoming disposable interactive entertainment? Does this differ with regard to participants from one conflict to another, i.e. combatants in the Second World War (1939–45) or in the First Gulf War (1990)?

03 Are video games any different to any other visual medium, i.e. print, TV, or film, when being used as a promotional tool?

GAMES AS SOCIAL POLITICAL COMMENT

Video games offer players a neutral and preloaded vista of the world that they inhabit. Known for their capacity for escapism, games as a visual language, shared through many commercial iconic markers, have the capacity to acknowledge the frailty and beauty of life. As a medium, they have furnished a narrative space in communicating significant world events.

The game artifact as an emotive journey is full of consumable and challenging responses. It is a common scenario for gamers to encounter questions of choice, conscience, or morality (visualized through a foreign policy narrative, or as an initiator to an act of terror; see *Call of Duty Modern Warfare II* Russian airport scene). Our escapism swings between playful bright futures to an assortment of bloody dystopian daydreams. Against this contentious backdrop of games imitating life, artists have found a new playground to challenge the viewer, a virtual arena to contend large societal ideas.

5.17
dead-in-iraq
A digital art intervention enacted through the *America's Army* online multiplayer game, which ran between 2006–2011. Logging in as Dead-In-Iraq, Delappe typed the names of the American war dead, as a fleeting memorial to military personnel.

5.18
Me and My Predator, Personal Drone System
Instructions on how to build the personal drone
project are on Instructables.com.

> **"**
>
> **BY APPROPRIATING CONTEMPORARY
> SHOOTERS I AM EXPLOITING THESE
> ENVIRONMENTS AND THE CONTENT THEREIN
> TO TWEAK OR RE-DIRECT SAID CONTENT
> TOWARDS ENGAGING CRITICAL DISCOURSE,
> DIALOGUE, AND THOUGHT.**
> Joseph DeLappe
> **"**

INTERVIEW
JOSEPH DELAPPE

● ●

Joseph DeLappe, professor of digital arts, reappropriates iconic game culture motifs of combatants into video, sculpture, and installation-based artwork. *The Terrorist Other, Paper Soldier, Taliban Hands* and *dead-in-iraq* engage the viewer in the most contemporary of mediums.

A key driver in your artwork, both intervention and installation, is the visual language of the 3D FPS game. What do you find compelling about these virtual worlds as a visual language?

What I found compelling regarding virtual gaming spaces and communities was both as the location of ephemeral works of intervention, and as sources for manifesting physical artworks in real life. I think what I am trying to do, beyond political protest, memorial or creative making, is to develop creative conceptual strategies to perhaps tease out just what these new virtual environments might signify beyond arenas of play or interaction.

I am very interested in moving my art out of the rarefied contexts of the gallery and museum system. Virtual game spaces provide a rich territory for artists to explore and in which to engage audiences, who might otherwise not be exposed to such content. For example, *dead-in-iraq*, could not have been accomplished without direct action within this government funded propaganda/ recruiting FPS. I took my action to the source—the *America's Army* game is a new type of federal property—literally one is virtually stepping into a US Army created simulation of war.

Whilst engaging global, political, and societal issues, do virtual environments ease the way to introducing serious political comment?

By appropriating contemporary shooters I am exploiting these environments and the content therein to tweak or redirect said content towards engaging critical discourse, dialogue, and thought. The works are intended as a kind of interruption of the tropes of contemporary war play; for example by inserting the names of actual dead soldiers into the *America's Army* game, or by realizing the hands of a Taliban shooter as large scale sculptural objects.

Both works seek to create a moment of engagement in meaning that breaks the third wall, or the "magic circle" of gaming immersion. I find these spaces, particularly FPS games, to be rich arenas for interventionist play, serious play.

The blank imposing figures (posed body parts) echo the virtual world, possessing an otherness and absence of detail. They indicate real narratives and global stories. Can you expand what is so symbolic about this iconic and generic form?

Certainly, in these works, there is a simplification of digital bodies as taken from a virtual context. The low-res polygon techniques used to create these objects serve both a practical and conceptual purpose. On the practical side, it would be nearly impossible to use such hand-made techniques to create full-resolution renditions of such data extractions. I take such objects from many thousands of polygons down to 500 or less. By magnifying the polygons, the very structure of digital is revealed. The terrorist other is created.

5.19
Cardboard Soldier—*America's Army* 2009
Digital content is simplified creating a low-resolution look sculpture. Scale as a device forces the viewer to consider the iconic value of the work.

5.20
Taliban Hands, 2011
This large-scale sculpture is described as an "interruption of contemporary war tropes, referring to the figurative or metaphorical use of cultural translations to recurring contemporary war themes." The Taliban Hands depictions are taken from the *Medal of Honor* FPS game by Electronic Arts.

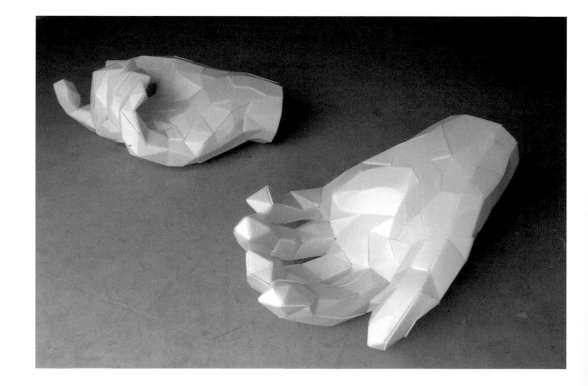

CHAPTER REVIEW

This chapter has presented and challenged ideas about social responsibility, what we consider acceptable and appropriate media content, and its wider influence. It has discussed the use and implementation of ratings systems. It has reflected upon the use of games across different media formats, and loopholes in legislation about the Internet. It has questioned the use of games in relation to advertising. This area of consideration can be defined as the examination and practical outworking of ethics in game creation.

Key Points

RATINGS: From arcade to console, video games have courted controversy, leading to some games either being banned or unrated. Globally, countries have opted to use a variety of systems to indicate the appropriateness of subject matter. The implementation of ratings systems provides a content guideline, identifying games as being suitable for different age brackets.

CAUSE CÉLÈBRE: The video games industry has become the latest pariah in a long line of media villains. It has attracted negative criticism and a culture of blame has arisen, especially after several notable global news stories, which reported on the use of firearms in planned massacres, where the perpetrator had a history of playing video games.

CULTURAL LENS: A method of questioning and thinking that considers the way that we see the world and which is influenced by the culture that we inhabit. In the context of video games, their content has broadened as the industry has matured and globalized. Who makes games and plays games is changing, and therefore the industry is now open to more questions about whose worldview is being presented, and who the content is for.

ADDICTIVE CONTENT: Digital culture presents society with new challenges, both corporately and individually. Lifestyle trends indicate that forms of digital media addiction are increasing, especially video games and Internet dependency. Video game addiction has yet to be officially recognized as a form of addiction.

6.1
Digging for riches.
Godus (2014) mining
settlement, 22 Cans.

6

THE BUSINESS OF GAMES

TOPICS COVERED
Industry Statistics / Mobile and Web Takeover / Propagating
Addiction / Crowdfunding / Branding, Franchises and
Intellectual Property / Story of an Extended Franchise

Video games are the new engine of growth for many economies employing many thousands of people in businesses large and small across the world. According to Statista.com it is a $102 billion (£65 billion) global industry that is now larger than Hollywood. How has this been achieved? What underpins it? Moreover, will it continue to grow?

In recent years a handful of video games have become famous for their record-breaking production costs. Games such as *Destiny* (2014) cost $500 million (£335 million) to produce while *Grand Theft Auto V* (2013) had a production budget of $250 million (£168 million). Both these titles have the commercial pull to recoup the full development cost either through pre-sales or from the first week sales alone. These titles are enormous and impressive feats of game design that have been driven into the public's imagination by colossal marketing campaign budgets combined with a little luck and a lot of incredibly savvy business sense.

Other video game super brands (see Branding, Franchises and Intellectual Property on page 182) such as *Call of Duty*, *World of Warcraft*, *Battlefield*, and *Halo* have production times, staffing, and budgets that are comparable to feature films. Large budget video games like *The Last of Us* have become cinematic undertakings for their depth and emotionally charged storylines. Others are defined by the use of A-list actors: the leading protagonist in the latest *Call of Duty* installment, *Advanced Warfare*, is played by Kevin Spacey through a motion captured performance. Video games continue to parallel feature films in their use of directorial input as well as their development and implementation of new technology (see Twenty-First-Century Gaming on page 30).

The games industry now needs to be viewed in its correct twenty-first-century context: as a business that has come-of-age in a world of ubiquitous technology full of consumers with a rapacious appetite for entertainment. The industry is still young compared to its media peers, and has the potential to become larger than any of them, employing more people and be more important to national economies.

INDUSTRY STATISTICS

What does the video game industry look like when we visualize the data? The data samples below highlight the economic breadth and power of the global video games industry.

All Sources: statista.com

DESTINY
2014

GRAND THEFT AUTO V
2013

STAR WARS THE OLD REPUBLIC
2011

CALL OF DUTY MODERN WARFARE 2
2009

FINAL FANTASY VII
1998

MAX PAYNE 3
2012

TOMB RAIDER
2013

DISNEY INFINITY
2013

RED DEAD REDEMPTION
2010

GRAND THEFT AUTO IV
2008

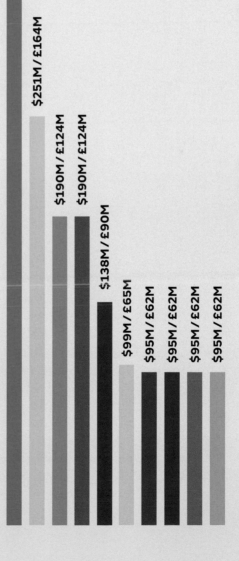

MOST EXPENSIVE GAMES OF ALL TIME
Estimated production budgets

$475M / £310M

$251M / £164M

$190M / £124M

$190M / £124M

$138M / £90M

$99M / £65M

$95M / £62M

$95M / £62M

$95M / £62M

$95M / £62M

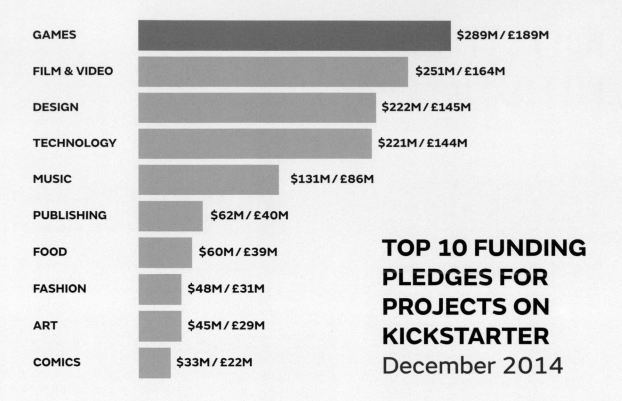

GAMES $289M/£189M

FILM & VIDEO $251M/£164M

DESIGN $222M/£145M

TECHNOLOGY $221M/£144M

MUSIC $131M/£86M

PUBLISHING $62M/£40M

FOOD $60M/£39M

FASHION $48M/£31M

ART $45M/£29M

COMICS $33M/£22M

TOP 10 FUNDING PLEDGES FOR PROJECTS ON KICKSTARTER
December 2014

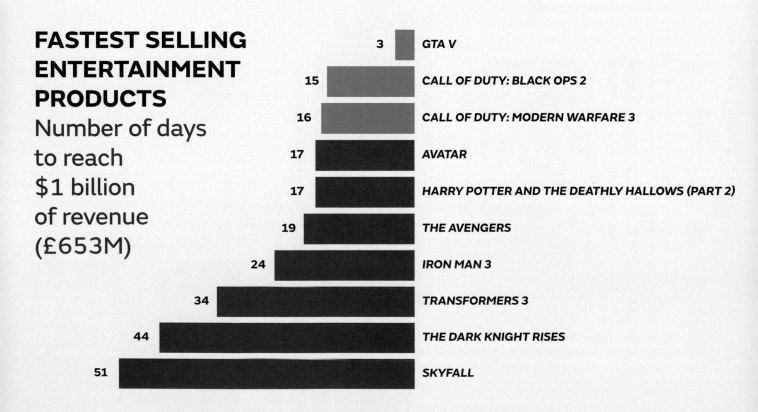

FASTEST SELLING ENTERTAINMENT PRODUCTS
Number of days to reach $1 billion of revenue (£653M)

3 GTA V

15 CALL OF DUTY: BLACK OPS 2

16 CALL OF DUTY: MODERN WARFARE 3

17 AVATAR

17 HARRY POTTER AND THE DEATHLY HALLOWS (PART 2)

19 THE AVENGERS

24 IRON MAN 3

34 TRANSFORMERS 3

44 THE DARK KNIGHT RISES

51 SKYFALL

TOP CATEGORIES IN MOBILE APP STORES

Worldwide Downloads February 2014

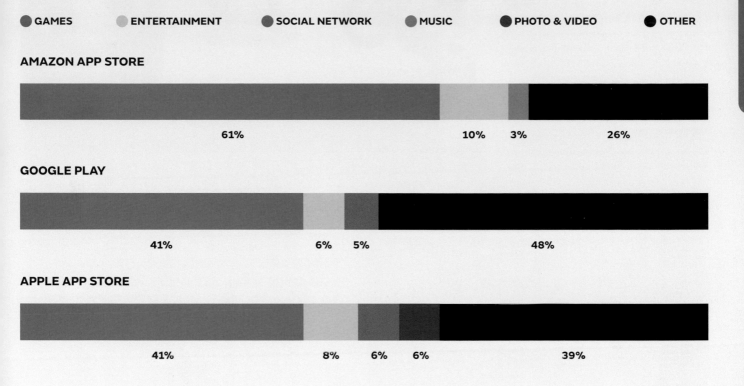

● GAMES   ● ENTERTAINMENT   ● SOCIAL NETWORK   ● MUSIC   ● PHOTO & VIDEO   ● OTHER

AMAZON APP STORE

61%   10%   3%   26%

GOOGLE PLAY

41%   6%   5%   48%

APPLE APP STORE

41%   8%   6%   6%   39%

MOBILE AND WEB TAKEOVER

It is tempting to consider web-based mini games as a poor relation of the established console-based titles, powered by cutting-edge technology and publicized at great expense by multinational game businesses. For decades, game consoles have held the center ground and therefore controlled the vast fortunes of the global games industry. However, this hegemony is being challenged by the rapid technological advancements and take-up of smart devices globally since the millennium. Combined with the expansion of online connectivity, this has marked the rise of the online gaming portal and the often irreverent, and creative, mobile gaming phenomenon. This rise has been extraordinary

and is often overlooked by the mainstream media. Mobile has fast become the unlikely champion of the once niche gaming culture (see Chapter 5 Games and Society, page 125).

Today, many workplaces would be incomplete without the quick "game-on" session, instigating an office wide button tapping frenzy to chase the next pixel-induced high. A notable example of the online and mobile gaming phenomenon is the Flash-based gaming hub Miniclip. In 2001 Rob Small and Tihan Presbie set out their virtual stall with their first mini game: *Dancing Bush*, a satirical jest featuring former US president George Bush Jr; it is still available on the Miniclip website www.miniclip.com/games/dancing-bush/en.

Now both a publisher and developer hosting over 800 Flash-based games and with over 451 million downloads to date (December 2014), Miniclip has moved beyond its undergraduate niche humor, to having an eclectic worldwide user base of over 79 million (for comparison Sony PlayStation has

6.2–6.4

A sample of Flash games published on Miniclip *Bike Rivals*, *Jelly Mania* and *Soccer Stars* (all released 2014), illustrate an intended universal approach to content whether the player is aged 6 or 60, games can be accessible and inoffensive, a business model that has been cultivated over time. As a hub, Miniclip publish a wide range of game and graphic styles to suit a broad global audience. (See page 169 Miniclip info graphic stats page.)

> ❝
>
> **FAMILIARITY IS IMPORTANT TO A GAME. YOU ONLY HAVE SECONDS TO GET THEM TO BUY INTO THE CONCEPT AS IT COSTS THEM SO LITTLE MONEY.**
>
> Rob Small, CEO and Founder, Miniclip
>
> ❞

110 million, Microsoft Xbox 48 million and Nintendo Network 27 million online: sources: Techradar, Microsoft). Its games are now translated into seventeen languages, with studios across Europe and North America.

Around three-quarters of the games hosted by the gaming hub have been published by Miniclip. This is in addition to the content produced by the company's development teams across Europe and America. It works with over 300 independent developers from a broad international pool of talent to procure the breadth of games it hosts. (See image 6.7, *Zombality*, which was created by and sourced from developers in Russia).

Depending on the scale of the project, size of team and its complexity, a game can take three months, six months or years to complete. To illustrate this Polytron (Phil Fish), developed the stunning game *Fez*, a 2D platformer set in a 3D world. Fluctuating between a one and two man team, it took Polytron from 2007 to 2012 to complete the game. It was released on the Xbox Live Arcade in April 2012.

A game's visibility and availability are directly linked to its profitability. An independent developer might consider releasing their game through a larger publisher or gaming hub, as it would offer a substantial and established user base, guaranteed levels of game visibility, and the opportunity for the game's monetization model to be realized and therein be a financial success. This is important when considering the numerous games that are released each month. Without a publishing deal, the indie developer risks his or her game being undiscovered and lacking recognition in the vastness of titles accessible via online stores.

Miniclip takes on the role of a curator of games to maintain and protect its corporate image, high standards of entertainment and to supply fully realized games. Being affiliated to a gaming hub also supports the wider purchases of new game upgrades and expandable or downloadable content (often referred to as DLC). This is a crucial aspect of a successful game's business model.

6.5

8 Ball Pool mobile (2013)
This game reached a record of nearly 200,000 concurrent users (196K), December 2014. *8 Ball Pool* has over 100m downloads, averaging 15.8m per month with daily and monthly active users of 7.3m and 40m respectively across mobile, miniclip.com and Facebook.

6.6

Themed pool cues the Zombie, Viking, or lightsaber
These themed pool cues can be purchased in the *8 Ball Pool* online shop. The pool cues are an example of how the success of a game can lead to "doubling down" and rewarding the player with increased content provision, keeping the user engaged, and thus helping to prolong the game's shelf life and improve its revenue stream. These cues and other game assets, or upgrades, can either be bought using the in-game currency, derived from the player's winnings or by purchasing the product like any online transaction. Also see image 6.12, Spin and Win.

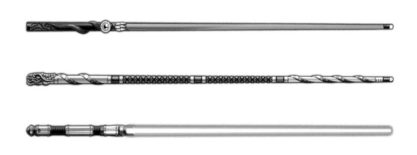

6.7

Zombality (2013)
Zombality by Yuri Shapkin and Vladislav Kim, independent developers, published on Miniclip. *Zombality* is a 2D platform game where the player is locked in a house full of zombies. It combines several classic gaming genres creating platform-style puzzle levels where the player gets to shoot, bash and kick an array of quirky looking 2D zombies whilst trying to solve puzzles and find a way out of the house fighting room by room. The game employs contemporary vector graphic characters and environments, and draws upon the survival horror genre. Zombie narratives attract a huge global following, and have been repeatedly reinvented in film, TV, and games.

INTERVIEW

ALEX WILLIAMS

● ●

Industry role: Alex Williams is Head of Web at Miniclip and is well placed to discuss the origins of Miniclip, its strategic decision-making processes and business model, and how it has achieved over a decade of success.

As a games company, is Miniclip predominantly a developer or a publisher?

Since we started, a transition has taken place. We did start out evenly balanced between producing our own games and publishing games from third-party developers. Over time, it has become easier for us as a publisher, and our network of developers has grown considerably. Additionally what they can do and offer has significantly grown, so that currently we are 85 percent publisher and 15 percent developer.

Miniclip is primarily a Flash-based gaming hub. How do you see its future with the emergence of alternate technologies and sections of the online industry ceasing to support Flash?

Probably 75 to 80 percent of our games are Flash-based. Over the last few years, we have been a strong supporter of Adobe Shockwave as a 3D option. We did look at using Unity3D early on, because it had benefits for the developing community, but it didn't really have any benefit for the users.

Every game you see in Unity, up until a couple of years ago, could still be made in Flash or Shockwave. Users didn't have the plug-in for Unity and so the penetration rate was quite low. There was no point in us moving to Unity at that stage because we would just have had to force our users to go through an install process.

However, Unity has grown up as a product and offers a lot more with significant benefits for the user. It's a very powerful tool. It's fantastic, because Shockwave and Flash were never designed for game making. Unity was designed as a game-building tool from the start and now has other applications. Flash was initially used for hotel websites and Shockwave for kiosks, CD-ROMs and elearning. Unity has none of those legacies that you have to work around.

6.8–6.9

Rail Rush (2012)

Rail Rush was created using Unity3D. Icons are employed as intuitive embedded instructions. The game's visual language taps into a pre-existing cultural cinematic motif, such as Indiana Jones, to engage the player. Clearly referencing populist media invites familiarity and in part engenders a sense of shared value and confidence in the product. The same is true of *Robot Rage* (image 6.11), another Unity game created by Miniclip where the concept taps into wider media knowledge, the international TV series *Robot Wars*.

> "
> **IT IS NOT ABOUT WHETHER THE GAME IS HARD-CORE; IT'S WHETHER THE USER IS HARD-CORE.**
> Alex Williams, Head of Web, Miniclip
> "

6.10
Concept art for the *Robot Rage* splash page
In this example, a battle narrative is illustrated through images of broken robot parts. In the end, this concept was not chosen, as a combat shot was considered a more exciting first impression.

When creating games for a universal audience, does this affect the design approach?

We try to have as little text in the games as possible. The instructions should be intuitive but if there is a need for instructions, we aim to have them graphically explained. We generally find nine out of ten people don't read the instructions. So, we try to have them embedded within the game. When playing a game, you don't want to lose your focus or have it taken away. It's better to take the player through a tutorial process, as simply as possible, rather than a tutorial that you have to complete before being able to proceed onto the game. Running along, you might get a little flag that says A for up and B for down. Therein level one, level two, and level three are effectively the tutorial, but you are actually learning and progressing in the game at the same time.

6.11
Robot Rage (2013)
Robot Rage was previously released on Miniclip as a 3D Shockwave game. Due to its popularity it was remade in 3D using the game engine Unity3D (loading screen pictured). Re-releasing the game in a new format has extended the life of the game, reengaged its original following, and the reboot has attracted new players to the company brand.

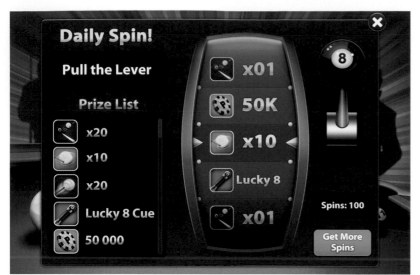

6.12
8 Ball Pool, spin and win
Loading screens can offer the
player an opportunity to receive
a new bonus every day. This is
an example of designed "hook-ins"
and incentivized engagement
that is part of a retention strategy.

**Is continuous growth sustainable or
is the industry oversaturated?**
We have noticed with mobile games that there was
a period when everybody was going into it, from big
businesses to individuals; probably thinking this is
the place to be. It got a bit saturated. People realized
that you still need a great product. Yes, it's easier to
develop the games and easier to have your game
published, but nothing gets away from the quality
that is required. We have seen many big companies
close their mobile divisions. There are companies
bigger than us, who have tried and failed in mobile.
There are individuals and employers who thought,
"we can do this ourselves," but after a year have
realized it is not quite as easy as they thought.

It is something we saw a lot because we
manage about 300 external developers sourcing and
providing games for the website. A couple of years
ago we noticed a fair number of them were saying,
"We are not looking at doing web stuff any more, we
are going to do mobile." There was the sense it was a
bit of a land grab. They could sell a game for £15,000
to £20,000 ($22,410 to $29,878) or alternatively
they can make the same game for a little bit more
and they can make £5 million ($7.5 million) on Apple!
Many people tried mobile, they weren't successful,
and then they came back to us. Obviously, we are
happy to take content as long as it's of a high quality.

We were relatively late to mobile, however,
our transition was at the best time for Miniclip and
our success compared to some web companies

highlights this. Other companies have tried HTML5,
however the major app stores aren't as interested,
as you are operating outside of their ecosystem.

With hindsight, the move to mobile was well
judged. Discoverability is important but you have
to have a quality game from the very beginning.
However, several quality games have not made it
because that market is so saturated. The cream
floats to the top! It is actually a very small
percentage of cream that actually makes it up there
through the dense thick app market milk.
Discoverability has been fundamental to the success
of many people now, and that's why we have been
successful as we have a website, which is a huge
driver of users. We can direct people to a web
version of a game that we are doing on mobile. At
one stage, we were in the top five referrers of traffic
to Apple. People were coming to the Miniclip website
and going straight to the iTunes store via Miniclip to
buy the games that we were suggesting.

We have web and mobile versions of the game,
both of which are fully featured. They are designed
for mobile with monetization hooks, and retention,
and engagement ideas. The intention is to make
them as similar as possible, but inevitably, the web
version is going to end up being an advert for the
mobile game. It is a free demo effectively. You can
still have a couple of hours' worth of fun, but it
does not have the same designed structure to drive
revenue or retention as you would on mobile. Good
fun but to get the full experience you'd go to mobile.

WALLED GARDENS

Apple and Google operate a "walled garden" approach to their apps. This means that the App Store and Google Play platforms allow users to download apps to devices powered by their respective technologies, but they are unavailable to their competitor's technology. The games offered through these services are stand-alone pieces of software and do not need to be viewed and played in a web browser like a Flash-based game. Therefore, Apple and Google have less of a commercial interest in the development of alternative web-based platforms that are open source.

Can you explain the role of advertising revenue in free-to-play and pay-to-play games?

There's a big issue with advertising on mobile; it's a very nascent market. The issue when playing a game is that you do not intentionally interact with an advert, but you may accidentally interact with it. The use of interstitial advertising is a far more enjoyable process for a user. When the game is finished, a visual ad appears. The user can then close it and progress to the score menu and then move onto the next level. I am not a fan of those tiny banners that pop up during the game. It doesn't add anything to the gameplay, in fact, it obscures it.

More recently, we've been looking at incentivized advertising. For example, in *8 Ball Pool*, if you want to play the game you need pool coins. Either you can buy them, or if you can't afford to, you can watch a branded video advert. Once you've watched the ad, you receive fifteen pool coins and you carry on playing the game. In that context, it works very well.

It is also possible to do deals where you get a link share. Passing through the website, then going

KEY TERMS

HTML5

HTML5 (Hyper Text Mark-up Language) is the next generation of the mark-up language that structures and assists in the presentation of web pages. It is an open format language and free to use to develop websites and applications. HTML5 allows more complex graphics, for example, games can be rendered directly into web pages without the need for third-party software like Flash. At the time of writing, games for HTML5 are few, and the technology is in its infancy, but it is likely that they will overtake plug-in based gaming in the future.

6.13
HTML5 logo

through an ad tracking tag, you can get affiliate money. However, the main revenue driver is when people buy the game. Alternatively, players get the game free on Apple or Android and then monetize within the game. Our aim is to make a great game, drive traffic to it, increase player engagement, and monetize it.

Having a web version that upsells to mobile is a key pillar of our marketing strategy. With around 700,000 apps on Apple, probably slightly more on Android, it is hard to be found. Therefore, unless you have a proper marketing scheme, you can understand why a company like King (of *Candy Crush Saga* fame) is rumored to be spending a million a day on marketing.

Miniclip started out pretty much 100 percent advertising funded, enough eyeballs and people will pay to have their adverts featured, which worked. Over time, we started to do third party deals with the likes of *Club Penguin* and *RuneScape* from Jagex. This made us less reliant on advertising until we got

to a pretty happy place of about 50/50; subscription revenue coming in from bigger, more engaging games and then the advertising revenue for the free games on the website.

Since the move to mobile, we've found that we are looking at the freemium model. Here the player gets the game free and where possible is encouraged to make in-app purchases. There's the paymium model, where the player pays for the game and also pays for in-app purchases, or there is the ad-funded model, which we use on Android because in-game monetization is less lucrative at this time than Apple. So, what we'll do is launch the game at 69p ($1) on Apple with no advertising and launch it free on Android with some advertising. Android is changing, as the market progresses. It is bigger now than Apple and there is more growth and more scope there. We will constantly look at what works and whether that audience can sustain a paymium model. As a rule, Apple makes a lot more money through app payments and purchases than Android.

6.14–6.15
Mobile gaming
Candy Crush Saga and *Candy Crush Soda Saga*, by King, and *Fruit Ninja*, by Halfbrick, have designed games specifically using the gesture functionality of the mobile touch-screen format. *Candy Crush* franchise games (*Candy Crush Saga* and *Candy Crush Soda Saga*) are played 957 million times per day on average, by 91 million daily active users (in Q4 2014). As an indicator of King's success in the app game market, King announced it had gross bookings of $586 million (£393 million) across all of its games for Q4 2014 (Q4 being a three-month period). Accessible yet complex level puzzle designs, accompanied by a playful whistling soundtrack, have enticed users into monetized cycles of gameplay. Purchasing extra lives and special tools to support passing complex levels (overcoming player spikes) have proved to be an extremely successful business model.

> **A GAME THAT KEEPS A SMILE ON THE PLAYER'S FACE IS A WONDERFUL THING. NINTENDO'S THEME WILL BE 'CREATE NEW FUN.' SPREAD THE FUN OF GAMES TO EVERYONE.**
>
> Shigeru Miyamoto, Nintendo

KEY TERMS

FREEMIUM

In the free-to-play model, players get the game free (online or via download), and are encouraged to make in-app purchases of enhancements and additional content.

PAYMIUM

In the pay-to-play model, players pay for the game (app download) and are encouraged to make in-app purchases of enhancements and additional content.

PLAY FOR FREE

The *Robot Rage* interface screen flow diagram demonstrates how to design for user retention, to engage the player in cycles of repeat play, options for splash page adverts to other products, and regular interaction with the online shop, as well as options to buy in-game currency. This flow model is designed to progress the free game user, either online or from an app download, into cycles of game interaction that generates income.

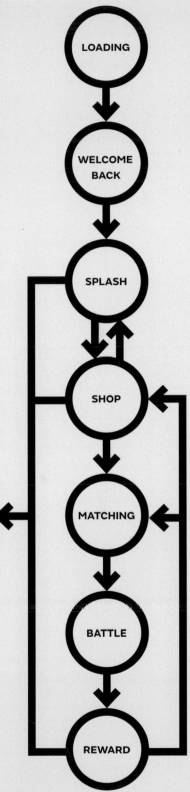

How do you perceive the emerging mobile market affecting user demographics?

The mobile market is effectively enhancing what Nintendo did with the Wii. The two main consoles were doing wonderfully with a hardcore audience playing in-depth strategic games. The Wii came out and made games accessible, like grandparents playing tennis in front of their TV. Nintendo created a family approach. Everyone has a mobile phone, whether it is smart or not, putting access into everybody's hands, meaning a much wider audience. Many people who aren't gamers got involved in a revolutionary democratizing of that market.

In the past, it used to be that you had to have all the kit. With the advent of tablets and phones, the play style is happening in the communal living space. Gaming has become a part of the social experience and the social a part of the gaming experience. I'm not locked away, headset on, I am still in the same room, chatting, and experiencing what's going on.

I went to a lecture at the GDC (Game Developers Conference) a few years ago and this person was talking about hard-core and casual and it is an obvious point. There are people who play *World of Warcraft*, which you would consider to be a hard-core game and they will play it casually half an hour a day and leave it there. He had friends who play *Minesweeper* in the office, and that's a casual game but on their stats they've played 70 or 80 thousand games, that's hard-core play! It is not about whether the game is hard-core; it's whether the user is hard-core. It is how you interact with the games you want to play.

Anyone can play these games! The market has changed and the accessibility to games has changed. They are no less clever, far more casual, light, and wildly intelligent at the back end but more importantly they are packaged to be accessible and monetize people.

I think it is a wildly interesting and exciting time in the market. One of the big things about mobile is that I can get snackable content wherever I am. I have a five-minute window and these games are expressed in little chunks of content. This allows me to flexibly fill my time. Everyone is competing for time and users wants to be involved with their games as often as they possibly can. I don't want players to dedicate a half-hour window in the evening; instead, I want to see interaction of 15 x 5 minute games over the course of the day.

> **"**
>
> **IN THIS MARKET, IF YOU'VE GOT A SUCCESS YOU NEED TO DOUBLE DOWN ON THOSE USERS AND REWARD THE PLAYERS WITH MORE AND MORE CONTENT. THEY FEEL BETTER ABOUT YOUR BRAND AND THEY FEEL BETTER ABOUT THE PRODUCT THEY'VE BOUGHT.**
>
> Rob Small,
> Founder and CEO Miniclip
>
>

MINICLIP IN NUMBERS
Mobile and web demographics
January 2015

79 MILLION MINICLIP USERS

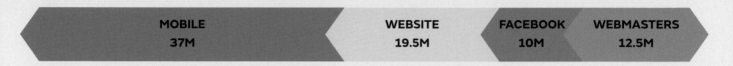

| MOBILE 37M | WEBSITE 19.5M | FACEBOOK 10M | WEBMASTERS 12.5M |

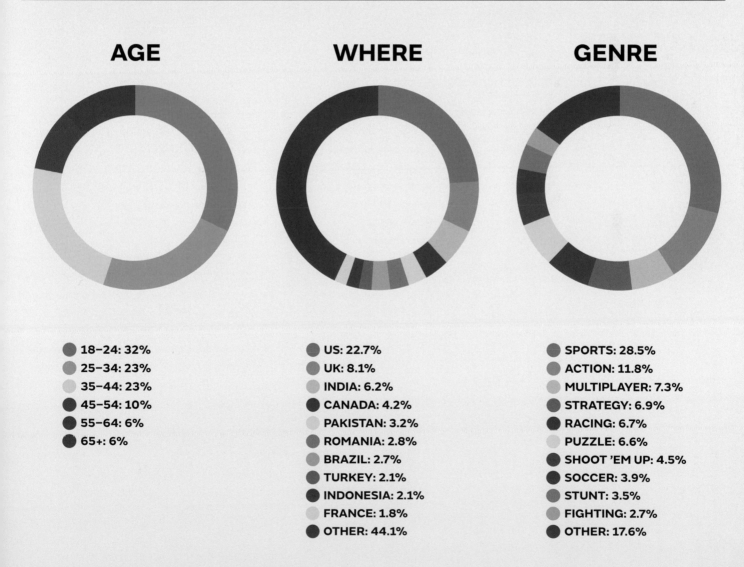

AGE

- 18–24: 32%
- 25–34: 23%
- 35–44: 23%
- 45–54: 10%
- 55–64: 6%
- 65+: 6%

WHERE

- US: 22.7%
- UK: 8.1%
- INDIA: 6.2%
- CANADA: 4.2%
- PAKISTAN: 3.2%
- ROMANIA: 2.8%
- BRAZIL: 2.7%
- TURKEY: 2.1%
- INDONESIA: 2.1%
- FRANCE: 1.8%
- OTHER: 44.1%

GENRE

- SPORTS: 28.5%
- ACTION: 11.8%
- MULTIPLAYER: 7.3%
- STRATEGY: 6.9%
- RACING: 6.7%
- PUZZLE: 6.6%
- SHOOT 'EM UP: 4.5%
- SOCCER: 3.9%
- STUNT: 3.5%
- FIGHTING: 2.7%
- OTHER: 17.6%

Happy Holidays! Play Games! ▶

6.16
Cultural contexts
The Christmas Takeover—seasonal
themes may be an additional consumer
draw in some regions.

TASK

Game Design Brainstorm

By Rob Small, CEO Miniclip

Use the ideas below to conceive and design an app
or mini game. Work in groups.

01 **DEFINE THE THEME.** Discoverability and
marketing: think about how you can make
your app design stand out in a congested
and competitive marketplace. Link it
to something topical (current affairs),
seasonal, or give it cultural relevance.

02 **DEFINE THE TECHNOLOGICAL FORMAT.**
Platform and controls: carefully consider
on which platform you want your app
published. Remember that this may affect
the target market you are looking to
reach. Make sure the control mechanism
works naturally with your platform of
choice, for example, swipe or gesture
controls work well on smartphones.

03 **DEFINE THE REVENUE STREAM.**
Monetization: there are many different
business models in the games industry.
How will your game make money, for
example, paid download, in apps sales, or
advertising?

04 **DEFINE CONNECTIVITY.** Social: the world
is becoming a more social and connected
place through technology. Think about
how your app idea can plug into this and
capitalize on people's motivation to play
with their friends.

PROPAGATING ADDICTION

Accessibility of content has enlarged the definitions of a hard-core gamer, heralding an expansion in gamer attitudes and appetites. Consumption, at unprecedented levels, indicates an industry metamorphosis is taking place. Free-to-play and pay-to-play gaming models, combined with the allure of anytime anywhere access, have led to young and old consuming game content at an unparalleled rate. Has this fluid digital revolution created a culture where eager young consumers can easily be preyed upon? (For more on addiction, see The Cost of Progress page 135).

THERE IS NO SIMPLE, SINGLE WAY OF 'CONTROLLING' OR 'TREATING' TWENTY-FIRST-CENTURY PROBLEMS SUCH AS INTERNET ADDICTION OR VIDEO GAME ADDICTION. ONLY A FULL, OPEN, AND INFORMED DISCUSSION BY ALL STAKEHOLDERS (PARENTS, SCHOOLS, OPINION LEADERS, GAMES AND TECH COMPANIES, AND TEENAGERS) WILL HAVE A LASTING IMPACT ON THIS CHALLENGING PROBLEM.

Dr Philip Tam, Sydney University,
The Nextweb.com

Access to Debt

During 2013, concerns were raised about the growing number of children amassing large debts whilst playing games on mobile devices, accrued over short periods. In the UK, a seven-year-old boy managed to create $5,106 debt (£3,000) in a weekend, after playing what his parents thought to be an innocuous mobile game app, primarily aimed at a family audience.

Touch-screens offer the illusion that they make life easier; swipe and it's done. Good game design aims to create a seamless experience for players between the narrative structure, and thought and action. (See Mobile and Web Takeover, page 159.)

A notable feature of good game design is how it subtly utilizes new technological formats. *Fruit Ninja* (see image 6.22), made by Australian company Halfbrick, is an example of an excellent design for a touch-screen device; the player chops or swipes through the fruit as it appears on the screen. A natural motion and desire equally fitted to both the narrative idea and the outcome, slicing things up with an imaginary sword; a seamless conjoining of format and game mechanic encapsulated in the player's gesture.

It is unsurprising that engaging, brightly colored games would appeal to a young audience eager to keep going as the fun escalates level to level. Many of these games are free-to-play but only up to a point. Their design is one that has been based around a monetized structure, focusing on areas such as apparel, tools, vehicle upgrades, and level expansions, as well as in-game currency: diamonds, coins, nuggets, and even doughnuts. When the player runs out of currency, a tap on an icon and the coffers are replenished, or the level extended, or a new character is unlocked. The cost of these items varies hugely, from pence or cents up to $100 (£60) a time or more. Widely accessible mobile Internet technology coupled with tech-savvy, eager-to-play children are causing concern. Is there a considered level of subterfuge by design embedded within these fun and clever games? The video games industry, after all, is a business and its aim is to make money.

There are various international bodies dictating how brands promote their products and interact with consumers. For example, advertising in the UK is watched over by the Advertising Standards Authority; it monitors certain types of endorsement or advertising, which should not be aimed at children. The ASA enforces an advertising code of conduct, which also includes non-broadcast advertising i.e. printed media. It is widely considered that children should be protected from manipulation by unscrupulous businesses.

In September 2013, the Office of Fair Trading in the UK (which later became the Competitions & Markets Authority, CMA in April 2014) began an investigation into in-app purchases. The discussion was based upon unfairly marketing games towards children. Currently no new legislation has been put forward in the area of children and online games. In January 2014, Apple reported it had refunded nearly $30 million (£20 million) to parents from purchases made by children. In response, the FTC (Federal Trade Commission, USA) Chairwoman Edith Ramirez said in a statement, "This settlement is a victory for consumers harmed by Apple's unfair billing, and a signal to the business community: whether you're doing business in the mobile arena or the mall down the street, fundamental consumer protections apply." At present many games have no in-app purchase capping.

Games companies or providers are not solely at fault for errant in-app prchases. Part of the issue is parental responsibility and education combined with an ability to control, where possible, escalating debt. Parents need to be aware what their children do with the technology they have access to and how it works.

6.17
CMA logo

. . . ADVERTISING MUST BE RESPONSIBLE, MUST NOT MISLEAD, OR OFFEND AND SPECIFIC RULES...COVER ADVERTISING TO CHILDREN . . .
The CAP advertising code, Cap.org.uk

Games and Advertising to Minors

UNESCO—the United Nations Educational, Scientific and Cultural Organization, defines early childhood as 0–8 years and the age of twelve is commonly considered a transition point where children can generally recognize advertising and apply a critical attitude towards it. The UK, Denmark, Belgium and Greece restrict advertising to children and advertising to children under twelve years of age is illegal in Sweden, Norway and the Canadian province of Quebec. In Australia the critical transition age is fourteen. The FTC (Federal Trade Commission) in the US takes an alternate view, where companies self-regulate their advertising to children in a multibillion dollar advertising industry.

However, brands have not given up trying to attract children as new consumers; they have moved their advertising campaigns from TV to the Internet. Part of this new corporate stratagem is proliferated through social media, widely used by young people. Although some well-known social media sites have an age restriction of 13+, many younger users are online accessing these sites. Manufacturers are using social media to directly attract new young consumers using adver-games, computer games that are all about subliminally promoting a brand.

The advertising industry spends $8.2 billion (£5.5 billion) a year on advertising. The move to online, by many soft drinks and confectionary companies, is in part driven by there being far less regulation and restriction than TV advertising. Children can watch animated adverts made by food companies to promote products high in fat, sugar, and salt, which would otherwise contravene legislation.

Kellogg's have utilized mini games aimed at children online for its Krave Chocovore Idol campaign, also linked to a live TV program. The game, *Pitfall! Krave* is a free-to-play mobile game where the player can collect pieces of a golden idol. Collecting items in the game enables the player to purchase promotional products and to be entered into a daily prize draw. A brand enticement process, which would not necessarily be allowed in other advertising mediums.

DISCUSSION POINTS

01 Should legal boundaries be put in place to protect children from advertising in games and/or the Internet, as they are in other media?

02 Is it OK for businesses to directly market products to children?

CROWDFUNDING

Development costs for video games are met in three ways. Firstly, the traditional mainstream titles are backed by the major publishers, and supported by very substantial investments comparable to feature-film budgets. Secondly, indie scene development teams are often self-financed. These micro titles do not usually attract risk-averse publishers. Last, but by no means least, there is the new kid on the block, crowdfunding.

What is crowdfunding? It is a platform—often online—used to advertise, engage, and mobilize the public to believe in a unique vision for a product, i.e. a video game. The process aims to rally potential investors to contribute enough funds to successfully realize the product. This form of collective financing has empowered entrepreneurs around the world and across a range of design disciplines.

The idea of crowdfunding stems from charitable giving—fundraising that is often based around community projects. In recent years, the Internet-based crowdfunding formula has proven to be a huge international success, allowing like-minded people to remotely support a project that has inspired them. It has tapped into the philanthropic desire to enable others to achieve their goal, whilst expecting little in return apart from the satisfaction of being involved with something new and exciting.

The individual or company proposes a project within categories such as "art, comics, dance, design, fashion, film, food, games, music, photography, publishing, technology, and theater" (this list is from Kickstarter, other crowdfunding sites have different categories). The project manager sets a financial goal and a deadline for reaching it. If the goal is achieved before the deadline, then they can add incremental stretch goals for additional investment. If the initial goal is not met then those who pledged do not make their payments. The backing structure has a tiered reward scheme; backers receive rewards for their support dependent on the scale of their financial contribution to the project. Proportionately, they range from being a simple thank you by email, to receiving signed original artwork, a product prototype, or to be flown out to major international events with the design team (note: your contribution needs to be in the thousands to unlock this level of gratitude!).

There are many crowdfunding websites aimed at a variety of different audiences or areas of interest. One of the most notable is Kickstarter, their crowdfunded projects have raised over $1 billion (£670 million), they have over 6 million backers and have successfully funded over 62,000 projects. These are extraordinary statistics from a single crowdfunding site. In 2012, video games attracted the largest amount of funding of all the interest areas. That year twenty-three projects successfully raised financial backing of over $1 million (£670,000).

A notable video game success story from 2012 is the Double Fine Productions adventure game, *Broken Age*. Veteran game designer Tim Schafer (*Grim Fandango*, 1998) along with Ron Gilbert (creator of the *Monkey Island* series) sought to create a game outside of the conventional publisher backed and controlled funding model. The Kickstarter campaign initially sought to raise $400,000 (£268,270) but went on to inspire 87,142 backers to raise a staggering $3,336,371 (£2,225,000) to fund the *Broken Age* project. The game was successfully

6.18
Broken Age logo
A Double Fine adventure game. Co-founder Tim Schafer, also known for games such as *Day of the Tentacle* (1993), *Grim Fandango* (1998), *Psychonauts* (2005) and *Brutal Legend* (2009), broke crowdfunding records with the Kickstarter campaign for *Broken Age*.

6.19
Valve's *Dota 2*
The International
Compendium 2015.

6.20
TerraTech (2015)
London indie developers Payload Studios used Kickstarter to help finance their off-world physics-based project. Players build extraordinary modular vehicles, harvest resources and battle other players and corporations for control of key territories.

completed and released in January 2014. Fundraising success stories are not unique to video games but are also shared by gaming technology. OUYA set out to make an affordable micro console based on Android open source architecture aiming to raise $950,000 (£637,000). OUYA went on to raise an amazing $8,596,474 (£5.7 million), nine times its fundraising goal.

People Power

Another noteworthy and different kind of crowdfunding phenomena is The International, which is Valve's *Dota 2* (*Defense of the Ancients*) Championships, (see the Steam esports documentary *Free To Play*, 2014). In 2011, The International took place at Gamescom, Cologne, Germany, where the tournament set a record-breaking prize-winning pot of $1.6 million (£1 million), a previously unheard of amount within competitive gaming. In 2014, this was superseded by the *Dota 2* tournament in Seattle, where the total prize pot was just under $11 million (£7 million).

The International has been based in Seattle (USA) since 2012 and hosts esports teams from all over the world. Valve utilized their Steam gaming hub to raise a staggering multimillion prize-winner pot by selling a digital *Dota 2* compendium ($9.99 or £6.56 each), funds from these sales supported the game and tournament. This competition has become a landmark in professional esports tournaments, offering the largest prize money ever. The viewing figures and prize money are greater than for many traditional international sporting events. The *Dota 2* Compendium 2014 included crowdfunding stretch goals and unlockable game components. Its initial $6 million (£4 million) goal was raised in less than two weeks, with stretch goals up to $10 million (£6.7 million) reached with relative ease. The compendium finally reached an astonishing $10,791,380 (£7,237,600), allowing Valve to offer a first prize just short of $5 million (£3 million).

TOP 10 HIGHEST EARNING ESPORTS TEAMS

Spring 2015

No.	Team	Prize Money
1	**NEWBEE** (China)	$ 5,525,714 (£3,697,376)
2	**EVIL GENIUSES** (US)	$4,188,876 (£2,802,867)
3	**NATUS VINCERE** (Ukraine)	$3,571,695 (£2,389,899)
4	**INVICTUS GAMING** (China)	$3,002,033 (£2,008,726)
5	**SK TELECOM T1** (South Korea)	$2,615,720 (£1,750,235)
6	**FNATIC** (Europe)	$2,609,224 (£1,745,888)
7	**VICI GAMING** (China)	$2,474,228 (£1,655,560)
8	**SAMSUNG** (South Korea)	$2,181,955 (£1,459,994)
9	**ALLIANCE** (Sweden)	$2,101,650 (£1406260)
10	**SK GAMING** (Germany)	$1,921,063 (£1,285,425)

Source: http://www.esportsearnings.com/teams

Resurrection Mode

A crowdfunding trend in recent years has been for game designers to revive a classic gaming title from the past. In terms of a viable business model, these projects stand a good chance of being funded, because they have a proven track record, and a loyal, nostalgic fan base.

Crowdfunding is resurrecting pre-loved titles, companies, and careers, across a variety of gaming genres. The 1984 classic genre defining game *Elite* created by Frontier (David Braben and Ian Bell) was the first ever 3D game for home computers, and the first ever sandbox style game. It was reincarnated in 2014, as *Elite Dangerous* after an extremely successful crowdfunding campaign. Similarly, the 2003 cult-console classic from Harmonix, *Amplitude* was successfully backed, after being reimagined over a decade later for the PS4. Cyan Inc., founded by brothers Rand and Robyn Miller, the company behind the 1990s' award-winning 3D adventure game titles *Myst* and *Riven,* have also successfully funded their new adventure game *Obduction*, raising over $1 million (£670,000) for the project. One of the most successful Kickstarter projects was the reinvention of the 1999 Interplay RPG title *Planescape: Torment*. Initially seeking $900,000 (£603,620), *Torment: Tides of Numenera* generated a substantial $4.18 million (£2,803,500), to realize seventeen of its stretch goals in 2013.

Peter Molyneux, creator of the first god game title *Populous* (1989) through his studio Bullfrog, used crowdfunding to back a re-imagining of the genre with a new game, *Godus*. Proposed by his new games company 22Cans, the campaign surpassed its initial target of £450,000 ($670,000) and raised over £526,000 ($886,000).

Crowdfunded video game projects have offered the backers, gaming enthusiasts, and game design students, a unique insight into what it takes to make a computer game. The developers, whilst navigating the development process, inform the backers through video updates and forum Q&A, and reveal the numerous hurdles and difficult choices along the way. This process is normally hidden from the public eye.

22Cans opened up the iterative design process by asking backers what they wanted to see in this re-invention of the god game. There were online discussions about gameplay, and what had worked in prior games. In addition, backers were offered early access to the Beta development process (an opt-in strategy on Steam) whilst the game was still in the formative stages of development.

In spite of the notable success stories in recent years, project pitches that have reached their crowdfunding target and beyond offer no guarantee of their successful completion.

Kernel Panic

Despite its many successes, crowdfunding is becoming a contentious source of financing for video games. It is estimated that nearly two-thirds of successfully funded games, that have met their funding targets, do not go on to complete the game that was pitched to online investors, and backers do not always receive the promised rewards.

Why are indie developers failing to meet these self-imposed project targets? It will be for several reasons. Some will be due to poor project management, or for others the project was designed around a bad business model. However, we should also reflect on the crowdfunding model itself. To attract investors, the pitch is often highly polished with engaging short films, impressive concept artwork, and an attractive rewards system. This creates an environment where the developer can promise too much in an attempt to attract the start-up capital needed to be fully funded. This of course does not take into account any unforeseen, technical development issues, and how they might affect the project narrative as it evolves in an iterative design system. Or simply that elaborate, high quality games often overrun and thus cost more.

By comparison, many studios that use other funding streams such as publishers, develop in private and have historically begun to develop a game concept, only to shelve it mid-development. This can be for a variety of reasons, but gamers do not always hear about these unsuccessful cycles of development.

INTERVIEW
PETER MOLYNEUX

• •

Industry role: Peter Molyneux created the god game genre and is the founder of 22Cans. He discusses developing a game under the public gaze of the crowdfunding format. He explains how a small company has coped with working in an environment of substantial feedback from early-access backers.

Kickstarter has been a great way to engage the public and generate a user/fan base. What are the pros and cons of using Kickstarter to fund a games company?

The way games are being developed now is very different to what it was only three years ago before Kickstarter started. It's a viable option for a business to say to itself, I am going to start up with some seed funding, normally from your own pocket, I am going to get the company ready to do a Kickstarter campaign. I am going to have that crazy thirty days, I'm not going to panic, and by the end of those thirty days, I don't have a team of ten people or five people, in our case twenty-two people, I have a team of thousands of people! You have an audience of people, who started as fans and then when you release something, a portion of them thinks "that's not what I thought we were doing." Another portion thinks, "that's better than I thought we were doing," and yet another portion will be very indifferent.

Designing by committee—the iterative design process has probably presented more challenges, especially concerning forum discussions. Formerly a lot of development decisions would be behind closed doors and away from the public eye. How have you found this?

The fundamentally big problem is and—this sounds very scary—if you are truly embracing iterative games development at the heart of that is to implement something, normally not to a highly polished level, but to a medium level. Try it out, throw it out because it doesn't work, put a new feature in that maybe doesn't work, bring the old feature back and change it in some way.

You actually don't know the game you're creating until the end! It was not until the last four weeks that I really knew *Godus*. I know that sounds insane, but that's been true of almost every game that I have created. I didn't know what *Black and White* (2001) was going to be until the end of *Black and White*. I didn't know what *Dungeon Keeper* (1997) was going to be until the end. In fact in almost all of my games there is some amazing feature that feels like it should have been in there at the start of the game but wasn't included until the end.

In *Black and White*'s case, you couldn't pick up the followers and turn them into disciples until the very end. We implemented that feature in the last two weeks! In *Dungeon Keeper* the imps didn't tap on the blocks, you used to do it yourself. So, that changed the game completely. Even in the original *Populous*, you could not finish and have a knight in armor until the very end.

This is true of *Godus*. There is a raft of new features, which never existed before, and which should have been there from the start. Now that makes it insanely difficult to communicate a message to your community. Because you have to say that it is going to be fine, this magic feature will bring the whole game together. You need to immerse yourself in a game to find the feature that is unique. There are many features in *Godus*, which have come in but it's the journey from Kickstarter to early access, to where we are today.

I am like a proud parent of this game, it's the most amazing experience and no one had any idea what the game is until you play it now. It feels so relaxing, engaging, and thoughtful as it is now.

6.21
Godus
Specific settlements are directly responsible for managing resource collection. This is a key in-game mechanic that drives game progression i.e. to level up, unlock god powers, provide resources for building.

Would you recommend the crowdfunding route to all indie projects? Do you see it being appropriate for all kinds of game title start-ups or only for some?

It's right providing you get your mind-set in the right place. It took us a while to get our mind-set in the right place. It forces you to be very clear about what your concept is, and it forces you to do things earlier than you would normally. As long as you're clear about what the game is. It is a baptism of fire and it makes you answer questions that every game should answer. It makes you answer questions about who this game is for. What are the exciting features in the game? And I can't think of a game that wouldn't benefit from that, providing it's not too much like a game that already exists.

I think *Star Citizen* (due 2016) is something like how you make a triple A game with crowdfunding, but I cannot imagine there will be too many more examples like that. That feels like a unique event. The budget he (Chris Roberts) is going to spend on that game is going to be the equivalent to *GTA*'s budget, which is amazing. He's raised $40 million (£27 million) and that is awesome! I have no idea how he did that.

I would probably die from stress if I had that amount of money in the bank, because giving people value based upon $40 million (£27 million) is going to be incredibly hard to do.

6.22–6.23
Godus
Settlement images
from *Godus*.

Crowdfunding has changed the face of game design. Do you think that the old guard of publishers, the financial gatekeepers, have disenfranchised themselves in the industry? Has their day passed?

I think there is a realization that publishers need to take indie development seriously. When the new generation of consoles PS4 and Xbox One were introduced, suddenly the publishers started talking about indie development a lot more. Microsoft and Sony were talking about it. My criticism is that this momentum seems to have waned and gone away. I think they think, as they have before, that indie development is a waste of their time. Indie development is never going to be able to catch up to their AAA properties and compete with them. The games that make all their money, like *Call of Duty*, *Titan Fall* and *The Last of Us*. The titles that make the bulk of the publisher's revenue.

Now that we see some Kickstarter projects come through, they are interesting and different. I think that the gaming community likes indie development. There have been some unique titles like *Papers Please* (2013). Publishers are starting to realize that the indie community isn't going to disappear and there are some very interesting developments. Inevitably and perhaps sadly, the term "indie development," being defined as a start up, are those who will risk everything for the sake of originality and uniqueness. This will change over time. A company cannot be a start up or have the mentality of a start up for more than a few years. As soon as you have a successful product, you're not really an indie any more. Not in the truest sense of the word. People like Double Fine have proved they can still hold on to the spirit of being an indie developer without losing it. It's so different now, because games don't tend to get finished any more. If you look at *Minecraft*, it's an ongoing universe, which is ever expanding. Mojang (the makers of *Minecraft*) do a fantastic job with that.

BRANDING, FRANCHISES AND INTELLECTUAL PROPERTY

What drives people to buy video games? A reassuring logo glowing on the side of sleek looking hardware? An update to a sports sim with the latest players and stats? Or as another way to experience a popular movie after the credits have rolled? As individuals we develop emotional connections to, amongst other things, technology, sports teams, and alternate universes. The video game industry, like other popular media, encourages this connection to help sell more of their products. Therefore an insight into how businesses tap into these human urges is essential.

Brands, franchises, and intellectual property are key parts of the twenty-first-century economy. They are well-established concepts with legal underpinning, which successful businesses utilize effectively to develop and expand. To thrive in the world of video games you need to be aware of what they mean and how they are used. In the more mature creative industries, successful books, TV shows and films combine originality and technical excellence with compelling characters, plots, and settings that people want to spend more time with. Once hooked, those individuals might achieve this by repeatedly watching the DVD, or by reading new books and comics that expand the story, but today they are just as likely to play the tie-in video game.

For the relatively new kid on the block, the video game industry has long been successful in creating and exploiting original content—its intellectual property—but also equally strong in taking existing creations from other media and making games from them, i.e. extending a franchise.

The industry has been historically weaker in gaining consumer awareness for the creators, developers, and publishers of video games outside of the gaming fraternity. A successful business will have established a brand that is more than a combination of identifying graphics and memorable TV ads, but also one that offers something distinctive and trusted by consumers. Apart from a few notable exceptions, the names of the organizations and creators involved in the business of games rarely permeate into the wider public's consciousness, so they do not become trusted and recognized commercial entities as other brands do. The exceptions to this are the hardware manufacturers, but, other than Nintendo, their brands were established through other markets. With the ever-expanding might of the video game industry and the numbers of digital natives growing, this situation seems unlikely to continue for long.

Media Franchise

A franchise is a legal right or privilege. In the business world, it can refer to several different models of extending a brand including chain stores or restaurants. In North America, it can also refer to sports teams. A media franchise is a piece of intellectual property consisting of a story and its component characters and setting. They are usually fictional creations derived from literature, film, TV, or video games, which are extended across multiple iterations in a single medium. A media franchise can also be non-fictional, in the form of a game show or other TV format such as *The X-Factor*. Franchise owners can, and often do, authorize (license) the rights to their creations to other businesses and media, in order to create merchandising and marketing materials.

Transmedia

Transmedia storytelling is a process that occurs when a story and setting expands away from the original media in which it has been created. The new works that are fashioned in other media formats might then fill in the gap between episodes, or sequels, as well as providing additional information about the world and its characters. Some media franchises have evolved to become transmedia, while others have from the outset deliberately embraced a variety of formats to tell their story. The Pottermore website (www.pottermore.com) that expands the world of Harry Potter is an example of transmedia, as it develops elements of the setting that have not been dealt with in the original books or movies.

Brands

The origins of branding are found at the dawn of civilization. Identifying marks have been applied to livestock, or the products of artisans for millennia.

The origins of the word itself are linked with the act of literally burning symbols onto the objects or animals in question. These symbols indicating ownership and provenance have over time evolved to become what are termed today as logos. But a logo is not synonymous with a corporate brand in contemporary culture. In his book, the *Brand Handbook* (2008), Wally Olins, co-founder of the international branding agency Wolff Olins and a godfather of modern branding, instead broadens the definition beyond visual identity to "the tangible manifestation of corporate personality." The act of branding is now a global business activity with large agencies devoted to inventing new or developing existing brands and advising on brand strategy for their clients.

Where modern brands diverge from simple symbols on the side of a tin or sports shoe is in their mission to build up trust, earn loyalty, and become an indispensable lifestyle accessory. Brands achieve this by offering consumers compelling and engaging narratives and stories to buy into. Their aim is to skillfully communicate the brand's values, ethos, and worldview, in the hope that consumers will share these, and identify with their product or service in a much more emotionally engaged way. Over time, it is hoped the relationship between brand and consumer will grow stronger and therefore more financially profitable to the brand's owner. This approach is necessitated by the crowded marketplace where many similar products compete. Essentially, the brand makes the difference in the consumer's eyes.

Despite their intangible nature, brands can be assigned a monetary value and appear on a business's balance sheet. A brand's value can be far in excess of any physical asset that the business owns. A significant portion of the stock-market value of some of the world's largest technology companies, such as Apple, Google, or Samsung, are built on the value of their brands.

6.24
Logos
Contemporary and historical consoles, publishers and studios.

6.25
SEGA logo
The SEGA name is derived from Service Games, the name of one of the original parent companies. The modern logo came into use in the mid-1970s.

6.26
Original PlayStation logo
First seen in 1994, Sony developed the original PlayStation icon in-house.

6.27
Xbox One logo
JDK Design developed the branding, visual identity, packaging and a visual language for the Xbox One.

Branding and Video Games

We can see branding in action when gamers of all types respond to questions like: Mario or Sonic? PlayStation or Xbox? Kratos or Master Chief? While many will point out the reasons for their preference is because they enjoy the game, or love the technology, these creations are all calculated to reinforce an image that the company wishes to convey for its brand. As players and consumers, we all make choices like these. They are emotional choices, and therefore it is difficult to pin down, in an objective manner, why we prefer one console or character to another. But these choices are important. If you can't connect with your audience, your enterprise will struggle to survive.

The development of contemporary branding practices and the rise of the video game industry are both phenomena of the last fifty years. During that short period, many manufacturers, developers and publishers have emerged and disappeared and few of the pioneering brands survive. Amongst a large number of contemporary consumers the console giants of the twenty-first century, PlayStation, Nintendo and Xbox have strong brand awareness, but game publishers and developers are much weaker. This situation is borne out in part by research from the market researchers at Harris Interactive who, in 2012, conducted a survey in the UK looking at consumer recognition of video game brands. Fifty percent or more respondents had never heard of Capcom, Konami, Activision or 2K Games. In the case of Bethesda, the publisher and developer behind the best selling *Elder Scrolls* series, and in the business since 1986, a massive 75 percent were completely unaware of its existence. Maybe this does not matter?

Plenty of casual game players might never use, or possess, a console or desktop computer on which to play games, but, instead use their phones or other handheld devices; in these cases those consumers are more likely to be aware of the brand of their device or their mobile network. Conversely, many self-identifying gamers might recognize a platform

BRAND FAMILIARITY COMPARISON

A selection of video game brands and their familiarity among consumers in the UK in 2012.

Source: Harris Interactive.

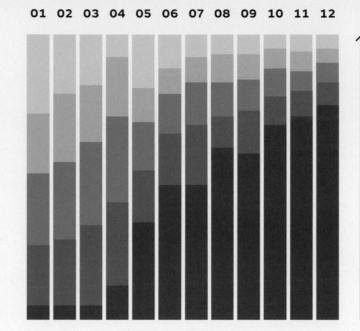

 I use this brand

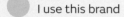 Very familiar

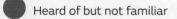 Somewhat familiar

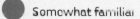 Heard of but not familiar

 Never heard of

01 **Nintendo**
02 **PlayStation**
03 **Xbox**
04 **Sega**
05 **EA**
06 **Ubisoft**
07 **Rockstar**
08 **Capcom**
09 **Konami**
10 **Blizzard**
11 **2K Games**
12 **Bethesda**

such as Steam, but it will have little impact on the public. Some studios and publishers—whether intentionally or not—have built strong brands through the consistency, creativity or originality of their output, or the individuality or quirkiness of the game. Rockstar Games or EA (Electronic Arts) both had wider recognition in the Harris survey compared to other publishers. In the case of the former, this could be partly due to the controversy that surrounds their games and their memorable advertising campaigns; and in the latter example the strong relationship with sporting titles, particularly the FIFA football series.

The first mega brand of the gaming world was Atari. During the late 1970s and early 1980s, Atari was the dominant name, particularly in North America, and led video gaming into pop culture and beyond. But by the middle of the decade, its heyday was over. Amongst gamers who grew up during

that period, it continues to be a highly recognizable brand. So much so, that many people have, over time, tried to revive the brand in order to try to tap into its large nostalgia value.

At the end of the 1980s and early 1990s, the top two brands in gaming globally were Nintendo and Sega. Their games had a distinctive look and feel, and they sought to appeal to different demographics. Sega aimed itself at a narrower, older male demographic of hardcore gamers in opposition to Nintendo's family entertainment. Then in 1994, Sony introduced the PlayStation and the market changed considerably. By the end of the decade, Sony's PlayStation was ascendant and had dumped Sega into third place amongst the consoles. Sega stopped making hardware in 2001, the same year that Microsoft launched the Xbox, and now exists only as a software brand that makes games for its once bitter rivals. PlayStation and Xbox are brands in their own right that have grown with each new generation, but at the same time they are a Sony or Microsoft product respectively and the percentage of their brand worth is factored into that of the parent company. It would be reasonable to assume that there will be consumers who are unaware of the connection.

In the second decade of the twenty-first century, the video game industry finds that despite its rapid ascent over the last forty years, the biggest brands in gaming don't have the power of those in the well-established world of fast moving consumer goods (FMCG). For example, fashion brands have built up decades of goodwill.

Brand recognition and loyalty is difficult to build. This challenge is highlighted by recent NYSE (New York Stock Exchange) debutant, UK-based mobile game developer and platform King, creator of the global mega hit *Candy Crush*. The company has struggled (at time of writing) to maintain its float price. This is largely due to the difficulty they have in convincing investors that they are not just one-trick-ponies. For companies like King, the problem is that although their games have market recognition, King's platform is not strongly enough associated with their product. To cement their future success, King's strategy is to build trust with consumers by producing a portfolio of games that is better than the competition.

As branding is largely about differentiation, the major console manufacturers have all tried to build a unique story for themselves. As well as hardware, modes of play, and exclusive content, they now encompass online and social elements. Both Microsoft and Sony were not solely built on the Xbox or the PlayStation. They are brands in their own right, with their own distinct identities and are not necessarily linked to their parent companies in consumers' minds. The only video game related brand to qualify was Nintendo.

The Nintendo Brand

Nintendo has built its brand by focusing on family entertainment, aiming to appeal to all ages, and to a broad demographic, specifically avoiding the lonely male stereotype. Nintendo is also the only solely video game brand that features regularly in countdowns of the world's biggest brands, based on their estimated value. In 2013, according to

OUR IP IS THE MOST IMPORTANT ASSET WITH WHICH WE CAN ATTRACT PEOPLE TO OUR OWN PLATFORM.
Satoru Iwata, President and CEO, Nintendo (2013)

Interbrand (the international branding agency) in their annual analysis of the world's largest brands, Nintendo's brand was worth $6.1 billion (£4.1 billion). At the time of writing, that was well over one-third of its stock-market valuation of $16 billion (£11 billion).

Early in the life of the company, Nintendo made the decision to allow other developers to create games for its consoles. At the time, this was a revolutionary practice. However, these developers

6.28
Nintendo logo
The Nintendo typeface has remained largely unchanged since the 1960s. The surrounding strip, sometimes referred to as the "racetrack," only came into regular use after featuring on the *Donkey Kong* arcade machine in 1982.

BRANDING CHALLENGES

Some challenges for a publisher or developer:

- How to create something that will appeal over multiple iterations.
- How to make games that are different from the competition.
- How to encourage players to try other releases from the same publisher.

Some challenges for hardware manufacturers:

- What differentiates the products?
- What types of games and extras are offered?
- How robust is the device?
- What technology should be used?
- What should the price be?

were subject to a veto. If Nintendo didn't like what they had created, it couldn't be released. This ensured Nintendo could avoid controversial content in its games, but also allowed them to demand changes to games to protect its family fun and values ethos. The price of Nintendo's products has also helped to construct their brand's appeal. While the pricing of any company's product might simply be a case of economics, it is not always that simple. Brands have inflated the cost of their products significantly above the actual costs of making and selling their products or services. When something is seen as expensive, it can create desire or exclusivity. This can work the other way too. In order to cement their family-friendly image, Nintendo have not always used the most cutting-edge technology, often producing machines that are not as powerful as their generational equivalents to keep the cost of their consoles down. Their continued success is built on their software, but Nintendo's future is not assured. Their Wii U, launched in 2012, has sold poorly and the company has been criticized for damaging their brand by confusing consumers as to what their new product was, and how it fitted into new gaming realities.

The exclusive video game titles and franchises available on consoles form part of the console's brand, and exclusive games exist on all platforms. Apart from simply adding to the differentiating features they also help to build the core identity of the brand—as well as helping to develop cult followings—and are often what consumers identify with and relate to.

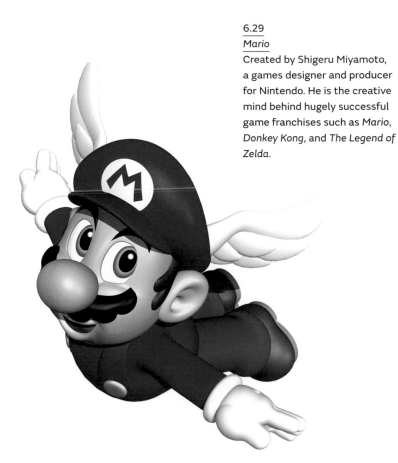

6.29
Mario
Created by Shigeru Miyamoto, a games designer and producer for Nintendo. He is the creative mind behind hugely successful game franchises such as *Mario*, *Donkey Kong*, and *The Legend of Zelda*.

Intellectual Property

Intellectual property, often abbreviated to IP, is described as "creations of the mind" by WIPO (the World Intellectual Property Organization) and concerns the rights assigned to the owners of artistic works, such as novels, film, and music, as well as industrial endeavor. These are the rights to be identified as the creator or owner and ultimately to benefit financially, i.e. make money from these creations. In most circumstances, these rights usually reside with the creator, but they can be bought and sold.

IP can be divided into two distinct types: copyright and industrial property. Copyright covers artistic output, while industrial property includes trademarks and patents for technological innovations and design.

Video Games and Intellectual Property

Intellectual property (IP) can be a controversial subject in software circles. The components that make up video games are, in most cases, covered by copyright. Copyright holders such as authors and artists, as well as organizations and business, who build up collections of copyright material will often allow their property to be used in media other than the one their imagination had worked in. (For further discussion on IP see Mike Bithell interview Chapter 4, page 114.)

When building brand loyalty, the console manufacturers have to use their IP to gain and maintain market share. Nintendo and Sega built their brands around the characters Mario and Sonic the Hedgehog respectively, both becoming mascots for the companies.

The role of copyright in video games is a complex one and has become more so as the games have advanced from rudimentary graphics and sounds to competing with blockbuster films. Like a movie, the contemporary video game can include many elements that are copyright protected, such as music, plot, and characters. Therefore, a game is protected in a variety of ways. However, in some circumstances these things are not automatically protected but rely on local laws.

The alternative to licensing IP is to keep it exclusive, this is another way of exploiting IP to drive your business. This has been massively important to Nintendo as a way of driving people to their products by not licensing out key titles like Mario and Zelda, which are among the most recognizable names in the gaming world. Exclusivity is their weapon of choice.

The dominant methods of enforcing IP in order for businesses to be commercially successful are being challenged and a brave new world of alternative models of collaborative creation is emerging. This includes crowdsourcing, and the involvement of players and individuals unconnected to the original rights' holders contributing to the development. Through legal frameworks like Creative Commons and open source platforms, video games can be developed using the gaming and software community, as individuals are not restricted by enforcement or protection of IP.

COPYRIGHTABLE SUBJECT MATTER FOUND IN VIDEO GAMES

Source:
The Legal Status of Video Games: Comparative Analysis in National Approaches
Produced by the WIPO (World Intellectual Property Organization)

I AUDIO ELEMENTS

1. Musical compositions
2. Sound recordings
3. Voice
4. Imported sound effects
5. Internal sound effects

II VIDEO ELEMENTS

1. Photographic images (GIF, TIFF, JPEG)
2. Digitally captured moving images (portable executable, MPEG)
3. Animation
4. Text

III COMPUTER CODE (SOURCE CODE AND OBJECT CODE)

1. Primary game engine or engines
2. Ancillary code
3. Plug-ins (third-party subroutines)
4. Comments

IV MISCELLANEOUS

1. Video game script
2. Plot and other literary works
3. Well-developed characters
4. Choreographies and pantomimes
5. Maps
6. Architectural works

LIKE A MOVIE, THE CONTEMPORARY VIDEO GAME CAN INCLUDE MANY ELEMENTS THAT ARE COPYRIGHT PROTECTED, SUCH AS MUSIC, PLOT, AND CHARACTERS.

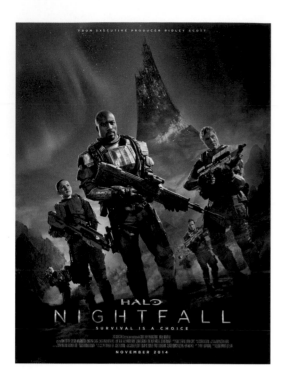

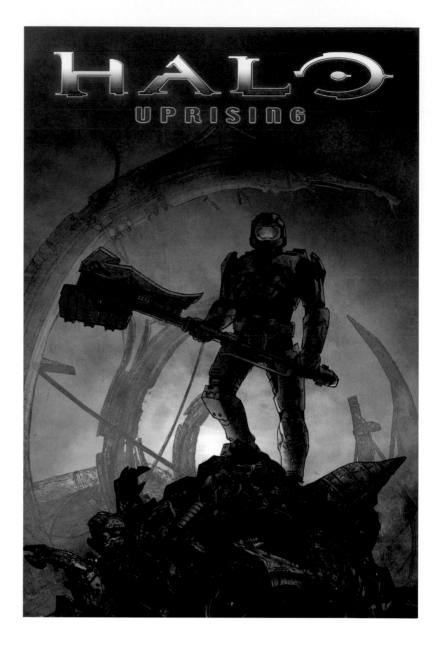

6.30–6.31
Transmedia identity
The *Halo* TV series—*Halo NightFall* and the Halo graphic novel—*Uprising*.

Video Games and Media Franchises

Some game narratives originally started out as a video game, whilst other ideas in the games industry began life in other forms of media, but franchises are an essential part of the industry. Over the years, video games have been fertile ground for the invention of new characters, worlds, and stories. Much of the industry has been built on these creations and some have proved so popular that they have spawned multiple sequels, and have subsequently crossed over into other media, particularly movies.

Recent years have seen movies based on *Hitman*, *Prince of Persia* and *Need for Speed*. The landmark science fiction FPS game *Halo*, has also long been mooted for the big screen. Instead, it has been realized as a science fiction TV series called *Nightfall*, and the Halo world has also been explored in various graphic novels.

An example of how a franchise can develop was discussed in a 2008 report by market researcher Nielsen. They identified the point at which a video game franchise became much larger and more well-known than its original inspiration. The American NFL commentator John Madden collaborated with EA to create the *John Madden Football* franchise of NFL sports sims in 1988, when he lent his likeness and voice to the game that bears his name. Since then, the name of the series has been shortened to simply *Madden* and the Madden

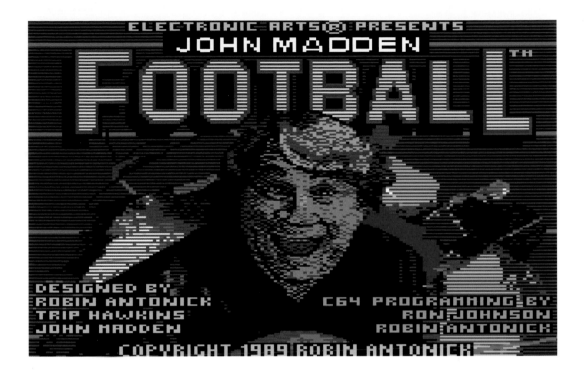

6.32
John Madden Football splash screen
The first version of the Madden NFL
video game was released in 1988.

brand has become bigger and more recognized than the individual, stretching across a range of other NFL related products.

Media owners use licensing agreements to extend their IP into other media, such as comic book characters appearing in movies. These crossovers can occur because of the challenges faced when creating original content. Why spend time and money inventing something new when you can look to existing books, films, comics and TV to provide ready-made universes and characters, already

popular with your audience demographics? Equally, these crossovers occur because they are a way to make money for the IP owners. Today, a cinematic franchise moving into the world of video games is commonplace, but it has been part of the video game world since the beginning of the 1980s.

Minecraft has become such a phenomenon that it has licensed itself to toy manufacturers. In a match made in heaven The LEGO Group released toys based on *Minecraft*.

AN EXTENDED FRANCHISE

In 2012, Disney bought Lucasfilm, the company behind the *Star Wars* films, TV programs and the LucasArts Entertainment Company (which at the time developed and published video games). A significant chunk of what Disney acquired for $4.05 billion (£3.1 billion) was the value of the IP possessed by Lucasfilm.

The wealth of the Walt Disney Company is primarily built upon utilizing intellectual property. Their most famous piece of IP is Mickey Mouse, the defining 1928 creation of its founder. Mickey is so important to the Disney brand that he is a registered trademark; his ears and silhouette are now a globally recognized visual shorthand for the company. As well as Mickey, Disney have, over the years, created more of their own characters or acquired rights to others either under license, or through buy-outs. Their continued business success is based significantly on their ability to make the most out of all the rights they own. As *Star Wars* is one of the best loved and biggest earning science fiction franchises of all time, Disney expect to be able to exploit George Lucas's universe for years to come; keeping their shareholders happy.

Unsurprisingly, it was not only Disney who recognized the value of the *Star Wars* brand. In

6.33

LEGO Star Wars
First released in 2005, *LEGO Star Wars: The Video Game* was a worldwide success selling in excess of 6.7 million copies. Its sequel *LEGO Star Wars II: The Original Trilogy* released in 2006 sold even more, and in the UK won the Best Gameplay award from the British Academy Games Awards. The success of the game is partly credited with helping reverse the fortunes of the LEGO group.

1999, long before Disney's purchase of Lucasfilm, the LEGO toy company began creating new construction sets based on the famous spaceships and characters. This was the first time LEGO had paid to license someone else's IP. Its success soon led to a new way of keeping plastic bricks relevant in an age of increasingly dominate screen-based entertainment.

LEGO Star Wars: The Video Game (LSW:TVG) was released in 2005 to great commercial success and to positive critical feedback. Although not the first video game based on Star Wars—there have been many titles over the years—it was the combination of the two pop culture giants that caught everyone's attention. Developed by Traveller's Tales, a UK-based studio that had begun to carve a niche for themselves fashioning games based on movies—most notably Toy Story—or working with other's IP such as Sonic the Hedgehog for Sega, LSW:TVG marked the start of a massive transformation in the fortunes and direction of the company. Traveller's Tales and its parent TT Group became part of Warner Bros Interactive in 2007, and now concentrate almost entirely on their work with LEGO. LSW:TVG has now been followed up by other LEGO-based video games including

Indiana Jones (2008), Batman (2008), Harry Potter (2010 and 2011), Lord of the Rings (2012), and Marvel Super Heroes (2013). Many of these tie in with the physical LEGO toy lines. Overall, the financial bottom line of all the businesses involved have benefited from extending franchises across mediums, and video games are now a key part of the transmedia landscape.

6.34

Angry Birds Star Wars

Star Wars has been linked with another piece of IP to create more best-selling video games. Rovio's *Angry Birds* was released in 2009 and became an international phenomenon by the end of 2010. By 2011, a new *Angry Birds* game had been created to tie in with a movie: the animated film *Rio*, which was swiftly followed a year later by another new game that combined Rovio's virtual characters with those of *Star Wars* into a webby award-winning title. With merchandising and toys based on the new game soon in the shops all the commercial opportunities of this crossover were being exploited. Once again, *Star Wars* had helped to keep another business, in business.

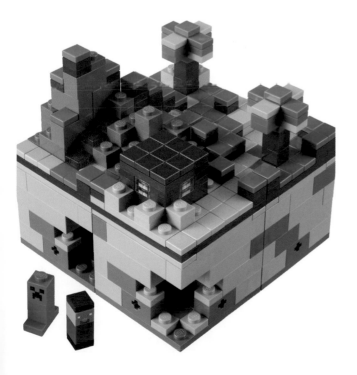

6.35

A Minecraft LEGO set

LEGO ® Minecraft was the first idea to receive 10,000 votes on the global LEGO CUUSOO website—a collaboration between the LEGO Group and CUUSOO Systems—passing the threshold required to put it into production. Here fans of the LEGO brand could vote on ideas for new LEGO sets or submit their own proposals for the public to vote on. This joint effort has since come to an end and LEGO has since launched its own similar service called LEGO Ideas, which can be found at: http://ideas.lego.com.

INTERVIEW
ARTHUR PARSONS

• •

Industry role: Arthur Parsons is Game Director at TT Games, he has been there for longer than he would like to admit and saw the start of the studio's relationship with LEGO. One of his most recent projects has been *LEGO Batman 3: Beyond Gotham* (LB3:BG). Below he talks about working with high-profile brands and franchises.

How did the connection between TT and LEGO come about? How did you feel when you found out?

Long before we started making LEGO games at TT, we were making hugely successful family friendly games. Games like *Crash Bandicoot: The Wrath of Cortex*, *Toy Story* and *Finding Nemo*; however, we were approached to work on a game that combined *Star Wars* and LEGO. At the time, I was on a different team and remember seeing the early prototype, and the entire studio just fell in love with what was on the screen. The rest, as they say, is history. The partnership between Giant Interactive and us obviously grew, but it all came about due to LEGO and Jon Burton, Jonathan Smith and Tom Stone, and the team that made the first title. Since then we have constantly worked to evolve and adapt the LEGO games, making sure each one is better than the last, but retaining core principles throughout. My first LEGO game in the series was the original *LEGO Batman*, and I've loved working on every title, as does the entire team here at TT.

As each new franchise landed with TT, from *Star Wars* to *Batman*, did you feel daunted by living up to the characters and worlds?

We never feel daunted by the new franchises. It's more an immense sense of excitement. Being able to delve into these different worlds is amazing, and making LEGO versions of these fantastic characters and worlds allows us to have so much fun, mixing things up in a very different way to any other video game. Obviously, there is always the pressure to deliver a fabulous title, but that is what myself and the team thrive on, being able to continually surprise people with what we do, we all count ourselves as being very lucky.

Once your collaborations are agreed, are you presented with instructions about how to use the material? Can you give an example of how you have used these to your advantage? Have any red lines become a positive?

The best thing about working on a LEGO video game is that we are entrusted with franchises; we are known for delivering an unprecedented fan service. Being able to come up with crazy ideas and scenarios, different interpretations of classic stories and characters is so much fun. Working with licensors becomes a fantastic collaborative process. Sure there are things that characters should or shouldn't do within given worlds, but this is never ever something that hinders us. Because we spend so much time researching our games, we know what we should and shouldn't do within a given brand, and licensors know this. For them, they can concentrate on working with us to pack the games full of exciting content, and that is why our partnerships are so successful.

LEGO games are renowned for having fun with their subject matter, being tongue-in-cheek and not taking themselves too seriously. Was that something that TT brought to the equation?

LEGO is all about fun and creativity, and as such, it is that ethos that has come from *LEGO Star Wars*. Being able to reinterpret the subject matter, putting a comedic twist on things, over-exaggerating character traits; it all adds up to fun. Again it is the amazing people I am fortunate enough to work with every day that make this possible, and our key word on every product is "FUN." If we make something that is fun and funny, then people will love it, no matter how young or old they are. So, that is what we concentrate on.

6.37

Wonder Woman

Each new LEGO Batman game has included more of the DC universe. In *LB3:BG* players have access to over 150 characters including well-known superheroes such as Wonder Woman, obscure individuals like Bat-mite and a cameo appearance by Adam West, the actor who played Batman in the 1960s TV show. Utilizing the depth of a franchise helps create games with replayability.

What do these franchises offer you as a studio that developing your own worlds does not?

In the past, I've been told that working within franchises on licensed games must be difficult and restrictive, however it really isn't the case at all. If anything, it allows you to really go to town and to take risks with the way that you design things. The way we look at it is that someone is giving you a load of fantastic ingredients to make a dinner with, so the challenge is using those ingredients to make the most magical dinner you can. We can explore pop culture, we can add layers of fan service that would not otherwise be possible, and we can explore every nook and cranny within the brands we are given. We leave no stone unturned when we work on a title, and have so much fun challenging ourselves to deliver brilliant games.

How do video games differ from the more established media such as movies, books, and graphic novels, when bringing to life these franchises?

Video games are all about interactivity and about giving players control of the situation, scenario, and characters. We need to ensure that we are constantly offering players something new, as they progress through our games, as we never want them to lose interest. Instead, we want players to be constantly wondering what is next, what character is going to make an appearance next, what locations are going to appear next, what vehicles they can use next, and that is how things differ. We need to engage our users, and really make sure that they cannot put the controller down.

CHAPTER REVIEW

This chapter began by visually exploring the context of a global games industry. We then presented a range of information about individual businesses and key aspects of the current sector. It has introduced funding issues and monetization models. It has examined the significant impact mobile gaming is having on the industry and discussed the importance of franchises. It has explored transmedia storytelling and branding in creating the emotional bonds that keep consumers spending.

Key Points

INDUSTRY SIZE: The video game industry now rivals or exceeds its media peers in revenue and looks set to continue growing. It has been transformed by mobile platforms and is the dominant force in drawing revenue from crowdfunding while providing good employment opportunities.

ACCESS TO TECHNOLOGY: Both Internet and mobile are seen in a strategic international setting. Focus is placed on the global marketplace, regional variance as well as cultural and seasonal contexts. Further attention is given to the emerging markets, which present varying stages of technological proliferation and development, which in turn affects content provision.

USER STATISTICS: These provide insights into genre popularity, download growth trends and demographics. This information is useful in understanding current and potential future trends for both the developer and publisher. Analyzing and understanding this information can potentially improve game design, refine monetization models, and lead to an improved end user experience.

MONETIZATION MODELS: At the time of writing, advertising on mobile devices is in its infancy. Several models for generating revenue are being explored, including advertising and subscription models that offer balanced revenue streams. Advertising can offer opportunities to earn rewards, i.e. additional lives or game currency, which can lead to retention. Advertising can also be delivered without obscuring gameplay at transitional points, such as level completion. Both of these models are used to engage and retain, rather than alienate the consumer.

UNIVERSAL DESIGN APPROACHES: The global marketplace for games, especially those for mobile devices, requires design approaches that avoid text heavy instructions, therefore increasing their global appeal and sidestepping issues related to language differences.

GAMING BRANDS: There is a large variation in brand recognition amongst consumers. Recognition is often strongest for hardware brands and weaker for publishers and studios. This is significant for some publishers, whose current success has been built on one or two games. A good brand is built on gaining and nurturing an emotional bond with consumers.

TRANSMEDIA FRANCHISES: Many games are now part of larger, imagined universes. The stories and characters depicted may have started life in comics, TV, film, books or games, but they have since spread to each other to develop the narratives and stories, allowing fans to have different ways of interacting with their favorites.

CONCLUSION

Video games were born out of a need to satisfy our human instinct to explore through play and the relentless march of technological development. As a legitimate pastime and exciting career option, it is unquestionable that the scope and breadth of the industry is far greater than most realize. Financially it has been shown and expressed through the diversity of games that exist, that contemporary video games are able to serve a variety of different markets and needs, redefining what video games can be. It is apparent that there is much more that could be said but we hope that you are now as excited as we are about the potential this global medium has and choose to investigate it further.

This is an industry that requires creatives who can realize a story, entertain and innovate, whilst making truly stunning content. An industry that requires highly skilled technicians who can bring video game concepts to life with all their complexities. Both kinds of people need a good education and a solid understanding of the industry if they wish to succeed.

For those wishing to forge a career in video games, we hope to have opened your eyes to the possibilities and potential that exist within the business of these virtual worlds. The games industry, as a part of the wider entertainment industry, continues to mature and is an exciting place to be right now. The professional and financial rewards can be significant and as seen in Chapter 2, there are many career routes to explore. Equally many of these roles involve transferable skills, applicable to other digital creative industries, particularly VFX in film and television.

Away from the immediate understanding of video games, this book has also examined the growing use of video games in the world of art, science, and education. Many of these new extensions to the medium are in their infancy, offering opportunities to discover new possibilities and directions. Knowledge of these areas is still limited to specialist interest groups but the expansion of computer-based gaming, away from its traditional core, will continue as technology develops, disrupts and evolves. These developments are aided by continuous research and debate, which takes place in companies and universities across the globe. Video games have become a significant area of study, as legitimate as film or literature.

We hope that this book has provided you with the confidence to consider taking on the business considerations of the industry, as well as its creative demands. Not since the early days of home computing have there been so many ways to become involved in the creation of video games. However, the industry is not without challenges. There are risks involved in regard to funding projects and reputations can be damaged as well as made. Likewise, there is considerable debate around the social and psychological impact of video games, which is likely to continue just as it has with other more established entertainment media.

It is unwise to precisely predict what the video game industry will look like in the coming decades. However, it is safe to say that people will still be playing games. Equally, we can be confident that technology will undoubtedly continue to develop and impact how people play and what they play them with. The only thing that is certain about the industry's future is that those studying for a role in it now, or just starting their career within it, will be the ones to shape it.

Online Magazines

edge-online.com
escapistmagazine.com
eurogamer.net
gamasutra.com
gamestm.co.uk
ign.com
kotaku.co.uk
polygon.com
rockpapershotgun.com

Useful Links

aana.com.au Australian Association of National Advertisers

arstechnica.com A technology news and information website

cinefex.com Journal of cinematic visual effects online and in print

dam-gallery.de Berlin-based gallery focusing on historical and contemporary digital arts

theesa.com ESA (Entertainment Software Association): The US video game trade association

esrb.org Entertainment Software Rating Board

fxguide.com Website dedicated to visual effects

gdaa.com.au Game Developers' Association of Australia

moma.org Museum of Modern Art, New York, US

nesta.org.uk UK innovation charity with strong links to the creative industries

pegi.info Pan European Game Information

pippinbarr.com/academic/Pippin_Barr_PhD_Thesis.pdf Video Game Values: Play as Human-Computer Interaction, a PhD thesis

publications.lib.chalmers.se/records/fulltext/111921.pdf Beyond the HUD, a PhD thesis

techradar.com A technology news and information website

ukie.info UK Games and Interactive entertainment trade association

Suggested Reading

ABOUT BEHAVIORISM
Burrhus Frederic Skinner, Vintage Series, Vintage Books, 1974

ART, TIME AND TECHNOLOGY
Charlie Gere, Bloomsbury, 2006

GRAND THEFT CHILDHOOD: THE SURPRISING TRUTH ABOUT VIOLENT VIDEO GAMES AND WHAT PARENTS CAN DO
Lawrence Kutner & Cheryl K. Olson, Simon & Schuster, 2008

JOYSTICKS: AN ILLUSTRATED HISTORY OF THE GAME CONTROLLER
Winnie Forster, GamePlan (Language: German), 2nd Edition, 2004

LEVEL UP! THE GUIDE TO GREAT VIDEO GAME DESIGN
Scott Rogers, John Wiley & Sons, 2nd Edition, 2014

MEDIA THEORIES AND APPROACHES: A GLOBAL PERSPECTIVE
Mark Balnaves, Stephanie Hemelryk Donald & Professor Brian Shoesmith, Palgrave Macmillan, 2008

REALITY IS BROKEN: WHY GAMES MAKE US BETTER AND HOW THEY CAN CHANGE THE WORLD
Jane McGonigal, Vintage, 2012

THE SPEED BOOK
Aram Bartholl, Gestalten, 2012

THE WORLD OF DIGITAL ART
Wolf Lieser, H. F. Ullman Publishing, 2010

GLOSSARY

AAA Refers to big budget blockbuster video game productions.

ALPHA A software development stage, performed by the QA team and engineers that aims to identify and fix the most critical issues prior to the beta stage.

API An application-programming interface is a programming framework that controls software component interaction.

ARCADE/ARCADE GAME A venue specifically devoted to video games where the games are played on coin-operated machines and usually are housed in upright cabinets. Very popular in the early years of the industry but now a niche concern.

AUGMENTED REALITY (AR) Technology which places visual interventions on top of the real world by using location data (GPS) gathered by mobile and portable devices.

AVATAR The graphical representation of the player within a game, or an image representing a user on a forum, or other social media.

BETA A software development stage, following Alpha, where the software's main features are stable and complete with few bugs so that real users can provide feedback.

BETA KEYS A code that is redeemed online to gain access to beta software i.e. a game that has not yet been finalized for sale.

CACHE Memory used for temporary storage of data.

CACHE MISSES A failure to find the required instruction in the cache.

CGI Computer generated imagery used across the various screen-based media.

CONSOLE A computer designed primarily to play video games. Usually requires a TV to display the game.

CPU Central processing unit, the microprocessor at the heart of a computer.

CRAFTING A process of gathering in-game materials and combining them to make a new custom object, or to upgrade an existing in-game asset.

CROWDFUNDING Funding a project by raising small amounts of money from many people, commonly associated with the Internet.

CUTSCENE A short cinematic film sequence used to break up gameplay, and to progress the game narrative.

DIEGESIS Related to narrative and storytelling within a game. In video games, interface elements are either integrated into the game world and can be seen/heard by the avatars as well as the player (these are diegetic elements) or are outside the game world, like an options menu (non-diegetic elements).

DRM Digital rights management is a software method intended to prevent software piracy.

EARLY ACCESS A funding model that is often connected to funding the Alpha stage of a video game; it often supports an unfinished game to completion.

ESPORTS Electronic sports are organized multiplayer video game competitions, they're often associated with the MOBA game genre (multiplayer online battle arena).

FPS A type of shooting game, and the acronym for first person shooter.

FREEMIUM A business model, often found on the Internet where gateway content is provided free and players are then encouraged to pay to unlock additional levels or features. Many app games use this model.

GAME ENGINE A piece of software that aids the creation of video games by providing a suite of tools for developers.

GO-BAN A Chinese term for a board game surface or play space.

GPU Graphics processing unit or VPU visual processing unit; a specific type of circuit dedicated to producing computer graphics.

INDIE GAME Video games made by small teams of independent developers, often without the backing of a publisher.

LET'S PLAY (LP) A video or series of screenshots accompanied by subjective commentary documenting a play through of a video game. They can be humorous, irreverent, and critical. They are not intended to show how to progress through a game objectively.

LUDOLOGY The study of games and gaming from the Latin ludere "to play." It is most commonly associated with the study of video games.

MAINFRAME A large, fast, and powerful computer that often supports a network of other machines and peripherals.

MILESTONE A defined point of time or stage in a project to be reached, which may have a conditional outcome attached.

NPC Non-playable character in a video game.

PAYMIUM A business model, where the user is required to pay for content; the opposite of freemium.

POINT CLOUD Data points derived from the Cartesian coordinate system (X, Y, Z) that describe the external form or surface of an object. See Crytek's *Ryse: Son of Rome*, page 96.

POST-INTERNET GENERATION Defined by the generations born after and growing up in an Internet saturated digital culture.

PUBLISHER A company that publishes and funds video games. Some are developed in-house and others externally by another developer.

RAY CASTING A method for rendering constructive solid geometry models in computer graphics and computational geometry.

SANDBOX A form of non-linear gaming associated with MMORPG games.

SCRUM A form of team project management, used to reflect upon project progress and setting short-to-medium goals.

SERIOUS GAMES 3D simulations of real-world environments often utilized by the army for scenario simulation.

SFX Special effects, used in digital entertainment such as Film, TV and Video Games, is the process of creating an illusion of reality using physical and digital means such as props, animatronics, camerawork and computer graphics. Also see VFX.

SHOUTCAST Internet live commentary, commonly associated with MOBA team based games; involves a lot of shouting.

SPRINT A short period of time, often 1 or 2 weeks in length, where achievable project goals set by scrum team management, are met.

STUDIO Organization in which video games are designed and developed.

TRANSMEDIA/TRANSMEDIAL Storytelling using narrative structures across multiple platforms and formats using digital technologies.

TRIBAL MOTIF Members of a community defined by an image, a specific design, or style (see Avatar).

VFX Visual effects where images are created, altered or manipulated via multiple layers (a composite). A process also known as compositing.

VR Virtual reality is a 3D environment simulation, generated by a computer. The user interacts using electronic equipment fitted with sensors, such as a headset with screens inside and gloves.

WWW World Wide Web based on the Hypertext Transfer Protocol (HTTP) referring to the browser-based technology created by Sir Tim Berners-Lee in 1989 at CERN, the European Organization for Nuclear Research.

ZERO PLAYER GAME A type of game run by a computer program that uses generative processes and doesn't require human players.

BIBLIOGRAPHY

Print-based media

THE ART OF GAME DESIGN: A BOOK OF LENSES
Jesse Schell, A K Peters/CRC Press, 2nd edition, 2014

THE BRAND HANDBOOK
Wally Olins, Thames & Hudson, 2008

DIGITAL REVOLUTIONS
Editor Neil Mconnon, Conrad Bodman and Dani Admiss. Barbican International Enterprises, 2014

THE ENCYCLOPEDIA OF GAME MACHINES
Winnie Forster, GamePlan/Hagen Schmid, 2nd edition, 2012

FUN INC. WHY GAMES ARE THE 21ST CENTURY'S MOST SERIOUS BUSINESS
Tom Chatfield, Virgin Books, 2011

FUNDAMENTALS OF GAME DESIGN
Ernest Adams, New Riders, 3rd Edition, 2013

HARMFUL CONTENT ON THE INTERNET AND IN VIDEO GAMES
Tenth Report of Session 2007–8, Volume II House of Commons , Culture Media and Sport committee

THE LEGAL STATUS OF VIDEO GAMES: COMPARATIVE ANALYSIS IN NATIONAL APPROACHES
Prepared by Mr Andy Ramos, Ms Laura López, Mr Anxo Rodríguez, Mr Tim Meng and Mr Stan Abrams World Intellectual Property Organization, 2013

NEXT GEN REPORT
Ian Livingstone, Alex Hope, Nesta, 2011

THE PRINCIPLES & PROCESSES OF INTERACTIVE DESIGN
Jamie Steane, Fairchild Books, 2014

REPLAY: THE HISTORY OF VIDEO GAMES
Tristan Donovan, Yellow Ant Media, 2010

Web-based publications

BEYOND THE HUD—USER INTERFACES FOR INCREASED PLAYER IMMERSION IN FPS GAMES
Erik Fagerholt and Magnus Lorentzon, 2009
http://publications.lib.chalmers.se/records/fulltext/111921.pdf
Last accessed 20/08/2014

COMPETITION AND MARKETS AUTHORITY (UK)
www.gov.uk/government/organisations/competition-and-markets-authority
Last accessed 03/11/2013

COPYRIGHT AND VIDEO GAMES
www.wipo.int/copyright/en/activities/video_games.html
Last accessed 13/08/2014

"CRAMMING MORE COMPONENTS ONTO INTEGRATED CIRCUITS" BY GORDON E. MOORE
www.cs.utexas.edu/~fussell/courses/cs352h/papers/moore.pdf
Last accessed 20/08/2014

CREATIVE INDUSTRIES: GAMES
creativeskillset.org/creative_industries/games
Last accessed 05/01/2015

HERE-ARE-THE-SALES-NUMBERS-FOR-WII-U
http://uk.ign.com/articles/2015/01/28/here-are-the-sales-numbers-for-wii-u
Last accessed 17/04/2015

"HOW KING DIGITAL ENTERTAINMENT'S CEO CONQUERED THE GAMING WORLD"
theguardian.com/business/2014/jun/06/king-digital-entertainment-ceo-riccardo-zaconni
Last accessed 17/06/2014

HISTORY OF BEAT 'EM UPS
tiki-toki.com/timeline/entry/53472/History-Of-Beat-Em-Up
Last accessed 03/11/2013

LEGO® MINECRAFT™ MICRO WORLD DETAILS UNVEILED

http://www.lego.com/en-gb/aboutus/news-room/2012/february/lego-minecraft-micro-world
Last accessed 10/04/2015

LUDOLOGY.ORG/

Last accessed 20/08/2014

MOORE'S LAW: HOW LONG WILL IT LAST?

www.techradar.com/news/computing/moore-s-law-how-long-will-it-last--1226772/1
Last accessed 18/08/2014

ONE NATION UNDER MADDEN: HOW THE MADDEN VIDEO GAME FRANCHISE BECAME BIGGER THAN JOHN MADDEN

www.nielsen.com/us/en/newswire/2008/one-nation-under-madden-how-the-madden-video-game-franchise-became-bigger-than-john-madden.html
Last accessed 24/06/2014

PLAYSTATION4-PS4-SALES-SURPASS-202-MILLION-UNITS

prnewswire.com/news-releases/playstation4-ps4-sales-surpass-202-million-units-worldwide-300045019.html
Last accessed 17/04/2015

A QUIET KILLER: WHY VIDEO GAMES ARE SO ADDICTIVE

thenextweb.com/insider/2013/01/12/what-makes-games-so-addictive/
Last accessed 19/01/2015

THE STORY OF THE INTEL® 4004

www.intel.com/content/www/us/en/history/museum-story-of-intel-4004.html
Last accessed 20/08/2014

A TIMELINE OF VIDEO GAME CONTROVERSIES

ncac.org/resource/a-timeline-of-video-game-controversies
Last accessed 18/12/2014

VB GAMESBEAT

venturebeat.com/2014/10/08/candy-crush-saga-not-ps4-or-xbox-one-dominates-ads-on-the-airwaves/

XBOX ONE SALES DECEMBER 2014

www.microsoft.com/investor/Events/Presentations/2014/ShareholderMeeting2014.aspx?eventid=151407&Search=true&SearchType=0
Last accessed 17/04/2015

INDEX

ACKNOWLEDGMENTS

Picture Credits

Thanks

Andy Bossom

To Alexandra, Gabriel, Sebastian, Francesca, and Jude, and to our families for their steadfast love and support. Special thanks go to the Coopers, Gallants and Barks families for being there when the phone rang.

Ben Dunning

To Sarah, Alfie, and Tilda, and to all my family. My deepest thanks for all your support, encouragement and supreme patience, particularly when I kept saying I was nearly done.

Both

A huge thanks to all our contributors: Ian Livingstone CBE; Rob Small, Alex Williams, Ricardo Serrazina and Jeremy Wadia of Miniclip, Mike Bithell, Dylan Beale, Peter Molyneux OBE, Jas Purewal, Luke Whittaker, Matt Warshaw and Eliott Johnson, Henrik Fahraeus, Anna Marsh, Arthur Parsons, Chris Brunning, Gianni Zamo, Professor Joseph DeLappe, Aram Bartholl, Chantal El-Bikai, Malsara Thorne, Susannah Clark, Will du Toit, John McCarten, David Bowman, Julia Hardy, Karen Stanley, Joseph Ryan, Mariusz Włodarczyk (Vlodarius), Wermilion, Aleksandrs Skudnevs, Matthew Price, Ricardo Serrazina, Tim Dixon, Steve Allison and Derek Siddle. Their willingness to help and generosity towards the undertaking of this book has been amazing.

We would also like to thank all the team at Bloomsbury/Fairchild, particularly Georgia and Miriam, for firstly giving us this opportunity and then their faith and encouragement throughout. Finally, the book would not look as it does without the efforts of Sharon McTeir in helping us track down our choice of images.